Three
Philosophical
Filmmakers

Books by Irving Singer

Three Philosophical Filmmakers: Hitchcock, Welles, Renoir

Feeling and Imagination: The Vibrant Flux of Our Existence

Sex: A Philosophical Primer

Explorations in Love and Sex

George Santayana, Literary Philosopher

Reality Transformed: Film as Meaning and Technique

Meaning in Life:
The Creation of Value
The Pursuit of Love
The Harmony of Nature and Spirit

The Nature of Love:
Plato to Luther
Courtly and Romantic
The Modern World

Mozart and Beethoven: The Concept of Love in their Operas

The Goals of Human Sexuality

Santayana's Aesthetics

Essays in Literary Criticism by George Santayana (editor)

The Nature and Pursuit of Love: The Philosophy of Irving Singer
(edited by David Goicoechea)

Three Philosophical Filmmakers

Hitchcock, Welles, Renoir

Irving Singer

The MIT Press
Cambridge, Massachusetts
London, England

This book was set in Palatino by The MIT Press and was printed and bound in the United States of America.

Renoir image: Courtesy Atheneum Press. From *My Life and My Films* by Jean Renoir, 1974.
Hitchcock image: Courtesy Editions Cahiers du Cinema. Originally published in *Hitchcock at Work* by Bill Krohn.

Library of Congress Cataloging-in-Publication Data

Singer, Irving.
Three philosophical filmmakers : Hitchcock, Welles, Renoir / Irving Singer.
    p. cm.
Includes bibliographical references and index.
ISBN 0-262-19501-1 (alk. paper)
1. Hitchcock, Alfred, 1899–1980—Criticism and interpretation. 2. Welles, Orson, 1915–1985—Criticism and interpretation. 3. Renoir, Jean, 1894–1979—Criticism and interpretation. I. Title.
PN1998.3.H58S54 2004
791.4302'33'0922—dc22   2003066630

To my friends, new and old, at MIT and Harvard

Contents

Preface

Since readers of my writings on film have wondered how to categorize them, a few words about my intentions may be helpful. Some reviewers have characterized *Reality Transformed: Film as Meaning and Technique*, the prequel to this book, as an essay in philosophical "humanism." That terminology is, however, somewhat misleading and in need of clarification. In this book, as in its predecessor, my humanism is mainly an attempt to show the many means by which cinematic art depends upon the creative expression of different insights into the human condition. My own perspective may presuppose a focused doctrine or general world outlook, as would anyone else's, but more immediately I wish to see how it can elucidate this art form and the possible ways of experiencing it.

The burden of the book is quite straightforward. Beginning with my previous claim that in art as a whole, and in film specifically, various problems of aesthetics and ontology disintegrate once we recognize the extensive interdependence between meaning and technique, I apply this approach to the work of the three filmmakers. I have chosen them because, in part, they are quite diverse among themselves. Moreover, all three are valued nowadays as masters of their craft. After the first chapter explains more fully why they interest me, the chapters that follow deal with their individual thoughts about the movies they made, the nature of art, the lives they led as filmmakers, and the world in which they lived. The productivity and the history of these men can, and should, be studied in other ways as well. My way of studying them is philosophical and humanistic insofar as I seek to understand their ideas and their vision as consummate artists.

Other filmmakers make a cameo appearance in my story, and I sometimes include analyses of their work. The Welles chapter, for instance, contains a lengthy discussion of John Huston's *The Dead* and its source in James Joyce's novella with the same title. Some people may think of those pages as an interlude within the harmonic texture of the book. I have no objection to their being read in that fashion. But they also serve an essential function in relation to the multiple strands of thought indigenous to my argument. Digressive as such excursions may sometimes seem, they play an integral part within the enterprise as a whole.

Among the people whose comments on this material have been of help to me, I am especially grateful to Herbert Engelhardt, Alvin Epstein, John Hildebidle, Richard A. Macksey, Martin Marks, Anne W. Singer, Ben Singer, Emily S. Singer, Josephine F. Singer, Saam Trivedi, Michael Wager, and David F. Wheeler. I am also grateful to students in my courses at MIT who lived through earlier drafts, sometimes contributing unknowably to them; and to Michael Shinagel and Marjorie Lee North, formerly master and co-master of Quincy House at Harvard, who allowed me to test my developing ideas about this and other books in talks to members of their Senior Common Room.

I. S.

Some Preliminary Remarks

In *Reality Transformed* I sketched a critique of formalist as well as realist theories of film. In the last hundred years they have had many followers among sophisticated writers about cinematic art. The contrasting emphases in these different perspectives have often nourished fruitful controversy. Throughout my book I sought to adjudicate among the varied versions of the two positions while looking for a way of harmonizing them that might preserve the reasonable claims in both. My concluding chapter outlined an alternative theory of film in an attempt to show how realists and formalists can benefit from each other's point of view. What follows here augments that effort without presupposing that the reader has much familiarity with its earlier formulation.

In moving from the earlier book to this one, I apply my speculations about the aesthetics and ontology of film to the work of three of the most renowned practitioners in that art form. I chose them in accordance with several criteria. First, I wanted representative "auteurs," directors whose mind and character retain a discernible identity throughout their output, sometimes to a greater extent, sometimes less so, but usually evident and ongoing. Since films are the product of many people who collaborate in their making, they can rarely be ascribed to a single auteur who is comparable to an individual poet or painter or composer. Above all in relation to the "studio system" and the invasive, though subtle censorship that distributors and producers impose in the name of the bottom line, no one on the set may possibly have the degree of autonomy that is still available in those other media. Nevertheless, some outstanding filmmakers have managed to mold their creations in ways that make them recognizable as more or less their own.

The auteur question will recur as we proceed, but I confess in advance that I may have prejudiced my case by choosing filmmakers whose achievements are obviously unique and plausibly judged as uniform in their totality. Given the nature of my quest, it is not surprising that the three directors I am studying usually served in several capacities—as screenplay writers or adaptors of literary texts, as directors who could be producers as well, and not infrequently as actors who also participated in the cinematography, the lighting, and the contribution of the art department. With this kind of versatility, they attained a power to show (with variable success) whatever vision of the world they wished to convey. They expressed their personal sense of reality through techniques that were available at the time and that they were especially proficient in deploying. By focusing on the general outlook of these filmmakers, who were also talented theorists, we can see how pervasively their methodologies transcend the disparity between realism and formalism. Or rather, how their transcendence of this disparity is manifest in their separate kinds of harmonization within the parameters they set for themselves.

One might additionally argue that these three are correctly thought to be "great" filmmakers *because* of their preeminent ability to unify realist and formalist attitudes. They do so in a manner that is idiosyncratic to each; and yet, they are alike in developing from film to film recurrent, though evolving, ideas they cared about as creators and as human beings. By considering what they found meaningful in life as well as the techniques by which such meaning had structural importance in their films, we may be able to detect the philosophical significance in at least a considerable part of the work they did.

Like many other artists, the three filmmakers I have selected would probably recoil at the notion that they had "philosophical" pretensions. Quoting the words of Henry V in Shakespeare's play, they might well exclaim: "We are but warriors for the working-day." That is true, and it is certainly the case that none of them pontificates about eternal verities or the analytical niceties of academic philosophy. They usually think of themselves as storytellers, as dramatists, as technicians in visual imagery, and above all as craftsmen trained to fashion and present cinematic effects. But none of this precludes their also being philosophical inasmuch as they infuse their productions with a profound perception of, and concerted interest in, the human condition as they knew it. As in all creative endeavors, the criterion of ultimate value depends upon the fecundity of their inventive imagination.

Moreover, Alfred Hitchcock, Orson Welles, and Jean Renoir are particularly intriguing because they left behind writings about film that have not been studied much thus far. Collected in recent books, these writings normally purport to deal with their own movies and their involvement in them. As a matter of fact, however, the filmmakers also comment on the nature of film itself, on other art forms, and on civilized as well as natural phenomena in life. Unlike the majority of other great or near-great filmmakers, they articulate beliefs that reveal the remarkable breadth and depth of their speculative minds. What I find most encouraging, their theorizing is almost always concrete, not abstract, and grounded in their own cumulative history of acquired knowledge within their chosen field.

Beginning with Hitchcock, I argue that he is much more than just a formalist enamored of the technical devices that he employs so effectively. In his hands they attain a meaning, whatever it may be, that lesser filmmakers do not achieve. At the opposite extreme from Hitchcock, I end with Renoir because his use of cinematic artifice constantly furthers his pre-occupation with thematic meaning while preventing it from becoming tendentious or prosaically realistic. Welles has a niche somewhere between Hitchcock and Renoir. While being what he called "a man of ideas" like the other two, he arrived on the scene much later than they did and progressively synthesized the film experience of both.[1] I do not mean that Welles sums up or completes their accomplishments, or is a better maker of movies. Despite his coming last, he can be seen as a bridge between them. While remaining an authentic originator in himself, he incorporates the formalist components in Hitchcock as well as the realist elements in Renoir.

Discussing the thinking of these artists, my initial point of departure is what they explicitly maintain on one or another occasion. In view of their influence and undoubted stature, even their casual remarks are worthy of our attention. All the same, I realize that the essays and interviews on which I draw were sometimes written long after these artists finished the movies they are interpreting in later years. Also one can never be sure that their accounts of what they did, or even of what they thought they were doing in the sometimes distant past, are entirely reliable. I am willing to take that risk because the relevant productions are so engaging and so clearly the offerings of very exceptional, though possibly representative, exemplars of their time and place. Apart from the utility of the filmmakers' statements as windows into their individual existence, these statements function—in one fashion or another—as valuable clues about the content of their films and the culture from which such artworks emanate. For that reason alone, what these three said and allowed to be printed warrants continual investigation.

With this as my basic principle, I analyze aspects of their movies in conjunction with the filmmakers' comments, without any necessary assumption about the validity of these comments. Only occasionally do I give an exhaustive treatment of the films themselves. In relation to most of the movies I discuss, a vast and often detailed critical literature has come into being with that aspiration. My book presents itself as an addendum to the excellent work that has already enriched this ever growing branch of film studies. I cite a few of its important instances in the three middle chapters, and in the family portrait I try to see how my previous discussions can be integrated with some of the suggestive books and articles about Hitchcock, Welles, and Renoir that others have published thus far.

In view of his manipulative intent, Hitchcock's work might be considered the product of a Frankenstein or proto-fascist who is extremely talented in arousing emotional responses by means of film technology. One may even think that the artistic purity Hitchcock sought is *inherently* dehumanizing.

Alfred Hitchcock

Throughout his interviews and writings about his films, Hitchcock often describes himself as someone who merely provides entertainment to an interested public. He is being truthful in saying this, not unduly modest. But then, we may ask from the very outset, does that prevent his being considered an artist whose aesthetic goals are worthy of serious investigation? Received opinion holds that entertainment, however successful it may be, is oriented toward the purveying of pleasure (in the broadest sense) rather than providing relevant and possibly profound insights about humanity as it searches for values that give meaning to life. That is what art does, we have often heard, as distinct from entertainment.

If we accept this view, if we believe that art and entertainment are inherently incompatible, or at least separate from each other, it might seem foolish to think that Hitchcock's films have philosophical scope and can be studied for their conceptual value. We may recognize the technical adroitness they often manifest, but that alone would not warrant treating his movies as anything more than highly effective divertissements.

In opposition to any such approach, I suggest that it contains a confusion about what is or is not philosophical as well as being misguided in relation to both art and entertainment. Art need not be dreary or coldly didactic, and there is nothing in the idea of entertainment that necessarily excludes the presentation of a meaningful perspective as one of its legitimate possibilities.

In great art the philosophical, also in the broadest sense of the word, not only accompanies whatever elements that entertain a receptive audience but also permeates the aesthetic fabric of the work itself. Art becomes philosophical when it offers probing insights into our reality that are valuable to people who have learned how to appreciate them. Not always but not infrequently, entertainment is capable of awakening our susceptibility to new ideas. It does that through an immediacy of comprehension that causes them to be quickly digested and fully savored. It may even evoke reactions that generate in the recipients personal yet appropriate ideas of their own.

When this happens, entertainment is integral to the achievement of artistic truth while also being a vehicle that conveys this type of truth. In that event, the formal structure through which a film (or any other work of art) succeeds in entertaining becomes the expression of an outlook that has conceptual import over and beyond the profundities that may or may not belong to its referential content. Hitchcock's art is worth studying because it shows the worthlessness of commonplace dichotomies between form and content which have been ordained or assumed by most traditional aestheticians.

To say this much, however, is to say that we can disregard Hitchcock's ritual statements about his intentions. In one place he repeats Sam Goldwyn's assertion that messages should be sent by Western Union, not by the movies his studio makes.

One need only reply that communications—whether aesthetic or otherwise—involve much more than just the sending of "messages." That term signifies a very special kind of communication, and therefore only a meager portion of what is significant on any level in both art and entertainment.

One theorist from whom Hitchcock originally learned his craft as a director was Sergei Eisenstein. From his formalistic approach Hitchcock attained a refined awareness of how cinematic effects can exercise great influence over the reactions of an audience. Eisenstein sought to use the artificial devices of film as a means of disseminating the director's ideological perspective through techniques that manipulate the feelings of a moviegoing public. Like other formalists of his period, he extolled the capacity of films to *do* something to the mind and responsiveness of their patrons. For Eisenstein this usually meant enunciating a political program by means of the mesmerizing technology in film, which is incessantly transforming reality toward that end.

Hitchcock does not try to impart overtly propagandistic ideas, though he often inserts a vaguely democratic aura within his formal design. What he gleans most notably from Eisenstein is the conviction that a filmmaker's subtle use of the camera can grip the impulses and even purposive attitudes of almost anyone who observes the finished product. Eisenstein did what he did in the hope of getting people to engage in action that would have importance to them as moral and social beings. Hitchcock does not think of his audience in that way. He treats them merely as individuals who can be induced to undergo strong emotions that may have little relevance to either their political beliefs or communal involvement. In this sense, Hitchcock is a more puristic formalist than Eisenstein himself.

In a documentary about Hitchcock, one of his associates recounts a conversation in which the director says to him: "What we're doing is, we're playing we're sitting at an organ and we're pressing this chord which makes an audience go 'oooh,' and then we press this chord which makes them laugh. And we're just playing on them. . . . Someday we won't need the movie. We'll be able to wire them so that we can just sit at the organ and make them have all the sensations that they have seeing the picture." This is reported by Ernest Lehman, who wrote the screenplay of *North by Northwest.* In a later documentary about the making of that film, Lehman repeats the anecdote but somewhat changes the words he ascribed to Hitchcock.[1]

❂

Eisenstein used the term *montage* to designate his technique for affecting audience response through cinematic communication. His thinking about this phenomenon developed over a period of years and finally comprised an intricate network of disparate notions. For us it will suffice to focus on remarks that Hitchcock made about montage in several contexts. He speaks of it as the basis of the "pure cinema" to which he himself subscribed. In discussing *Sabotage,* he says the following about the scene in which Sylvia Sidney kills her husband:

It was a supper table. The man complained about the color of the greens. All I did was to show the close-up of the woman, about ordinary bust size, and the man the same. Sometimes the man from her eye-line, sometimes the woman from his eye-line. That was all we were concerned with. The most important aspect of the scene was her hand. It was essential to play up to her using the carving knife. She carved meat with it, and then found herself helping him to vegetables with the carving knife. She realized what was wrong. Then I showed her hand dropping the knife, trying to get rid of it, and then having to pick it up because more meat needed carving—and dropping it with a clatter. Then immediately a close-up of the man hearing the clatter. Then the woman's hand clasping and unclasping over the handle of the carving knife. All we saw was a foreground of a table, glasses and cutlery, and her hands hovering. Then back to him. He got up, and the camera tilting up with him. He realizes his danger. I never bothered to show the room, and I allowed that man to go right past the camera towards the woman; and then again he comes to her and he looks down, and the camera goes right from him, following his thought, down to the knife and her hand still hovering over it. And then he makes a grab and she gets it first. Then the two hands: her hands win. And then all you see is two figures, and the man gives a cry and falls.[2]

Hitchcock explains his reliance upon montage in this scene as the way in which he can make the murder seem "inevitable without any blame attaching to the woman. I wanted to preserve sympathy for her, so that it was essential that she fought against something stronger than herself."[3] Hitchcock claims that this revelation of the character's feelings requires an approach on the part of the director that is radically different from the usual procedure. Instead of recording a continuous succession of events that would be shortened and reunited in the cutting room, the director must have a prior conception of the response he wishes to achieve and how it can be evoked: "To have shot all that in a long view would have been useless. It had to be made up of these little pieces. With a first-class director the final cutting is a simple job, if he has constructed the scene in his mind in advance and knows what he wants to create."[4]

Several things are worth noting as at least implied by this method. It places upon a director the responsibility for controlling not only the overall shape of the film he makes but also every detail of its contents and construction. Instead of reproducing the world as it is or as a backdrop for telling a story or providing a message, the director presents an event in the narrative through a process that only cinema can have. The director chooses and orders the "little pieces" of cinematic material in accordance with his prior decision about the motivation of some character he has imagined—the uncontrollable sense of inevitability experienced by the woman in relation to the knife that will then kill her husband. Finally, the director imposes an interpretation, in this case a moral judgment about the culpability, or lack of it, in what the wife does. She is to be seen as fighting blamelessly against "something stronger than herself." All this is arranged to stimulate specific feelings of the audience. Our sympathy for the murderer is to be preserved while we remain engrossed in the observation of a brutal event that has upon us a cathartic effect issuing out of the particular situation and its place within the narrative.

As a further illustration of Hitchcock's ideas about montage, consider Tippi Hedren's ordeal in the attic of the besieged house in *The Birds*. After slowly climbing the stairs to the top floor in a scene of isomorphically mounting tension, she is suddenly attacked by wave after wave of birds. They are mainly seagulls like the one that had wounded her in the rowboat. That strike served as a momentary jolt to prepare us for the longer sequence that now unfolds. As in *Sabotage* the event in the attic lasts several minutes. It consists of a large number of discontinuous close-ups organized to simulate continuity. In its sensory power and rhythmic forcefulness, it becomes an emotional climax in the plot.

Hitchcock says that his employment of such montage defines the nature of pure cinema, as opposed to the simple filming of a novel or the photographing of a stage play: "Pure cinema is complementary pieces of film put together, like notes of music make a melody. There are two primary uses of cutting or montage in film: montage to create ideas, and montage to create violence and emotions."[5] He refers to *Rear Window* in demonstrating both types of montage: the first occurring in that film's ability to manifest ideas by cutting back and forth to what James Stewart sees (and shows in his facial expressions) as he watches what is happening outside his window; the second, in its manner of depicting violent behavior and emotional turmoil during Stewart's struggle with the murderer who has burst into his room. If the camera had viewed the latter from a distance or in continuous shots, the fearfulness of the encounter would have been much diminished. By juxtaposing small bits of imagery in close-up and precisely organized among themselves, Hitchcock tells us, he was able to involve the spectator's feelings most emphatically. When Stewart is pushed out of the window, Hitchcock shoots that "from a distance, the complete action," and without any montage. There was no longer a violent or emotional confrontation in the narrative, and therefore no further need to arouse a strong response.

In *Psycho* there are two familiar scenes that exemplify Hitchcock's use of montage. One involves the detective walking warily up the stairs in the Bates house. We feel the suspense of his approaching the room in which we know that danger lies. Suddenly the camera lights upon a menacing figure of someone who storms out of this room. The camera zooms to a close-up of the startled face of the detective as he is being stabbed. We seem to see the knife enter his body, though in reality there is only a series of simulated jabs that are filmed to appear consecutive. Particularly since the detective is a likable, at least innocuous-looking, person, our feeling is highly reactive to this close-up of the horrific assault he endures.

Even more famous is the shower sequence in *Psycho*. Janet Leigh is sitting at a desk in her room in the Bates Motel. On a piece of scrap paper she calculates how much she still retains of the $40,000 she has stolen. She tears up the paper, walks to the bathroom, throws the pieces into the toilet, flushes it, and then casually removes her dressing gown. She is now naked, but we see only her shoulders and her legs. When she steps into the bathtub for her shower, the camera is positioned outside the shower curtain. Once she is in the shower—and thereafter for most of the scene—the camera is also inside, watching at first her upturned face as she enjoys the flow of water on it. Shots of the water descending from the shower spout augment the sense of comfort and abandon that she is experiencing.

Our anxiety is aroused when we notice a darkened shape on the other side of the curtain. She does not see this, but we know it must be a menacing individual who has now entered the bathroom. There has been no sound thus far except for the rushing of the water. When the intruder quickly pulls back the shower curtain and begins to slash at the naked woman with a kitchen knife, loud and high-pitched screeching noises provide an eerie and relentless accompaniment to the rhythmic thrusts. While they continue, we watch the attack's effect upon the victim from outside the bathtub—in other words, from the point of view of the assailant.

The woman shrieks in pain and terror as the knife strikes her repeatedly; when the attack stops and the murderer leaves the bathroom, her back slumps against the porcelain wall and she collapses in the bathtub. Her last act consists in a desperate gripping of the shower curtain, which is torn down by the sheer weight of her body. The darkened water flowing into the circular drain at the base of the bathtub is her blood. With an almost clinical fascination, the cinematography studies in close-up her now immobile face, the eyes open, fixed, lifeless. The camera focuses on one of the eyes and then moves slowly around it in an arclike movement that is almost but not quite circular. The camera then creates a transitional closure to the scene by swinging around and panning out of the bathroom and into the adjacent bedroom. In a lingering shot, whose meaning is evident to us, it stares at the desk on which the stolen money lies hidden in a folded newspaper.

In an interview in which he states that "pure cinema is pieces of film assembled," Hitchcock gives a brief analysis of this scene to substantiate his belief that "*Psycho* is probably one of the most cinematic pictures I've ever made." He then goes on: "Because there you had montage in the bathtub killing where the whole thing is purely an illusion. No knife ever touched any woman's body in that scene. Ever. But [despite] the rapidity of the shots, it took a week. The little pieces of film were probably not more than four or five inches long. They were on the screen for a fraction of a second."[6]

When he discusses the assault on the detective as he walks upstairs in *Psycho*, Hitchcock describes his use of montage in a similar fashion: "I took the camera very high, extremely high. So that he was a small figure. And the figure of the woman came out, very small, dashed at him with a knife. And the knife went out, and we're still very high, and as the knife started to come down, I cut to the big head of the man. . . . So the big head came as a shock to the audience, and to the man himself. His surprise was expressed by the *size* of the image. . . . In music going high would be like the tremolo of the violins and suddenly the brass goes GRRR! as it comes out with the big head expressing his shock. Now that's juxtaposition of pieces of the film to create emotion."[7]

Instructive as these remarks surely are, much more is at stake. Particularly in the shower scene, Hitchcock's camera is in fact controlled by considerations that exceed the bounds of what he calls pure cinema. In various writings he acknowledges that public opinion, and his own concern about censorship, made it imperative that the erotogenic zones of the unclothed female must not be shown on screen. Though Janet Leigh's stand-in, and at times she herself, was naked or topless during the filming, the sequence artfully avoids any lurid exhibition. As Hitchcock mentions in the statement from which I quoted, the knife never touches the body of the actress. The intensity of violence and implicit sexuality is left to the imagination of the spectators, with the preconceived purpose of arousing different affective reactions in them. One reason Hitchcock made the film in black and white was his belief that the sight of red blood flowing down the drain might be more than the audience could take. He rightly surmised that he would better attain the emotionality for which he strove by cleverly manipulating the little bits of film in his suggestive montage rather than by the more sensationalistic use of color.

�֍

The aesthetic success of Hitchcock's approach becomes evident if we contrast his *Psycho* with its 1998 remake. Gus Van Sant, the director of the later project, tells us that his is not the usual kind of remake. Although it changes the narrative date from the 1950s to the late 1990s, employs color (sometimes vivid color) instead of black and white, and substitutes actors who inevitably project personae somewhat unlike the earlier ones, 95 percent of the shots are more or less the same as Hitchcock's. Some of the 5 percent that are Van Sant's alone are quite significant. For instance, when Norman Bates spies through a peephole upon his new client at the motel as she undresses in her room, the movement of his arm indicates in this version that he is masturbating. For the most part, however, Van Sant wanted to *re-perform* the Hitchcock film instead of making it over. As in the art of music different orchestras can give their own rendition of a symphonic or operatic composition, he informs us, so too was he trying to re-present Hitchcock's cinematic masterpiece as faithfully as possible, even though he was making his own movie almost forty years later.

Before questioning the degree of fidelity that Van Sant may actually have attained, we may well wonder about the analogy between music and film that he proposes. We generally think of remakes as different films, just as film adaptations of a novel are recognized to differ from their literary source in ways that are fundamental to each art form. In music, the situation is not comparable. A symphony or opera remains basically the same despite its variability from performance to performance because its character is explicitly defined by what the composer has written out. He or she specifies the notes to be played, the instruments to be used, and usually the tempi and expressive elaborations to be followed. Much is, and has to be, left to the discretion of individual performers onstage and in the pit; but too great a deviation from the musical essentials would lead one to conclude that the integrity of the original composition has been violated.

As a consequence, Van Sant's analogy is indefensible. Film is not a living art of the sort that music is. Both originate with artists who are alive, and both are subject to mechanical duplication through recordings that are more or less identical each time they are played. The film we watch on television is the same as the film we watch on the much larger screen of a movie house, and this relationship is unquestionably analogous to hearing a symphony on a receiver at home and hearing it in a concert hall. But the movie differs from the symphony or opera in being an aesthetic artifact that exists only as an entity *on* film (or some equivalent). Each time the film is played, the mechanism of projection causes it to be the same; and apart from its capacity to be projected in one circumstance or another it is not a movie. For music this is not the case. Though symphonies and operas can be read on the page or heard in an indefinite number of equally valid interpretations, each performance is a personal *rendition* of a composer's score. Nothing like that belongs to cinematic experience. Every remake is literally a different movie, including Van Sant's despite his attempt to duplicate almost all of Hitchcock's shots.

The second *Psycho* is especially interesting because it reveals, inadvertently of course, how much greater was Hitchcock's technique in all the replicated shots. The new version of the shower sequence does contain modifications that are entirely befitting—the figure being calculated at the desk is now $400,000 instead of $40,000; the present actress, Anne Heche, walks to the bathroom in more flamboyant sandals than before; the shower spout is octagonal in shape rather than round; and the accoutrements of the room are those of a modern motel equipped with up-to-date lighting. But even these minor variants, meager as they might seem, alter the previous effect. Together with the bright illumination, they curtail the creepiness and outlandishness that Hitchcock instilled into the Bates Motel, isolated and abandoned as it is in its period because the world has built a new highway and so deprived it not only of clients but also of routine contact with human beings in general.

These revisions are accentuated by other changes that Van Sant introduces. The murder of the girl in the shower is both more realistic than the original and less so. More realistic because so little is left to the imagination. We now see a few seconds longer, and presumably the victim does as well, the large knife that the assailant holds aloft before using it; we see the many wounds it inflicts on the back as well as the front of the victim's body, whereas in Hitchcock only one is shown and that very briefly; we see the streaks of blood that smear from the woman's back as she succumbs and then slips down against the tile wall; we see a great deal more blood flowing down the drain; and we see all this in living color, and therefore in the fashion of a current action film providing audiences nowadays with what they demand as proof of authenticity in the portrayal of human butchery. But this portrayal has become so habitual to us that our emotions are less engaged than they were, and still are, in Hitchcock's somewhat restrained and vastly stylized treatment. His less is more.

The emotional effect in Van Sant's filming is further diminished by unfelicitous shots he has included on his own. As a correlative to the fading of consciousness that occurs while the woman is being stabbed, Van Sant flashes an image of clouds slowly moving in a darkened sky. Later we see an image of her pupil totally dilated just before she passes out. One can only wonder why Van Sant inserted these additions. They not only go beyond Hitchcock but also serve as a needless distraction from what Van Sant presumably wished to reenact.

When the blood is rushing down the drain at the bottom of the tub, Van Sant takes further liberties that are counter-productive. He follows Hitchcock in showing the open eye (no longer dilated), but then he has the camera circle twice around it. In Hitchcock's film the camera barely suggests this iso-morphism in shape between the drain and the open eye. Throughout his movies he often uses circular movements by the camera to call attention to some affective affiliation, usually an attachment of one sort or another between people in love. His deft presentation here, in this contrasting event, of murder rather than love, registers as a sharp, even bitter, commentary on the fragility of what we value in life. In Van Sant's movie the accentuation of this idea seems grossly overdone, and such as to make us question the coherence of his intention. Had he forgotten how minimal was Hitchcock's turning of the camera? Was he afraid that his audience would miss the point? Or was he trying to express the fact that he responded more acutely to this event than Hitchcock did?

In both versions the scene ends with the camera traveling from the open eye to the folded newspaper on the desk. This reminds us of what the deceased had lusted for all along, and so the shot sustains our desire to know what will now happen to the money in the newspaper. In Van Sant's movie, however, the lifeless body has splayed itself across the low wall of the bathtub. We are given a view of the actress's naked backside looking like an ineloquent slab of meat, and doubtless that is what Van Sant meant to suggest when he made this alteration.

But the posture is such that we can't imagine how her head could have turned to the requisite angle of alignment with the newspaper in the next room. As a result, Hitchcock's masterful transition from eye to money is completely undermined.

In the detective scene it is crucial that the juxtaposition of the shots on the stairs be balanced precisely. The ones that are "very high" must not be so high that the figure of the ascending man seems tiny, while the close-up of his face as he is struck must be unexpectedly large. Hitchcock is able to shock the viewers at this moment because he has presented the succession of tremolo and GRRR!, in his analogy to music, with great finesse. In the Van Sant remake the ratio of size has been tampered with. The high shot is not equally high and the close-up is not as close as in the Hitchcock. Moreover, the rhythm of this entire sequence is thrown off, when the detective is stabbed, by the odd and slightly ludicrous inclusion of a cow in pasture and then a nude shot of Anne Heche looking into the camera. One is not offended by the fact that Hitchcock did not use these images, but rather by their being a pointless dampening of the acute violence in the sudden attack.

Some of the other changes that occur in the remake have less importance than one might have thought. Though it matters that the two principal females—the murdered woman and her sister—are brought into the present moment, along with the setting as a whole, not much is affected by their being depicted in the current feminist mode and therefore different in their personality from what they were before. The homicidal operation of Norman Bates's mind is made neither more nor less understandable by the suggestion that he is secretly enraged by liberated women. Hitchcock pointedly remarks that there is little characterization in this film. In answer to a

question that suggests that in *Psycho* he was directing the audience more than the actors, he replies: "Yes. It's using pure
cinema to cause the audience to emote. I think that in *Psycho*
there is no identification with the characters. There wasn't time
to develop them and there was no need to."[8] Though one might
question the accuracy of Hitchcock's denial that there is much
characterization in *Psycho*, his expression of intent can be
applied to Van Sant's production as well as to his own. But only
the earlier film is able to carry out that guiding principle with a
singleminded ability to manipulate the feelings of an audience.

❁

Hitchcock's adherence to the concept of what he calls pure
cinema shows itself in the relish with which he describes his
cleverness as a technician. He is always preoccupied with
questions of how to use his tools and available technology for
the sake of achieving some effect. The remark that he quotes
himself as having used to help different actors who experience
problems in their performance—"It's only a movie!"—speaks
volumes about his approach to his art form. The human reality
that enters into film creativity at various levels is, for him,
subordinate to the technical solutions he manages to reach. He
does not see the real as an ultimate and possibly unknowable
entity that art must seek to penetrate, to disclose, or even to
explicate. The world that Hitchcock portrays is recognizable as
the one that we encounter daily, and yet for him it exists
mainly as something in our experience that lures us into the
artificiality of his aesthetic construction. It is never allowed to
deflect us from the business at hand, which resides in the
evocation of emotions that are usually muffled, or submerged,
in life.

One might reply that since Hitchcock's cinematography is so thoroughly realistic he enables us to view the world as any traditional realist would. But even to the extent that this idea can be defended, there is very little that Hitchcock wishes to tell us about the world, either through perceptual or conceptual means. I will later modify this statement, when I discuss Hitchcock's ideas about "the ordinary." Apart from them, however, Hitchcock works from virtually no polemical or ideological stance, and no meditative or analytical probing into the facts about our ontological being. Though he is often charged with having had an excessive interest in sexuality, possibly resulting from his repressed upbringing, he studies its problems only to a minimal degree. He exploits sex in his art, using it primarily as something that a contemporary audience cares about. But even sexual violence—as in the brutal scenes of *Frenzy* or *The Lodger* or *Marnie*, where the husband rapes his wife on screen—is for him just a common event whose showing can be expected to shock the observers.

Throughout his very long career, Hitchcock retained a precise intuition of who these observers might be. He knew that moviegoing men and women do not go to "the pictures" in order to be educated or uplifted. They go to be delighted and excited, exhilarated by the comedy and enthralled by the drama, especially when the two are interwoven. Above all, they want to see a picturization of themselves and their endangered ideals, provided that neither is articulated too laboriously. To satisfy this broad-based demand, Hitchcock films often concentrate on the life and amusements of the majority of any population, those who belong to the middle and lower strata of society, as in the music hall scenes at the beginning and the end of *The 39 Steps*. But he can also reach higher if the plot requires it—as in *Suspicion* or *Notorious* or *North by Northwest*—yet not so high either socially or intellectually as to risk losing the interest of the mass audience he has in mind. Despite his frequent cynicism about the rectitude of those who wield power and influence in the world, he is scarcely concerned about the political problems of either upper-class or lower-class people.

Nor is investigatory psychological realism his forte. He pretends to accept and express psychoanalytic ideas in various films—notably in the pathological aspects of *Rope, Vertigo, Rear Window*, and above all *Spellbound*, in which he includes Salvador Dali's surrealistic reminders of Freudian dream symbolism. He tendentiously tacks on that tedious explanation by the psychiatrist at the end of *Psycho* in order to explain why Norman Bates behaved as he did. In *To Catch a Thief* he artfully develops the notion that the family jewels are attractive to a former thief like Cary Grant because they represent Grace Kelly's sexuality, as in the explosively orgasmic fireworks scene. But in every case it is the filmic use of these alleged realities that he cares about rather than any clarification of them or their human circumstances. From that point of view Hitchcock can be taken as a half-hearted realist, and radically different from the authentic ones who wish to *examine* reality through their cinematic techniques. For him, reality is only a convenient, albeit necessary, setting for some formalist aspiration that matters most to him.

Hitchcock's ideal of pure cinema is best illustrated by his television programs, which have been played and replayed for decades, at once becoming an important part of American culture. Each program was sculpted as a carefully crafted sequence, an hour or half-hour in length, superficially realistic with respect to situations drawn from ordinary life, but in fact serving as devices by which Hitchcock and his assistants could captivate the public through subliminal procedures that he controlled so well. His unequaled success is gauged by the endurance of the entire series through reruns that continue to mesmerize millions of people across the globe. It keeps them glued to their TV screen from one commercial to the next.

*

In view of this manipulative intent, Hitchcock's work might be considered the product of a Frankenstein or proto-fascist who is extremely talented in arousing emotional responses by means of film technology. One may even think that the artistic purity Hitchcock sought is *inherently* dehumanizing. When I was young, I held that opinion. I tended to agree with Welles when he said at one time that he "detested" Hitchcock's use of the camera, and on another occasion concluded that "his contrivances remain contrivances, no matter how marvelously they're conceived and executed."[9]

Hitchcock tried to justify his type of film by saying that it enhances the social and affective life of the spectators without indulging in excessive sensationalism. He claimed that he satisfied a deep and pervasive need that many persons have— a need to be frightened. He likened his movies to roller-coaster rides, for which people give others money so that they themselves can be scared under conditions in which there is little or no danger: "Fear and fear not, that is the essence of melodrama."[10]

Hitchcock defends this approach in several places, but most explicitly in an essay entitled "The Enjoyment of Fear." He says that while few of us seek fear "in the real or personal sense," millions do so vicariously in the darkened ambience of a theater or moviehouse: "They identify themselves with fictitious characters who are experiencing fear, and experience, themselves, the same fear sensations (the quickened pulse, the alternately dry and damp palm, etc.), but without paying the price."[11]

The two propositions in this quotation are both essential to Hitchcock's argument. To explain the very concept of *enjoying* fear as that which underlies his aesthetic and presumably moral goal in the art of film, he emphasizes the human need to experience this response in a situation that does not involve actual suffering or harm. But we may ask: "Suffering and harm to whom?" Not counting the villains or ne'er-do-wells who end up badly in his movies, the Hitchcock heroes or sympathetic characters with whom we identify often suffer very much. As protagonists in the narrative, they undergo real and harmful distress. Among those in the audience, this is true only of the unsatisfiable movie critics. All the rest have bought tickets in the hope of enjoying the sight of fearful occurrences being displayed out there on the screen.

These events may in fact be frightening to children, whose absorption as they watch can be emotionally overpowering, but usually not to grown-ups. Having been asked by an interviewer whether he himself experiences fear while watching movies, Hitchcock honestly replies that he does not do so frequently. When *Psycho* first came out, there were reports of young women who said they were afraid to take a shower for some time after seeing the film, and possibly some of these women had sweaty palms during the movie. Nevertheless one can't believe that they were representative of the audience as a whole. In a subtle and intriguing way, Hitchcock misconstrued the nature of the responsiveness he was so adept at eliciting. It may have registered as fear only rarely and in few observers.

For one thing, the analogy of the roller-coaster or any other thrill that people relish is fallacious. Attending a movie, even a "thriller," is not the same as confronting real dangers in the world. The point about activities like walking a tightrope, auto racing, mountain climbing, or big-game hunting—just to mention Hitchcock's other examples—is the fact that *in them-selves* these all induce fearfulness. They cultivate feelings of fear that can be surmounted, and even enjoyed, although the conditions in which they arise are truly perilous. When we watch a movie, however, we enter into another kind of circumstance. There is nothing inherently frightening or immediately dangerous about watching films. We know that we can always walk out of the theater if we so desire. We also know that the characters cannot, however much they may resemble us. Within their fictional world, they are forced to face some grim reality they may or may not be able to escape. Even when the spectators feel excited by events that make the *movie* exciting, the two types of excitement are not the same. Throughout the performance the viewers are there to have a good time, while the characters, in their own reality, may be going through hell.

For this reason we need to describe spectatorial response in a manner that contravenes what Hitchcock says. The specta-tor's enjoyment of fear to which he refers is an enjoyment of someone else's fear, that someone else being the fictitious personage who represents people that are indeed real and yet not as any of these characters are. Viewers whose highly sensitive imaginings are ensnared by dangers within a movie may feel what is fearful for the characters so strongly that they experience a comparable fear themselves. But this will not happen to most people, or even very many, and it cannot be a criterion for the common and aesthetically relevant appreciation of cinematic effects.

Finally, there is something wrong in Hitchcock's repeated confession about his failing as a director when he allowed the boy in *Sabotage* to be blown up by a bomb he was carrying unawares on the streetcar. As a corollary to his claim that the enjoyment of fear is a consummation his art makes possible for millions of men and women, Hitchcock insists not only that the clientele must feel safe while enjoying their fear but also that the fictional characters with whom they identify must not pay too high a price for being participants in whatever fearful events befall them. As a consequence of this reasoning, Hitchcock feels that he violated his own artistic principles in having the boy killed. But does he mean to suggest that only nasty or evil characters with whom one cannot identify should die in the senseless way that the boy does? Hitchcock's powerful and beautifully constructed *Frenzy* derives much of its strength from the fact that the two women who are brutally murdered in it are likable, even generous and warm-hearted, persons with whom a contemporary audience can readily identify. And even *Sabotage* would have lost much of its authenticity without the death of the young boy. That is what leads his grief-stricken sister to avenge him by murdering the brutish husband who was instrumental in his death.

❀

This confusion on Hitchcock's part is compounded by difficulties I discern in an ambitious and far-reaching distinction that he makes among alternate types of movies. In his interviews, he mentions differences among a suspense film, a thriller, a mystery, and a whodunit; and in one of his articles he maintains that his own movies are not horror films. Describing the first of these five genres, he asks us to imagine two men who are sitting at a table, talking and having a drink. We are also to imagine there is a bomb under the table that is timed to go off at any moment. This is paradigmatic of suspense. It requires us, the imaginative spectators, to know in advance the factual setting of the unwelcome condition these two men are in. We feel anxiety for them, Hitchcock says, though they themselves do not realize the risk they are running just in being at the table and calmly conversing with each other.

According to Hitchcock, for there to be suspense it is crucial that the bomb not go off. If that happened, we would have nothing further to wait for apprehensively. The audience might experience shock, but suspense as a cinematic effect would no longer exist. This point is relevant to Hitchcock's self-criticism for having the boy in *Sabotage* die when the bomb explodes. Not only does Hitchcock feel in retrospect that he violated the principle of "fear and fear not," but also he remarks that the entire structure of suspense was vitiated by this termination to it. I myself find it hard to know what he means in this connection. The suspense would have had to end eventually, one way or another, and the shocking culmination he chose for this sequence is the kind of melodramatic climax he uses quite successfully in many of his films. I return later to this problem.

At the opposite pole from the suspense film, Hitchcock places the whodunit. In that genre the audience does not have prior knowledge of the facts in some beguiling situation. The pertinent details are disclosed at the end, not at the beginning.

Clues are made available from the start, but they are merely tantalizing and do not create suspense. Though Hitchcock does not say much about his own employment of whodunit effects, these often serve as major components in his films. They occur in the search for the guilty man in *Young and Innocent* who blinks his eyes but is otherwise unknown; for the identity of the murderer in *Spellbound* who appears in Gregory Peck's troubled dream but is unrecognizable; for the person who occasioned the fatal trouble with Harry; for the cause of the suspicious disappearance of the sick woman across the courtyard in *Rear Window*, or of the lady who vanishes in that earlier film; and so on. The bits of evidence about some homicide, as it usually is, are fundamental to the story, but only at the denouement do we learn what they signify and who has dunit.

Extrapolating beyond Hitchcock's few remarks, we can envisage the mystery story—in contrast to the whodunit—as a narrative about some unknown occurrence in which there may not be any criminality at all. Watching *Spellbound* we are puzzled by the strange but not illegal behavior of Gregory Peck, whose hidden agony Ingrid Bergman must try to unearth. She is a practicing psychiatrist but her expertise shows itself as a form of detective work. In *Vertigo* James Stewart, who is a professional detective in need of psychiatric help himself, seeks to clarify the bizarre activities of Kim Novak. Mysterious elements, like the phrase "39 steps" or the arcane meaning of pi in *Torn Curtain*, frequently pervade Hitchcock's movies and readily interweave with the suspense that results from the search to comprehend them.

The thriller movie uses suspense but does so for a special end that goes beyond it alone. Suspense is an affective state that ranges from a sense of mounting terror, at one extreme, to feelings, at the other, that are much more tranquil: inquisitiveness about a problem that has been posed, idle but engaged curiosity about an odd event and its consequences as they unfold in the plot, concern about the welfare of fictional persons whom we find interesting for whatever reason, or just aesthetic involvement in a fascinating story. For a film to be a thriller, however, or to have the distinctive ingredients of one, it must keenly vivify our sensory experience through carefully timed excitation that occurs at crucial junctures in the narrative. Given the nature of film, these are visual or auditory, though sometimes kinesthetic, components of our consciousness. The images reach out and activate our sense organs in ways that can be unpleasant at the moment though quite acceptable and even welcome as artful contrivances that make it possible for us to enjoy the movie. The thriller plays upon the fact that in the proper context everyone likes to be thrilled.

Horror films are somewhat different from thrillers. In a 1936 essay entitled "Why 'Thrillers' Thrive," Hitchcock contrasts the two. Thrillers he commends on moral as well as aesthetic grounds. He argues that our natural state is such that we human beings need to have "shake-ups," or else "we grow sluggish and jellified." Since civilized existence does not provide sufficient thrills, "we have to experience them artificially, and the screen is the best medium for this."[12] Particularly if it is what Hitchcock calls "a well-made film," a thriller can get members of the audience to feel as if they too are participating in the exciting events while also knowing that they themselves are not in any danger. But the horror film works too hard at this and is therefore repellent, Hitchcock insists. He finds "unnatural" the excitement it creates: "The term [*horror*] meaning 'extreme aversion,' has been loosely applied to films, which to supply the desired emotional jolt, exploit sadism, perversion, beastiality, and deformity. . . . This is utterly wrong, being vicious and dangerous. It is permissible for a film to be horrific, but not horrible; and between the two there is a dividing line which is apparent to all thinking people."[13]

By making this distinction, Hitchcock would seem to be invoking criteria of good taste or what is morally permissible. He gives us no reason to believe that the horror films he describes cannot deliver "the desired emotional jolt" as productively, and with as much safety for the audience, as thrillers that do not go to such lengths. In his own career one observes a development in the direction of ever closer proximity to the horror films that he is here condemning. We need only compare *The Short Night* with *The Lodger* to see how much he finally deviated from the rigid demarcation asserted in this early statement.[14]

Throughout his work Hitchcock often invokes a *sense* of horror without allowing it to turn his thrillers into horror films. We undergo a feeling of instant dread when Cary Grant is strafed in a cornfield in *North by Northwest*, and when he drives drunkenly at the edge of a cliff, toward the beginning of that film, and later when he and Eva Marie Saint dangle from another cliff. We have similar feelings when sudden and sometimes fatal stabbings occur in Hitchcock films. In *The 39 Steps* a horrifying burst of adrenalin occurs when the hero Hannay is shot point-blank in the heart, followed by a rapid cut and moment of blackness on the screen that makes us think this is his end. The combination of horror and thrill is wonderfully captured earlier in that movie when the train that carries Hannay to Scotland goes through a tunnel and its whistle shrieks in synchrony with the cleaning woman's open (but silent) mouth as she screams upon discovering the dead woman in Hannay's London apartment.

At the same time, it is also true that Hitchcock employs the element of horror only sparsely and within special, limited parameters in which it can have its greatest effect. In the archetypical horror film that Hitchcock reviles, the emotional impact is often impaired, and usually lacking in aesthetic quality, precisely because it is overdone. It either excludes any other mode of imaginative presentation or else is too gross in itself, too thoroughly oblivious to the subtleties of human affect. On Hitchcock's palette, horror is but one among other instrumentalities that he blends within the artistic and highly variegated complexity of his narratives.

Complementary to his sophistication about these five genres, there is in Hitchcock's methodology a supervening attempt to integrate and harmonize the values of them all. That requires accommodations among them that he understands very well. He emphasizes that a director always has to adjudicate between the suspenseful and the shocking. These follow different paths and are incompatible in any single moment of the film. Since it is predicated upon prior knowledge the audience has been given, suspense is incapable of creating the shake-up that comes from being startled by the unexpected. Resulting from a sudden thrust upon one's sensory faculties, shock eliminates the possibility of any simultaneous suspense. In combining the two within the totality of a film, Hitchcock remarks that he devotes two-thirds of the movie to suspense and only a third to events that are shocking.

Hitchcock distinguishes between two types of suspense. What he calls "objective suspense" occurs when the audience observes an engaging but unresolved occurrence that is portrayed as happening in the outside world. For "subjective suspense" to exist, the audience must be shown what arises in the mind, or appears to the eye, of one or another character. *Rear Window* presents itself from the perspective of a man who is immobilized, with his leg in a cast. Correspondingly, the suspensefulness of this movie is predicated upon the cinematic subjectivity that largely consists in revealing the man's thoughts and perceptions as he stares out the window. The audience is led to wonder about the significance of what he sees at any time, about the evidence of a possible crime that he accumulates from his detached but prolonged vantage point, and about the imminence of dangers that he too runs when his passivity turns into active involvement.

The core concept in *Rear Window* is the same as, or similar to, the theme in the film *I Am a Camera*, directed by Henry Cornelius, based on the stage play with the same title by John Van Druten, and drawn from writings of Christopher Isherwood. In a major portion of his *Berlin Stories*, Isherwood depicts the state of a young and alienated intellectual who tries to find his place in a hostile and evil environment that systematically rejects him because of his foreign nationality, his deviant sexual orientation, and his professional being as one who watches, reports, and endlessly analyzes practical realities to which he does not, cannot, belong. The protagonist must ask himself whether it is justifiable, or morally sufficient, for him to live as he does, resembling a camera that looks but does not intervene in whatever it registers.

Hitchcock's film delves into the meaning of the underlying metaphor in all this. Hitchcock uses a real camera, or several, in a way that makes us think about the aesthetics and the ontology of the art form that depends so much on this visual equipment. He acquaints us with a character who is himself a working photographer, currently incapacitated and therefore able to ponder at leisure over his role in life while also remaining in position to use the tools of his profession—long-distance lenses in particular—to remotely scan his neighbors' lives. He becomes immersed in their existence not by protesting against brutal thugs, the Nazis, as in the Isherwood original, but by helping *through his powers of observation* to protect his and their community from a similarly destructive constituent of it. As an outcome of the romance that furthers this narrative theme, the detached personification of the camera rejoins what is normal in the human race by finally marrying the sexually desirable woman he has been eluding thus far. Their harrowing but successful pursuit of the murderer has made the difference. The evasive male is able to accept the bonds of marriage now despite the sacrifices that it may entail in relation to his creativity as a photographer (or filmmaker?).

Deliminating this generic problem through his inclusion of subjective suspense, Hitchcock relies on the kind of montage that he referred to as a means of "creating ideas" by filming, back and forth, first James Stewart's facial expressions and then the objects or events that Stewart sees. Hitchcock resorts to this technique in all his films, and above all when he has the camera record a conversation through successive over-the-shoulder shots, in which each participant is first the talker and then the listener. Most of the time, however, Hitchcock's suspenseful scenes are not subjective in this way, and only partly constructed by montage. Whether his characters are clambering over Mount Rushmore or climbing the Statue of Liberty or hiding from the police on a Scottish moor, the action arouses in us feelings of objective suspense frequently resulting from little or no montage.

Hitchcock perceives, as well as anyone has, how functional a chase can be for sustaining the objectivistic kind of response. Yet chases do not lend themselves to the rapid cutting that montage involves. A chase is a continuous event in nature that the camera can follow by focusing on the mere skin of whatever and whoever is active in it. Being objective, which only means that our attention is directed toward what is out there in the world rather than residing in the recesses of someone's mind, the spectacle ratifies our condition as an audience that passively looks at moving images on the screen. Moreover the chase is by its very nature the perfect embodiment of suspense. A chase cannot occur unless there is an unresolved effort by one or more persons to reach a conceivable goal or destination, or to snare some individual who tries through ongoing maneuvers to escape capture or detection. That state of affairs is always entrancing, and a possible source of enjoyment at every level.

In his interview entitled "Core of the Movie—The Chase," Hitchcock defines this mainstay of the cinema as follows:

Well, essentially, the chase is someone running toward a goal, often with the antiphonal motion of someone fleeing a pursuer. Probably the fox hunt would be the simplest form of the chase. Now if you substitute a girl for the fox, and put a boy in place of the hunters, you have the boy-chases-girl variation. Or substituting again, the police chasing a criminal. So long as a plot has either flight or pursuit, it may be considered a form of the chase. In many ways the chase makes up about 60 percent of the construction of all movie plots.[15]

Later in the essay Hitchcock embellishes this description by emphasizing the value of double chases—for instance, when the hero is being pursued by the bad guys as well as the police, or when the hero is pursuing the bad guys and the police are pursuing him. Hitchcock's concept of the chase is broad enough to include conditions that are not especially physical or even visual. He mentions detectives, also Hamlet, as characters who are in pursuit of truth, and Jack the Ripper in *The Lodger* as a man who is on the run psychologically. Though he draws the line at the idea that Macbeth is involved in a chase because he is an evildoer pursued by fate, Hitchcock denies that all characterization undermines the aesthetic purity of the chase. On the contrary, he argues that D. W. Griffith's chases were rudimentary because they did not include either mental action or the development of character. "In the ideal chase structure," Hitchcock says, "the tempo and complexity of the chase will be an accurate reflection of the intensity of the relations between the characters."[16]

Hitchcock maintains that in the best plots several chases are going on at once. This enables the audience to identify alternatively with the chaser and the chased, and that augments the level of suspense. Through the final physical chase in which many Hitchcock films terminate, the total pattern of suspense is, as he puts it, "crystallized": "You see, as the picture approaches the climax of the tension, everything should begin to move faster. The threads of the plot become tauter and I even change the style of acting, broaden it. The tension is then released into the final physical chase, which must be short and breathtaking, to avoid the error of anticlimax."[17]

❋

While depicting the development and release of tension as the basis of suspense, Hitchcock also notes the advantage of relieving the heaviness of melodramatic events with an interspersed variability in the general atmosphere: "It is important in a story with sinister implications to use counterpoint, great contrast between situation and background."[18] Two of the agencies that contribute to contrasting effects of this sort are the realistic portrayal of ordinary life and the inclusion of humor that is blended into the melodrama.

I will return to those factors later in this chapter. Here I want to touch upon a distinction between types of shock effect that Hitchcock suggests in conjunction with his differentiation between the two kinds of suspense. Explaining the incompatibility at any single time of shock and suspense, he sometimes characterizes the former as "terror." In itself that response undermines the possibility of suspense because it entails a sudden and usually visceral confrontation with the unknown, whereas suspense is based on the trepidation caused by what we have already been told. But at other times, Hitchcock talks of "surprise" of any sort as a source of shock. Without necessarily being terrified, we are startled by something we had little reason to expect. The numerous turns in the plot of *The Trouble with Harry* or *Suspicion*, or the revelation that Charles Laughton is the villain in *Jamaica Inn*—these create beneficial surprise as opposed to suspense, but they do not evoke terror.

Most important throughout Hitchcock's account of his methodology is his recognition that unification among the conflicting techniques he wishes to harness can only result from some "compromise" the director must administer. Does this mean that we should see Hitchcock as just an expedient pragmatist, an artist who has no fixed ideas about which elements in his method should dominate on any specific occasion? He himself offers a more plausible interpretation of what he means, and what he does, when he speaks of cinematic orchestration, and even counterpoint analogous to what happens in the creation and performance of music.

As opposed to what Van Sant says about movie remakes resembling performances of musical compositions, Hitchcock's analogy seems to me both apt and insightful. The great virtue of formalist approaches to film resides in their understanding of the ways in which technical innovations contribute to an interactive dynamism within each work. The interaction occurs in a continual responsivity among the cinematic components that is indeed similar to the harmonic patterns that constitute the art of music. The putting together of the "little pieces" of montage is a part of film's compositional panoply. And beyond that, the plot itself is normally a narrative representation of differing possibilities in life, differing interests and experiences that human beings can have, all of them generating a variety of interwoven problems that need to be resolved.

As possible solutions develop in the plot, characters who are separately in some pursuit of them systematically react to each other. That is the source of any dramatic progression that is capable of eliciting feelings and creating suspense in viewers who watch but cannot otherwise participate. The ricochet sustains our attention from moment to moment in the story, and this enables us to identify with the personages who are living through it in their fictional realm. In the hands of a master like Hitchcock, the requisite inventiveness does indeed resemble the creativity of musical composition and performance. If all art constantly aspires toward the condition of music, as Walter Pater said, we have further reason to believe that cinematic constructions such as Hitchcock's are preeminently artistic.

❀

From this point of view, we may also perceive the nature of Hitchcock's virtuosity in the gripping and climactic culminations of his films. For instance, think of the sequence near the end of *Strangers on a Train* that begins with the tennis match and ends with Bruno, the psychotic murderer, recovering the cigarette lighter at the amusement park. Bruno has told the tennis champ that he will find some means of incriminating him. The champ has lost his cigarette lighter but suspects that Bruno is in possession of it and may well use it against him. In order to get to the amusement park as quickly as possible, the champ throws himself into playing a professional tennis match with reckless abandon that will hasten its completion.

As we watch several minutes of the match, projected in considerable detail, our suspense mounts while the players fight ferociously through game after game. The fierceness of their contrapuntal exchange is accentuated by the presence in the stands of spectators whose heads move quickly left and right, from side to side, in rhythm with the shots being played before them. Since the movie audience is viewing in its own fashion both the observers in the stands and what those people are likewise watching, the isomorphism of the situation creates enriched suspense at progressively higher degrees of intensity. All of this then becomes an ingredient in the extended counterpoint that results from interlarded shots of Bruno's frantic actions at the amusement park.

Bruno arrives there exactly at the moment the tennis match begins. He intends to plant the cigarette lighter close to where the dead woman's body was found, as evidence that the tennis champ is the guilty party. By accident Bruno drops the lighter into the upper catch of a sewer drain and then has to put his arm through the grill in a difficult attempt to retrieve it. By cutting back and forth between the two situations, the tennis match and Bruno's efforts to grasp the cigarette lighter, the camera orchestrates them into a single dramatic event. Both occurrences, at the game and at the sewer, are themselves spectacles being seen by fascinated onlookers. Just as the tennis match is followed with rapt attention by the empathetic people in the stands, so too does Bruno have his own audience at the sewer. He succeeds in recovering the cigarette lighter about the time that the tennis match ends. In both cases the multiple tensions that have been aroused in us, the theater audience, are simultaneously quieted but retained as preparation for the next pattern of suspense, which pervades the grand finale.

Hitchcock can orchestrate these effects as artfully as he does because of the brilliance and intelligence of his camera's movements from one perspective to another. But in turn this achievement issues from a unifying motif that binds everything in the story as whole. The dual tensions in what is happening at the tennis field and at the amusement park run parallel to the tensions that we have experienced in observing the contortions of the two men who are pitted against each other throughout the narrative. The relationship between Bruno and the tennis champ is a clash of different personalities, a game in life not entirely different from tennis, in which each word or deed—each idea or individual move—must be parried responsively by the other person until some final factuality like death terminates their relentless exchanges. The notion of "crisscross," which comprises Bruno's scheme of reciprocating murders, and which is visible in the crisscrossing of the train tracks, recurs throughout the cinematography of this film.

At the beginning Bruno had shown himself to be a tennis aficionado who nevertheless cannot play the game himself. He therefore challenges the champ in a contest of imagination and ruthless will-to-win that is deeper in human instinct than tennis or other civilized sports. It is a struggle for mastery by any means, including murder, and it reaches beyond the conventional and therefore merely superficial aspects of our being. In this game the playing field has been leveled. Despite his madness, Bruno is capable of winning if only he can get the champ to forfeit his sense of right and wrong. The champ refuses and we all side with him. But he is a rather dull and uninspiring person, while Bruno is alluring and inventive. Hitchcock knows that we who monitor the film like judges at a tennis match will see this disparity in the two characters, and that this will contribute to the alternating feelings that he arouses in the patrons he has ensnared with his hypnotic visual music.

The aesthetic potency of all this derives from the quick and unsettling, but exquisitely controlled, busyness of the camerawork. At the same time Hitchcock's success is also due to his use of real music in the film, which relies on it much more than any musical composition—even the opera—can possibly rely on film as an ingredient in its sonic art. In his score for *Strangers on a Train*, Dimitri Tiomkin supports the augmenting conflict through sounds that are abrupt and sometimes staccato, though sufficiently subdued for us to be largely unaware of their agitated presence. Even if we realize that we are being manipulated by the cinematography as well as the music, we can only relish the cleverness and the intricacy of their magnificent design. We accept Hitchcock's bravura and can no longer distance ourselves from its artificiality. At this point Hitchcock and his composer duplicate the achievement of Verdi in his greatest works. Though opera may only barely incorporate cinema, movies like this one show how film can become cinematic opera at its best.

✺

The presence of dramatic music, scenically involved rather than vaguely in the background, yields much of the emotive effect that Hitchcock is aiming for. The sound is always highly integrated with the plot, strictly geared to the evoking of suspense, and conducive to the affective responses he persistently keeps in mind. Under his orchestration or conducting, the outcome succeeds in molding feelings as he wished. Thanks to what he wrote for Hitchcock movies, Bernard Herrmann earned a reputation as a composer who fully understood what the role of film music should be. His Hitchcock scores have been extolled by many critics. I myself hated them in earlier years, though I liked the music he contributed to the first two movies of Orson Welles. His work for Hitchcock made me feel as if I were being forced to undergo something that I did not want to experience under the circumstances. I thought of myself as an inoffensive spectator who was spending money to be entertained and, ideally, delighted by a work of art. I saw no reason why I should submit to being prodded and jabbed by nervous noises that only made me uncomfortable.

A good example of what I am talking about occurs during the credits and opening minutes of *Psycho*. Herrmann's music is jarring, rude and maniacal in its determination to arouse anxiety that may well be suitable when something in the plot appears on screen. But as yet we have no reason to feel suspense; there is nothing in the preliminary images to justify any emotion whatsoever. It is as if a willful demon has chosen to poke us in the ribs, persistently and rhythmically in a sadistic gesture designed as preparation for what will follow. Or as if the heat in the hall had been turned up to an intolerable degree in the hope that this will make everyone sympathetic to the sufferings of the characters in the coming melodrama. I could not see that as a model of good film music. Nor do I now, so many years later.

In the decades that have followed, I overcame much of my resistance to Herrmann's Hitchcock music, and in general to the fact that everything in these thrillers serves a manipulative purpose. I gradually acquired the ability to relish Hitchcock's formalist genius as well as the philosophical depths that it probes within the dimensions of his art. Eventually I began to appreciate how appropriate Herrmann's frenetic music is, not for all films but particularly for the ones by Hitchcock for which it was crafted. In *Psycho* itself, there are stretches in which the irritating assertiveness of the score is entirely correct. For instance, after Janet Leigh has stolen the money, we watch her drive her car through town on her way out of state. Looking in through the windshield, we see her face as she sits at the wheel. She is presumably reflecting on her escapade, and nothing of importance happens for a while. She drives calmly but with an edge of concentration, though we do not know as yet that she is starting to feel guilty for the crime she has committed. The music tells us that more is going on than meets the eye.

This induced inquisitiveness envelops us in a feeling of concern for the young woman. We have previously seen her in an explicit, and possibly illicit, sexual relationship in a seedy hotel room, and that awakens our intuitive sense that she is headed for trouble, which many in the audience might think she deserves on moral grounds alone. But she is so fetching and erotic to look at that most of the spectators are likely to be apprehensive about her welfare. Music is needed in these moments because little if anything is being said or done, and Hitchcock wisely wants to limit as much as possible his use of voiceover soliloquies.

The scene is important because Leigh's boss happens to cross the street in front of her car. He stops only for a second, but we can tell that he notices her and is surprised to see that she is not at home as she said she would be. This will later lead the investigators to suspect her involvement in the theft. While that link in the story justifies the previous moments of inactivity, Hitchcock knows that he has to keep the audience's attentiveness simmering throughout. Herrmann's worrisome music solves that problem for him. It supplies an equivalent substitute for something in the narrative that would evoke the proper level of suspense. It not only arouses anxiety in us but also facilitates imaginative inferences about the woman's mounting sense of guilt and fearfulness that Hitchcock would like us to entertain without his having to spell them out at length. In sequences such as this one, and in other Hitchcock films—for instance, *Vertigo*—Herrmann's music has a major role in the development of the kind of film that Hitchcock made his specialty.[19]

❋

The greatest of Hitchcock's contrapuntal feats consists in his orchestration of the "sinister," as he calls it, and the comedic. In one essay he even says that all of *Psycho* should be taken as merely humorous. He means that since there is little character-ization in this film, what takes place in it is there just for the fun of shocking and frightening the audience. In other words, the analogy of the roller coaster again. But his remarks may also help us explore the extent to which the humorous in different guises bolsters not only Hitchcock's own technique but also his view of what is generically fundamental in cinema, and even in human life itself.

We can begin by noting his celebrated cameo appearances in most of his later movies. He is always an extra in them and usually somewhat brash, portraying a pushy little man who insists on taking snapshots, or stepping down from a train while carrying a cello almost as big as he is, or showing exas-peration when a bus shuts its door in his face, or staring rudely at Jane Wyman when she mutters something to herself in the street, and so on. These are all whimsical vignettes that afford fleeting amusement that contrasts with, and slightly lessens, the weightiness of whatever drama is at hand. Only occasion-ally do these shots have much narrative importance, though sometimes they are relevant to the plot. An example of this sort is Hitchcock's cameo at the beginning of *The Birds*. In it he is shown walking out of a pet store, two small dogs on their leashes leading him into the street. If, as I argue later, that movie expresses ambiguous ideas about man's relationship to other species, we may take Hitchcock to be asserting in this scene that he at least is an animal lover.

For the most part, however, Hitchcock's signature appearances can be taken as meaning something else, something pertinent to his conception of himself as a filmmaker. Being aware of his need to control audience response and to dominate every aspect of film production (which he did more than anyone else had since Chaplin), his pretending to be just another extra on the set serves as a compensatory statement and even an expression of his selfless devotion to the technological wonder which is his cinematic art. In the tiny, insignificant roles he enacts, he seems to be saying: "I may be the director and producer, the one who tells everyone minutely what to do, but really I too am just a cog in the machine, a humble servant of the great enterprise that engulfs me as well as everyone else." At the same time, of course, he knows that he alone is the dictatorial celebrity whose face and figure were recognized throughout the world by millions who awaited his brief but imaginatively varied presence in his films. That combination of whimsicality, childlike prankishness, and self-deprecation mingled with willful self-promotion is typical of Hitchcock's humor.

His comedic strain infuses all the genres Hitchcock employs from film to film. It plays its part in the texture of even his darkest plots. It modulates their structure while adjusting an audience's attunement, prolonging suspense and keeping the strongest feelings in reserve and readiness for some appointed moment in the story. The orchestration and counterpoint that Hitchcock employs requires precise timing in the succession of events that can evoke whatever emotional reaction he intends. Through the element of humor, he beguiles the spectators until he reaches an occurrence in the narrative that

will startle them and increase a primordial tension that has
been developing unawares. The humor primarily exists as a
linchpin or transitional inducement that furthers the overall
melodramatic pattern. The pleasantry in Hitchcock's comic
effects is almost always a by-product of something else, something beyond itself and generally sinister.

I can illustrate what I have just said by scanning a long and
central sequence in *Family Plot*. This film, the last one
Hitchcock finished, is especially outstanding in its studied
combination of comedy and drama. No one is murdered in it,
but the possibility that someone has been murdered, and the
fear that the agreeable and even funny young protagonists
might be, blends all five of the Hitchcockean genres into a
human comedy that occasionally makes us laugh at the same
time that it causes us to sit on the edge of our seats.

In the scenes I have in mind the amusing couple, who are
living lustily in premarital sin but also behave with each other
like middle-aged married people, agree to meet one of the bad
guys at a roadside café halfway up a wooded mountain. They
drive through the vernal landscape on a sunny day that
makes us feel at peace with the world. But then we see the bad
guy secretly watching them as they pass by. That snaps the
natural beauty into its specifically dramatic role. In the café
the couple wait anxiously for the bad guy and eventually
drive off when he does not appear. They do not know that he
has already arrived and has tampered with their car in the
parking lot, releasing the brake fluid. While they wait, they
and we are entertained by the occurrence of a clandestine
assignation between a single woman and a man of the cloth
who is seemingly there as the shepherd of some Sunday-
school children.

The lightness of this mild sexual divertissement, like the beauty of the forest setting, is presented at a fairly slow tempo, which is then speeded up by the nightmarish reality of the couple leaving the café and finding themselves in a car that is rapidly going downhill without brakes. The horror of this situation builds as the tires squeak at every turn of the mountain road, as autos and motorcycles scurry to evade the wildly runaway vehicle, as the distant views, seen through the windshield, show us the gorges into which it might plummet, and as exterior shots reveal how close to the edge its wheels are. But, in typical Hitchcock fashion, the terrifying suspense is cushioned by a comical counterpoint within the car itself. In the passenger seat the young woman loses control of herself, and of her flaying arms and legs. She sits, or rather contorts, in utter panic next to her virtual husband, who is trying to steer them to a safe landing. She blindly grabs him around the neck, throws her legs across his abdomen, thereby preventing him from firmly holding on to the steering wheel and all but causing them to have a fatal crash.

Though this is hilarious in itself, and similar in its sheer farcicality to Cary Grant driving while drunk at the beginning of *North by Northwest*, there is also a formal function to it. It mitigates the agitation we are sure to feel by lessening our sense of both the terror and the suspense, and it does so for two reasons: first, our identification with these likable characters would be unbearable if the tension kept rising in proportion to the ever greater danger in their precipitous descent; second, our strongest emotions need to be preserved until the sequence is terminated by an authentic disaster that occurs shortly afterward. When the car comes to a halt and the couple climb out, the bad guy drives up and then recklessly pursues them. His car goes over an embankment and explodes. We witness the enormity of this event, which culminates and resolves our concern for the couple we care about while also bracketing the catastrophe with our feeling of poetic justice. Horrible as the accident is, we self-righteously extend little sympathy to the repulsive and somewhat ugly bad guy.

By constructing the sequence out of the visual/aural interplay of these comic and melodramatic components, Hitchcock elicits and adjusts the responses of his audience, shunting them back and forth as he did in the tennis match scenes of *Strangers on a Train*. His genius consists in captivating us with this fictional concoction that is so vivid cinematographically, so realistic in its detailed depiction of events taken from everyday life in this age of death by automobile, and so entrancing in its ability to lead us step-by-step through the absorbing trajectory he has chosen for us.

In *The Trouble with Harry* the counterpoint between light and heavy appears in the contrast between, on the one hand, the lovely colors of autumnal New England vegetation as the setting for the quaintness of each of the characters, and, on the other hand, the revulsion we all have about someone being killed, or even being dead. This is humor on a par with Frank Capra's *Arsenic and Old Lace*, except that Hitchcock uses the corpse as more than just a prop or symbol of human mortality. For Hitchcock it is the consequence of unknown events that must be dug up and then covered over. That happens to the dead Harry several times in the course of the movie. The dynamics of this repetition perfectly suit Hitchcock's proclivity to orchestrate and to counterpoint, though now with a predominance of comedic effects. Bernard Herrmann's score, so different in expressiveness from what he wrote for *Psycho*, is one of his best.

Among the fifty-three films that Hitchcock made, *The Trouble with Harry* is the only one that is an outright comedy. But it is also, in part, a whodunit and a mystery story, though precluded by its good-natured humor from being a thriller. Even so, its preoccupation with the disposal of a corpse, and the possibility that the deceased may have been murdered, enables it to approximate the kind of suspense that exists in *Rear Window* under less benign circumstances.

Since Cary Grant was so versatile as a comic actor, the Hitchcock films with him as the male star are wonderfully enlivened by his unique combination of the sublime and the ridiculous: the charming, elegant, sexy man being forever poised at the brink of frantic absurdity and helplessness. Hitchcock said that *North by Northwest* was a "fantasy." Though this is true, that film is also a romantic comedy, like *Notorious,* and equally spiced up with spy stuff and all the trappings of a thriller. But even *The Birds,* with its ominous overtones of mass human destruction perpetrated by species whose native existence on this planet has been put in jeopardy by us, includes moments of visual humor that turn out to be integral to the plot. Riding in the back seat of Tippi Hedren's car, the two lovebirds she has purchased as a gift for the man she ostensibly wishes to humiliate sway back and forth in perfect harmony with each other like the spectators at the tennis match in *Strangers on a Train.*

The movements of these birds can be experienced as sheer divertissement, as they clearly are in *To Catch a Thief,* where the two policemen in pursuit of Grace Kelly's sportscar sway in a comparable rhythm when their own vehicle speeds around the sudden turns of the Grande Corniche. But in *The Birds* the comedic byplay tells us something significant about these gentle creatures who live in harmonious accommodation not only with each other but also with the manmade conveyance in which they are riding. The lovebirds introduce into Bodega Bay a type of oneness with humankind that the other birds try unsuccessfully to defeat. Just before Hedren goes up the stairs that lead to the attic in which she is violently attacked, she glances at the birdcage below with the two lovebirds in it. This alerts us to the contrast between inhabitants of the natural world who have goodwill toward the human race and those she will now encounter who do not.

The counterpoint that Hitchcock composes in this situation is hardly laughable. Though related to the humorous effect of the birds swaying in the car, it is a deft transition to the horror in the attic that we will presently observe. In the final moments of the movie, the little girl who has been traumatized by what the family has gone through asks to take the birdcage and its occupants with them in the car when they make their escape to safety. The closing shot, following the automobile as it recedes, suggests a bit of lightness, a ray of hope and even guarded optimism, as intimated by the expanse of open though leaden skies above the road. A comparable but much less developed meaning occurs in *Sabotage.* Just after Sylvia Sidney has murdered her husband, her eye falls on a bird sitting peacefully in its cage. In her consternation at what she has just done, the harried wife seems to draw some comfort from this symbol of another, better, way to live.

In all these films, Hitchcock's magnificent sense of timing is the key to his achievement. The pace is slow enough to lure

us into a feeling of what real life is like but fast enough to prepare us for the acceleration that soon leads into the suspense
and sometimes terror. This acuity about what is aesthetically
available through time itself, through the mere duration of
mundane existence, becomes a technique that Hitchcock draws
upon in many of his films. It is parallel to one that Mozart uses
regularly at the beginning of his piano concertos, when only
bland, or even pedestrian, music is heard until the solo
instrument enters, at which point it and the orchestral accompaniment begin to modulate extensively. Hitchcock displays a
rhythmic awareness comparable to the one that all
accomplished musicians have, whether they are performers or
composers. Leonard Bernstein once told me that his sense of
rhythm was the secret of his success as a conductor. Within his
own visual and representational medium, Hitchcock is a
supreme master for the same reason.

Hitchcock's statements in interviews and in his writings are
generally given as explications of his own approach to filmmaking. They tell us about his methodological procedures
while also clarifying the nature of what he achieves in his
movies. But they often reach beyond himself and offer expert
opinion about cinema in its relation to other arts, to modern
civilization, and to reality as a whole. From this aspect of his
thinking we can detect the influence of intellectual forebears he
never mentions but whose work he presupposes. His desire to
arouse and then direct the feelings of his audiences, and his
pronouncements about the state of "fear and fear not" that
serves as the affective goal of his endeavors, are reminiscent of
the Aristotelean conception of catharsis. In his *Poetics* Aristotle

names terror and pity as the appropriate audience response to tragedy—for which we may substitute Hitchcockean melodrama. The plight of Oedipus evokes terror in us, Aristotle suggests, because we fear that sufferings similar to his may be visited upon us as well. In his references to suspense emanating from our identification with a protagonist who faces imminent dangers, Hitchcock could have said the same.

He might also have agreed in relation to feelings of pity (or compassion, which differs from pity but is kindred to it). His dramas are so taut, so greatly filled with actions that arouse reactions and their further complications, that sentiments such as pity and compassion can have only a secondary role in them. Nevertheless Hitchcock is able to deploy these feelings as motors that propel our affective involvement in the plot.

When Cary Grant and Eva Marie Saint in *North by Northwest* have learned the truth about each other but need to be separated so that she can complete her assignment as a secret agent, we sympathize with them as star-crossed lovers— but only briefly. Grant has to be knocked out so that she can go on to do what she must; he, in the heroic mission fate has thrust upon him, has to reach the house on Mount Rushmore by himself in order to save her from detection; and so on, as the course of unrelenting suspense demands. In other films, there is sometimes more scope for pity and compassion, or other sympathetic feelings, as in *Notorious* when we watch Ingrid Bergman decline in health and beauty after she has been poisoned, or in *The Man Who Knew Too Much* when the boy's mother is almost out of her mind because her son has been kidnapped. What predominates, however, is usually the need to move on through one exciting development after another in their serial, but also interlocked, progression. While Aristotle could have characterized *Oedipus Rex* as a kind of chase, for Hitchcock the chase serves as the fundamental principle in his art.

In trying to formulate the aesthetic views assumed by Hitchcock's approach, it is also useful to place his thought in the context of literary theories that arose in England in the 1920s and remained in vogue for several decades. The writings of I. A. Richards are especially noteworthy. In books like *The Principles of Literary Criticism* and *Science and Poetry* (later expanded into *Poetries and Sciences*), Richards maintains that poetry consists of language that has little or no cognitive content but instead evokes tense and complicated feelings that are finally resolved in a manner that is internally consummatory, satisfying from within their formal structure as aesthetic components. The relevant emotions are therefore created by each work as a harmonious unity in itself, rather than being representational, or even indicative of what people experience in the real world apart from the fictive fabrication.

In effect, Hitchcock applies this outlook to the narrative employment of photographic images that move across the silver screen and have their impact on us by means that are primarily visual. At the same time, he deviates from the more extreme implications of Richards's doctrine (which Richards himself revised in later years) by stressing the importance of what Hitchcock calls "the reality effect." Explaining why glamour interests him not at all, he insists that "reality is the most important factor in the making of a successful film."[20]

Hitchcock's emphasis upon realistic detail, and much of his conception of reality, enters at that point. The world that he shows us is photographed to resemble as closely as possible the world we can all recognize as present in daily life. His films would not have had their great popularity if they lacked this

quotidian verisimilitude. It functions as a limiting contrast to
the suspenseful deviation from normality that Hitchcock's stories cultivate, his pervasive predilection for *bizzarria* (Verdi's
term to characterize a similar outlandishness he wanted in his
melodramas). In *Shadow of a Doubt*, as in *The Birds*, the routine
and uneventful serenity of a small town in California is the
calculated setting for the grotesque and egregious evil that
descends upon it.

In this vein Hitchcock says that maximum correspondence
to reality is something he must have for his kind of film.
Realistic photography is needed "to make it look as real as
possible, because the effects themselves are actually quite
bizarre. The audience responds in proportion to how realistic
you make it. One of the dramatic reasons for this type of
photography is to get it looking so natural that the audience
gets involved and believes, for the time being, what's going on
up there on the screen."[21]

All the same, Hitchcock realizes that one must include
many contrived and artificial devices in order to make something on the screen look natural. Moreover, he adheres to
"very, very strict rules" about the use of the camera: "For
example, never, never use a shot without its having a clear
dramatic purpose."[22] When he discusses camera movement,
the details of lighting, the creation of mood, the choice of setting and of background, he reiterates the importance of the
natural but always subordinates it to one or another dramatic
end that it can serve. Far from there being any necessary
conflict between the two, he envisages their combination as
another opportunity for orchestration.

Mood being apprehension, he says, he creates it by putting
some frightening event in a natural situation that is realistically

portrayed. That is what he means by "murder by the babbling brook." He then remarks, in reference to *The Trouble with Harry*: "Where did I lay the dead body? Among the most beautiful colors I could find. Autumn in Vermont. Went up there and waited for the leaves to turn. We did it in counterpoint. I wanted to take a nasty taste away by making the setting beautiful."[23] In films that were made mainly in a backlot or studio—*Torn Curtain*, for example—he carefully inserted bits of reality that had been photographed on location. They were designed to pin the melodramatic action to the unmistakable authenticity of something familiar in the natural world though usually minor in itself. This had to be done, he nevertheless realized, without slipping into some clichéd depiction of reality.

The most celebrated instance of this, and one of Hitchcock's favorites, is the crop duster sequence in *North by Northwest*. In that film "the girl sends Cary Grant to a rendezvous where we know an attempt will be made to kill him. Now the *cliché* treatment would be to show him standing on the corner of the street in a pool of light. . . . I said *no*. I would do it in bright sunshine with no place to hide, in open prairie country. And what is the mood? A *sinister* mood. There's not a sign of where the menace can come from, but eventually it turns up in the form of a crop duster airplane."[24]

Having made this decision, Hitchcock then manifests his fidelity to the reality effect by directing the action toward events that would naturally exist under these circumstances. Since the attempted murder will occur through the operation of a crop duster, not only does he have Cary Grant hide in the crops once he has been fired upon but also he has the plane dust crops, first as a deceptive maneuver and later as a way of flushing out the victim. As another illustration of this rule about using whatever activity a background would normally contain, Hitchcock cites the ballet Paul Newman goes to in *Torn Curtain*: "Who discovers him? A ballerina, in the middle of her dance. How does he get the idea to shout 'Fire!'? From a scenic fire on the stage."[25]

A similar effect appears in most of Hitchcock's films, though not always successfully. In order to build up the climactic suspense in *The Man Who Knew Too Much*, he makes us sit through long stretches of orchestral and choral music in the concert hall where the visiting dignitary is to be assassinated. With increasing anxiety we are supposed to listen for the clash of symbols that will muffle the gunshot. But in my experience, at least, Hitchcock's sense of timing fails in both versions of this plot because he makes us wait too long. The performance serves as neither a musical cameo, which it should not be in this place, nor as an ever tighter turning of the screw prior to the anticipated moment. Our attention wanders, and that diminishes the dramatic impact.

Hitchcock's desire to fit real settings and events into his various counterpoints, and to portray the normal functionality that makes them seem natural to us, explains his preferred choice of monumental landmarks like Mount Rushmore, the Statue of Liberty, Covent Garden, the United Nations Building, and so on. This kind of choice manifests in turn a broader principle he also espouses: namely, to use recognizable material objects to their fullest. Explaining why John Gielgud and Peter Lorre go to a chocolate factory in order to find their local informant, he remarks that the idea came to him because *The Secret Agent* takes place in Switzerland, renowned for its chocolates. Similarly, he regales us with their walk through the Alps and their murdering the wrong man there because we know that people not infrequently do fall off these cliffs. Though the sequence in the chocolate factory is masterful, the one in the Alps—which shows us what the camera sees through a telescope—is much inferior. It is not at all the equal of Hitchcock's use of the Scottish moors in *The 39 Steps*.

When Hitchcock describes his focusing on material objects in order to augment the reality effect, he says that they help him overcome the inexpressiveness of the human face. Returning to the murder scene in *Sabotage*, he claims that its "subject" is the knife with which Sylvia Sidney kills her husband. The task for the camera was to display her mind while also arousing spectator response that is direct and sympathetic, rather than detached as it would be in distant observers. Her thinking had to reveal itself through the movements of her hand, specifically in relation to the knife. "In an older style of acting Sylvia would have had to show the audience what was passing in her mind by exaggerating facial expression. But people today in real life often don't show their feelings in their faces; so the film treatment showed the audience her mind through her hand, through its unconscious grasp on the knife."[26]

This approach to *things*, to material objects as the basis of scene construction, is entirely coherent with Hitchcock's interest in "building up" a film by means of montage, bit by bit. It also underlies his conception of how a director should deal with actors. They are the conveyors of the psychological meanings without which there cannot be any dramatic tension or involvement of audience feeling. As persons, they represent the personhood that each of us has. That is why we undergo vicariously the experiences they enact within the narrative, and why we are able to care about them and even identify with them as protagonists in it. And yet, montage in film—like cubism in painting—breaks up the image of people's variable personalities and imposes visual perspectives that formalistically violate what we normally consider to be their reality.

Far from thinking that this is a shortcoming inherent in cinematic technique, Hitchcock revels in the freedom of imagination and creativity that it affords the filmmaker. It shows the inventiveness of "pure" cinema and embodies the difference between the screen and the theatrical stage. Plays must also subordinate the personhood of the actor to the exigencies of the fiction he or she enacts. But whatever the meaning of the play may be, it is always conveyed by a person who is there alive and mobile in front of us. In film that person has been transformed into a material object, a concoction of images produced by one machine, or several, and projected by another kind upon a two-dimensional surface.

One may accept that state of affairs as an essential constant in this art form and try to deal with it as best one can. But being the supreme technician that he was, Hitchcock saw the situation somewhat differently. He delighted in the opportunity it afforded him as a film*maker* to make something that no actor by himself can either represent or express. That is why Hitchcock insists that there can be no room in his films for the "virtuoso actor," the one who thinks his talent as a performing artist can enable him to reach an audience more or less on his own. "The screen actor has got to be much more plastic," Hitchcock says, "he has to submit himself to be used by the director and camera. Mostly he is wanted to behave quietly . . . leaving the camera to add most of the accents and emphases."[27]

Since the director controls the camera, this means, in effect, that he or she is inevitably a Svengali who dominates the actors' presentations of themselves. The director fashions their self-expression in ways they cannot alter, or even recognize until they see the final product. According to Hitchcock, the effect that persons in the real world have on each other can be registered in film only through the professional maneuvers of the director and the cinematographer. On the stage you can watch two people talking, but only in an over-the-shoulder shot can you see them as they participate in a conversation, either as the talker who is being heard or as the listener of what is being said. By overrunning one person's voice with another's face, the filmmaker can shape and even accelerate the action in a way that stage plays cannot. Hitchcock also mentions the unique ability of close-up shots to illustrate someone's instant response to an event that is being shown or just has been.

What Hitchcock does not take into account is the fact that exploiting this capability means treating people as visual artifacts whose personality is presented to us only as a fabrication out of the imagery that emanates from the camera's technical apparatus. Is this a defect or a virtue in the cinematic medium? To philosophers who think of the human soul as a transcendental being that exceeds the natural order, filmmaking must be inherently deceptive and even a desecration of our reality as spiritual entities. I am not of that opinion. For me the greatness and potential profundity of cinematic art issues from the infinite resourcefulness it has in rendering the world as we live in it, and as it exists in us, through points of view that no earlier art form was capable of transmitting to our visual and auditory senses. What Hitchcock prides himself on also applies to the

work of every other filmmaker. Though always describing
what he personally does as a director, he speaks as well for the
others in his calling.

�֎

Not all directors agree with Hitchcock's notions about the
human face, however, or about the need to express the mind
that lies behind it by material rather than psychological effects.
In my chapters on Welles and Renoir, I discuss their different
approaches to this question. Here it is only necessary to rectify
a common misconception of Hitchcock's opinion. In several of
his writings and interviews, he tries to rebut charges that he
loathes beautiful women, that for him all actors are like children or even cattle, and that he cares less about them as human
beings than about the imagery he can get from some thing or
other instance of physical nature that excites his imagination—
zooming in to show the key in Ingrid Bergman's clenched fist
in *Notorious,* or the razor in the hand of Gregory Peck in
Spellbound, or seeing someone through the bottom of a glass
in *The Lady Vanishes,* or showing a body that falls from a height
in *Vertigo* and *Rear Window.*

These complaints frequently result from misinterpretations
of Hitchcock's staged persona as an English showman who
utters outrageous quips for the benefit of the press, above all in
America. But sometimes his remarks are indeed worthy of criticism. For instance, consider his lamenting the need to work
with stars who have been schooled as method actors in the
theater and are uncomfortable with his demand that they
should do nothing before the camera (but, as he adds, do it
"extremely well").[28] Hitchcock shows indignation at the effron-
tery of Paul Newman on one occasion, and Montgomery Clift

on another, when they dared to express ideas about how he should direct a scene they were in.

The second case is especially instructive. It deals with a sequence in *I Confess* that happens after the end of the trial. The young priest makes his way through a hostile and jeering crowd outside the courthouse. Hitchcock says he then needed a transition from that spot to the Hotel Frontenac across the street, where the action would next occur. He solved the problem by putting a large placard with the word *Hotel* on it one flight up on the façade of the building, and by positioning at the windows a number of people who are watching the turmoil. He told Clift that while standing in front of the courthouse he should look up at these spectators. That would make the film audience see the placard and point their imagination to the location Hitchcock wished to lead it toward. To his surprise and annoyance, Clift answered: "I don't think I would look there."

Hitchcock informs us that he insisted that Clift do as he was told, and that when he did the transition worked as expected. But though Hitchcock recounts the story to indicate why actors cannot understand the technical problems that a director has to face, the fact remains that Clift was right. The reality effect is impaired by the priest's upward glance at that moment. Why would he look there? What could be going on in his mind? Had Hitchcock been less dictatorial, he might have thought about Clift's suggestion and easily improved the scene. He had only to tell the spectators in the windows of the hotel to do more than just watch, to shout above the crowd, and thus to catch the attention of the priest.[29]

Hitchcock often chafed at the way that stars are given prominence, and exorbitant salaries, in the movies. He saw no reason why he, as the director, should not be treated like a star himself. Eventually he succeeded, more than almost any other director, in becoming the superstar in his own productions, the name above the title, the image that everyone knew, and the icon that could always be counted on for the kind of entertainment sought by millions of people.

Though suspicious of the power that actors who are stars might want to have, demanding some leading man or lady, or telling the cameraman which profile to shoot, Hitchcock never lost sight of the commercial value they brought to their films. But for him this was only what he calls "camouflage—or, if you prefer it, as the jam round the pill."[28] He knew that, with the stars as a commercial cover, directors and producers could get away with making the innovations their artistic taste impelled them toward. The stars must not be allowed to dominate a production, but Hitchcock emphasizes how important they are as "magnets" who earn their keep by bringing in the public that identifies the film in its totality with them alone. What Hitchcock does not mention is the *reason* that stars can serve as magnets—their ability to embody the face and voice and questing human spirit that all members of the audience want to make contact with through the film experience.

A similar ambiguity or conceptual inadequacy belongs to Hitchcock's statements about actors as children or as cattle. He means that they cannot possess the mature authority that only an accomplished director has. But even children may be very inventive, and no cattle of any breed can perform as professional actors do. Hitchcock is obviously being facetious when he denies having said that actors are cattle and then adds: "My actor friends know I would never be capable of such a thoughtless, rude, and unfeeling remark; that I would never call them cattle. . . . What I probably said was that actors should be *treated* like cattle." Immediately afterward, however, he gets closer to what he really must have meant when he tells us: "I will admit that I have, from time to time, hoped that technology would devise a machine to replace the actor." He then says that in *Foreign Correspondent* he took a step in this direction by having Joel McCrea play a scene with a windmill, and in *North by Northwest* he shot the sequence that Cary Grant shares with the crop duster. That airplane, he states, "had real star quality, for it drew an amazing amount of fan mail."[30]

More than once, Hitchcock said he envied Walt Disney, whose actors could be redrawn or erased at will on the story board. Had he lived long enough to see computerized characters at work, he might have felt that they approximate the ideal he pursued. Like the machines that make them, they can be readily manipulated. They don't talk back or make ignorant suggestions. They wouldn't resist either his formalist design or his conception of reality. Beautiful women can do that because their good looks and seductive appearance tend to undermine the goals he has set. Not only does glamour have "nothing to do with reality," but the same is true of the female attempt to be ladylike: "I hate it when actresses try to be ladies and in doing so become cold and lifeless, and nothing gives me more pleasure than to knock the ladylikeness out of chorus girls."[31] For that reason, he says, Madeleine Carroll gets pushed about in *The 39 Steps* and makes her first appearance in *The Secret Agent* with cold cream on her face.

On the other hand, Hitchcock insists that the actresses he chooses to direct must be elegant women, even "ladylike women" he says in one place, rather than sexy fleshpots. He claimed to prefer Nordic types because their sexiness is deeply hidden in them and must be discovered instead of being flaunted. He thought that stylish actresses—such as Grace Kelly, Eva Marie Saint, Joan Fontaine, Madeleine Carroll, Kim Novak, and Tippi Hedren, to name only a few of that sort whom he directed—have the greatest range of cinematic expressiveness. But they too would have to be molded, even manipulated by him, in order to function as he desired. After Hitchcock's death, Tippi Hedren, most particularly, attested to his possessive and tyrannical attempts to control her private life as well as her acting.[32]

In Hitchcock's defense, one should note his belief that only in film can an actor have the stage "all to himself."[33] This happens through close-ups and other techniques that magnify the presence and the importance of a performer on screen. Moreover, Hitchcock voiced his pleasure at the versatility of actors like Cary Grant and Peter Lorre, both of whom he praises because they knew how to introject a gamut of humorous as well as dramatic nuances through slight gestures of a kind that the camera can use to advantage. Through their comedic and ingratiating talent Hitchcock wished to make his audience sympathize with the hapless individual who has been caught in some precarious situation.

Grant's debonair insouciance made him a perfect choice for such roles, and Lorre's clownishness in The Secret Agent was crude enough for us to feel assured that all the problems would somehow work themselves out. The dramatic development could then evolve through twists and turns that squeezed reality into whatever manifestations that would increase suspense on the part of spectators who identified with the protagonist. Hitchcock could not have attained this integration

of film possibilities if he had treated Grant or Lorre as cattle—
or, with one or two possible exceptions, any of the other stars
he directed.

❊

As another entry into Hitchcock's effort to harmonize the
formal and the real, we should also mention his admiration
for the silent films at a time when they were beginning to
become obsolete. He sees them, at their best, as vehicles of
montage, and more puristic in their artistry than talkies,
which dilute the visuality of films by mixing it with sound. By
the end of the 1920s he himself did the same, but always with
a sense that something fundamentally cinematic was being
jeopardized by this degree of reliance on reality. He implies,
though he does not say it, that the less realistic movies are (as
in the case of the silent ones), the more the audience must
depend upon the filmmaker to create images they can under
stand without spoken words, images he arranges to elicit their
feelings.

On the other hand, Hitchcock also tells an interviewer, at
least once, that he prefers color films to black and white *because*
the former are more realistic than the latter. He rightly realized
that he could find ways of mastering both. More telling, I
think, is Hitchcock's assertion that the ideal analogy to film is
short story telling. In a short story the sheer length prevents
one from delving too deeply into the reality of a situation.
Without being artistically superficial, the short story has to
skim some surface, snaring and retaining the reader's interest
until an evident culmination has been achieved. Hitchcock
tended to avoid adaptations of novels because he thought they

cannot be reduced to the smaller scale of film, and therefore do not lend themselves to the needed transformation of the literary into the visual. The greater the novel, the more likely is this the case. Even so, he did direct various adaptations of novels, and even entire plays—for instance, *Rope* and *Dial M for Murder.* These he filmed as replicas of staged performances and without montage.

In theorizing as he does, Hitchcock fails to recognize the extent to which short stories can and do succeed as realistic vehicles. While minimizing our involvement in, or concern about, some regions of experience whose surface they are skimming, great short stories often yield a sharpened awareness of the world, and even an epiphany of something fundamental in our humanhood. And yet they need not explore at any length the specific bit of reality that they help us perceive and possibly savor. Hitchcock's approach to film suffers from a disability similar to theirs, though it redeems itself by constantly providing an experience that even the greatest novels cannot duplicate.

In this connection it is worth comparing *The 39 Steps* with the bestselling novel by John Buchan that Hitchcock adapted for the screen. Without being weighty or presuming to have philosophical scope, his movie is one of the triumphs of Western art. It gets its inspiration from Buchan's mediocre mystery story about spies and such but fillets out of it a series of interrelated episodes that unite suspense with comedy and romance beyond anything its literary source attempts or would be able to encompass. All narrative clutter has been eliminated in the film, and every scene leads directly into the next one with an economy of visual means that sustains our enjoyment throughout. The novel seems totally dated nowadays, and one has to wonder why people in the 1930s gobbled it up. But the film is a delight, however many times one sees it. As with all masterpieces, one always finds something new and satisfying in it.

❀

In two of his essays, Hitchcock invokes the word *God* as a means of presenting ideas not about the origin or meaning of the universe but rather about the nature of suspense as it exists in his movies. In "Let 'Em Play God," he draws upon the colloquial expression to reinforce his point about audience precognition of the facts being essential for there to be suspense. The spectators are playing God inasmuch as they know in advance what the relevant dangers are. But in "Would You Like to Know Your Future?" Hitchcock suggests that if we had knowledge of the future, above all our own, "most of the zest would go out of living. . . . The unknown has its appeal precisely because it is mysterious." From this he concludes that in keeping the future hidden God "is saying that things would be very dull without suspense. . . . He is also being merciful. Because, if life would be dull knowing about tomorrow, it would also be terrible."[34]

The first essay is of interest because anyone who makes movies as Hitchcock did is also playing God. Formulating his argument, he refers to the structure of *Rope*. In that movie, which deals with the mentality of the two young men who play God by deciding to terminate the life of their friend, the film spectators know from the beginning who committed the murder. Nevertheless we in the audience do not know how and whether the perpetrators will be apprehended. Our feeling of suspense results from that rather than from any godlike precognition. The second essay, written eleven years later, is even more problematic. When Hitchcock says that God mercifully spares us from the boredom and the meaninglessness of a life without suspense, he seems to be interpreting divine motivation as a model for what filmmakers like himself try to achieve. His statement is another protestation of the virtue in what he does for so many people, another justification of his life-enhancing mission as an artist. This attitude is innocuous enough, and rather wholesome in view of Hitchcock's illustrious role as a consummate innovator. Unfortunately, the basic idea is internally confused.

For if suspense consists in giving the audience knowledge in advance, how can God be creating that effect by keeping us from knowing what our future will be? One might reply that suspense in life results from the fact that, while we know we will die, no one knows exactly when or how. In other words, the situation would seem to be the same as with the bomb beneath the table. But is it? We only *suspect* that the imagined bomb might go off, and thus our feeling of suspense is directed to the likelihood that this will happen as well as to the nature and the timing of what may actually occur. In life itself there is uncertainty of a different kind. We know not only that a bomb resides within our very being but also that it will definitely go off and kill us sooner or later, and often in some unpredictable outcome.

The suspense of being alive is therefore not the same as in a Hitchcock movie, where we may even feel confident that the good guy who is in a threatened position will surely manage to escape. Cinematic suspense consists in waiting anxiously to see how a sympathetic character deals with whatever it is that besets him or her in the narrative. Inclusion in a work of art, especially one concocted by Hitchcock, is an aesthetic phenomenon of a type that existential human anxiety is not.

The breeziness of Hitchcock's speculations about God's interest in suspense may be used to buttress the belief that Hitchcock was only a technician, as he himself suggests, and not a thinker with any real philosophic scope. I have been trying to show that this view does him an injustice, and that his creativity bespeaks a world view worth treating seriously. What holds it all together are ideas about "the ordinary" that appear in each of Hitchcock's films. They manifest his kind of realism and are basic to his use of formalistic methods. They contribute to an all-pervasive contrast that he always presents as the contrapuntal relationship between everyday facticity and the extraordinary, even incredible, events he recounts.

Hitchcock's conception of the ordinary permeates the action in his films not only as a grounding in reality but also as an affirmation of its hideous disregard for human welfare. Throughout his movies Hitchcock expresses a kinship to ordinary people—for instance, his mother and his father, who was a wholesale grocer in Covent Garden as it still existed when *Sabotage* and *Frenzy* were made. The milieu in which his father plied his trade is itself a character in those films, and in the second one it elicits some of his best cinematography in two pivotal sequences. In both films, and in both sequences, we observe how ordinary life can shelter turpitude that crushes the values that most people cherish. In each case, Hitchcock shows how much he can say about the world by means of his versatile techniques.

Among the movies Hitchcock finished, *Frenzy* is undoubtedly his most violent, while also being the most explicit demonstration of his great distrust of what passes for ordinary life. After the seductive but sexually demented murderer, a seemingly ordinary wholesaler, rapes and then brutally strangles the protagonist's former wife, he calms himself by eating an apple, in fact the one his victim had bitten into before he entered, as if the two of them were sharing it in an act of oneness like Adam and Eve. He is a professional dealer in fruit. He takes possession of them, and he consumes this one as if to attest—in his disturbed condition—to having possessed the woman whose life he has plucked for his enjoyment.

Having forced this upon us, the camera then positions itself in the alleyway outside. The murderer leaves, but we see the former husband try to get in through the outer entrance. He finds the door locked and moves on. The camera sits still. Then two women, probably office workers, walk toward it down the alleyway, chatting idly. Meanwhile the victim's secretary returns from lunch, unlocks the door, and goes into the building. We know what she will find; suspense is not a part of the sequence. Instead we are enthralled by the fact that there is now no action to intrigue us or music to divert us, and so we are left in silence for what feels like a long time under the circumstances. The scene before us is perfectly ordinary, the young women in the alleyway conversing as they walk in our direction at the other end of the camera. Finally loud screaming comes from the building. It means that the secretary has discovered her employer's mangled body. The women are alarmed by what they hear, and their hearing it terminates our painful wait in a resolution that issues from the recognition by others of what we have already seen. It ratifies the feeling that ordinary, common, and presumably uneventful life can contain within it terrible evil and pathological cruelty in which we vicariously participate as observers who bought tickets to watch all this.

The other sequence, also with no music and a measured, platitudinous pace that is native to Hitchcock's cinematography, occurs when a later victim enters the murderer's apartment. Having prepared us for the worst by letting us hear his guileful lying to the young woman, the camera backs away. It has decided not to film the kind of thing we saw in the earlier scene. It slowly moves down the stairs of the unprepossessing little tenement, out through the hallway, into the street and what lies beyond it—Covent Garden at its most bustling. When sound finally returns, we hear the hybrid noises that were common in this market area. It is as if we and the camera have shied away from the perfectly ordinary but upsetting apartment in which the director has mercifully refrained from showing us what we do not want, or need, to see.

By forcing us to remember the previous occasion on our own, Hitchcock awakens our imagination more effectively than by throwing the violence at us again. This is obviously a trick on his part, but a superlative one. It strengthens his idea that what happens in peaceful-looking moments of life can be ontologically as well as morally unspeakable. The sequence conveys that point of view without dialogue or music because the reality of it is beyond our comprehension. The ineffability of brute existence exceeds any language and defeats our understanding or communication. It can only be shown.

A similar perspective exists in all of Hitchcock's work. In *Rear Window* James Stewart's courtyard looks like one he could have photographed himself in a middle-class neighborhood in which a murder would never be expected. In *Shadow of a Doubt* a comparable theme is encased within a post-Romantic and quasi-incestuous version of the myth of Beauty and the Beast. In *The 39 Steps* the governing idea occurs in the demeanor of the master spy with the missing joint in his finger. He gives every appearance of being a respectable member of society, and his wife and daughter act as if his business with Hannay is completely ordinary and aboveboard, though they undoubtedly know about its criminal nature. Even the cute and innocent-looking maid in their house in Scotland lies so convincingly to the police that we can only conclude that we too would never be able to see through the deceptiveness of this seemingly reputable household. It's not only skim milk that masquerades as cream, Hitchcock implies, but *all* of the everyday life that we naively take for granted as our native habitat.

Hitchcock never develops the epistemological ramifications of his skepticism about the ordinary. Instead he deploys it as a means of orienting the story in each film toward whatever emotional effects his technology can evoke. By instilling anxiety about events we normally experience as indicative of the real world, he fosters an underlying paranoia in everyone that intensifies the fearfulness his method expresses melodramatically. As Ernest Lehman says in that documentary to which I referred at the beginning of this chapter: "Paranoid is the word for Hitch." Lehman was describing Hitchcock as a managerial boss scrutinizing every detail of a production, and in his relations with his coworkers.

Beyond this, the comment applies to Hitchcock's vision of the world as a whole. It is an outlook that issues into a philosophical, though also pragmatic, framework for thrillers that may help us cope with the hideous aspects of our existence. But comedy and romance are also means by which human beings can overcome their subliminal dread. That is why Hitchcock drew so heavily on them as well in virtually every movie he made.

For the [film] experience to ring true, and for movies to *be* true in themselves, the final cut must show forth not only the ambiguities of life but also the ambivalences of the filmmaker. This dialectical goal, paradoxical as it may sometimes seem, is present in everything Welles did as a director/actor/scriptwriter for film, theater, or radio.

Orson Welles

At various times Hitchcock refers to his idea of the "MacGuffin." It is a mysterious object of pursuit that sustains audience attention throughout the trajectory of a movie. As such, it is the basis of whatever suspense Hitchcock creates within a particular film. But, as he remarks, the MacGuffin is in itself a thing of no great significance. It is a secret document, perhaps, but one whose contents do not interest or preoccupy the spectators and may never be disclosed to them. At the very end of *The 39 Steps* we do learn the formula that the spies were trying to take out of the country; and in *Torn Curtain* Paul Newman finally tricks the German professor to write on the blackboard, for our uninformed inspection, the meaning of pi. But the fact remains that Hitchcock's entire effort as a film-maker consists in arousing our curiosity about something that hardly matters to us. It is just an aesthetic thread that leads us on, knitting together our concern about the perilous experience of protagonists to whom it does matter for one reason or another. They become entangled with it, and that propels the suspense from scene to scene.

Hitchcock reveals the cunning of his device by recounting an anecdote that embodies the original MacGuffin idea:

There are two men sitting in a train going to Scotland and one man
says to the other, "Excuse me, sir, but what is that strange parcel you
have on the luggage rack above you?" "Oh," says the other, "that's a
MacGuffin." "Well," says the first man, "what's a MacGuffin?" The
other answers, "It's an apparatus for trapping lions in the Scottish
Highlands." "But," says the first man, "there *are* no lions in the
Scottish Highlands." "Well," says the other, "then that's no
MacGuffin."[1]

I mention this now because it serves as an entry into Orson
Welles's different approach to the nature of film. He writes,
produces, directs, and often takes a starring role in melodramas
that bear a variable resemblance to the ones that Hitchcock
made. But he approaches them with a mindset that is quite
remote from Hitchcock's. Welles's work is haunted by a sense
of the past which Hitchcock does not have. For Welles the all-
embracing MacGuffin in life is the constantly evolving fragility
of our temporal being, the past enduring as a nonexistence that
somehow remains present to us, but without the vital immediacy it had when it was the present.

As Hitchcock's anecdote suggests, the meaning of the word
MacGuffin—"an apparatus for trapping lions in the Scottish
Highlands"—is used to thwart our attempt to get whatever
information we may have sought. The anecdote is therefore a
wry and amusing commentary on the human inclination to
hide some truth from the prying noses of other people. In
Hitchcock's employment of this notion, the MacGuffin
becomes a contrivance for arousing curiosity and directing it to
the predetermined unfolding of his story. For Welles the equivalent device serves as an aesthetic exploration into the fundamental character of our temporal reality, our lives as we exist in
time. If Hitchcock can rightly describe himself as a maker of

thrillers, so too might Welles be characterized as a maker of mystery stories, even detective stories, about the past in its possibly unfathomable nature and in its evasive continuance in what is now real to us.

In *Citizen Kane* Welles establishes this problematic at the very start and then uses it as the basis for his investigation into the departed life of Charles Foster Kane. Not only is Rosebud something that belongs to Kane's earliest years, but it is also a reminder of goodness that has always eluded him. Though elaborations of this theme in later movies that Welles wrote and directed go far beyond its function in *Citizen Kane*, the search for vanished origins—not all of which are highly cherished—recurs in many of them. His relentless probing becomes for Welles a philosophical tool that Hitchcock never felt he needed.

❀

There are various means by which we might approach the vision that Welles articulates in relation to his conception of what the past is and what its disappearance implies. One way is to look for relevant symbols in his movies. He himself scorned this as a modus operandi, above all when it seeks to disclose autobiographical data about himself as a human being. In his discussions with Peter Bogdanovich, Welles says that throughout his creative life he never concerned himself with symbols of any sort: "I hate symbolism. . . . I never sit down and say how we're going to have a symbol for some character. They happen automatically, because life is full of symbols. So is art. You can't avoid them."[2] But if you purposely insert them, he tells us, the aesthetic results are disastrous.

Even in the case of *The Trial* Welles claims there "isn't a single symbol in it," although the subject matter might make us feel that we ought to be searching for symbols. When Bogdanovich says that the children tormenting K at the end of that film must be a symbol of something, or else "what's the point of it?," Welles replies: "What's the point of a dream? . . . Yes, it's a dream—a particular nightmare—inspired by Kafka. It's surrealist, if you want. But the good surrealists aren't symbolists."[3] Welles doubts that Kafka himself was interested in symbols. His film remains true to the spirit of Kafka, he says, because that was "a spirit of hauntings and anguish and all kinds of feelings that stir in the bloodstream of the race, and they're far above and beyond and too essential, too noble, to be reduced to shoddy . . . symbolism."[4]

We need to study the ramifications of this view. But first I want to compare it to something that Ingmar Bergman said about symbolism in his own work. Answering a student who asks whether the symbols that occur throughout his films are intentional or rather read in by one or another spectator, Bergman replies:

I have never made a symbol in my whole life! . . . And if I *find* a symbol, I kill it because to me, my pictures are like my dreams. Of course, you know we have learned that our dreams are full of symbols. I don't mind. If a train goes in a tunnel, I say, "Okay." But I don't *use* that symbol. . . . So, no, there are no symbols in my pictures. What I hate most of all in art is the self-conscious symbol, the symbol that is put here like a strawberry on the ice cream. I think that's terrible, terrible![5]

Though Hitchcock consciously used the train going into a tunnel in the last shot of *North by Northwest* as a symbol of now authorized (since marital) sexual consummation, Welles and Bergman consider this kind of effect too facile. Neither denies the occasional presence of symbols in his own movies. In saying that they do not *use* them, both are making assertions about the relevant and fundamental meanings in their work as well as about their own intentions. Whatever differences separate these two filmmakers, they are alike in realizing that their productions thrive in a manner and at a level that no type of symbolism can approximate. Hitchcock would undoubtedly agree, while savoring the naughtiness in his mildly humorous reference to carnal completion. Moreover, he could rightly insist that the symbolism of crisscrossing railroad tracks in *Strangers on a Train* has organic import within the narrative of that film.

In relation to what I have suggested as the underlying theme in much of Welles's work, we may ask ourselves: What is, or might be, symbolic of the past? The search for remote beginnings of a person's life, as in *Citizen Kane*, or the reminder of what American culture was like before the invention of the automobile, as in *The Magnificent Ambersons*, or the buried criminality of the protagonist's former activities in *Mr. Arkadin*, and its progressive discovery in the present? But these elements of the Wellesean films are not merely symbolic. They are themselves constituents, active motifs, of their respective stories. They belong to the fictional world that the filmmaker has imagined, and that we as spectators must reimagine. They are part of the artist's attempt to express a view about the world, about persons and events as they exist and are valued in our reality. Symbols, whether self-conscious or not, are generally desiccated by their own abstractness. The works of filmmakers like Welles or Bergman have greater vibrancy than that. They are more personally conceived and more inclusive of the human complexity that fiction penetrates.

In one place Welles says that the camera is a kind of litmus paper that registers the authenticity of what is being enacted, the "presence or absence of *feeling.*"[6] In themselves, symbols can hardly tap this capability, above all when the feeling that is being photographed incorporates someone's experience in and about the past.

❀

Much of Welles's approach to Shakespeare's plays—his directing as well as his acting in them—devolves from this preoccupation with what has been lost or retained through the passage of time. That point of view shows itself most strikingly in *Chimes at Midnight*. The first bit of dialogue, repeated later in a slightly altered form, occurs in reminiscences exchanged by Falstaff and Shallow. They are both old men now, prolonging life in themselves by fondly regurgitating moments in their past that they relish in the present as happy times that are no more. Shallow is emotional about them, so much so that he can only repeat his exclamation: "Jesus, the days that we have seen!" Falstaff, played by Welles, is less sentimental. Though smiling and with a focused look of intelligent appreciation, he says in measured tones: "We have heard the chimes at midnight, Master Shallow." In their deceptive sparsity, these words evoke the splendor of former delights and late-night revelry that the two friends cannot reexperience but will never forget.

Welles presents Falstaff as a refugee of the good old days whose passing Shakespeare laments. According to Welles, this bespeaks a special goodness in Falstaff. He even asserts that he is "one of the only great characters in all dramatic literature who is essentially *good* . . . his goodness is basic—like bread, like wine. He's just shining with love; he asks for so little, and in the end, of course, he gets nothing." Welles then says:

Even if the good old days never existed, the fact that we can *conceive* of such a world is, in fact, an affirmation of the human spirit. That the imagination of man is capable of creating the myth of a more open, more generous time is not a sign of our folly. Every country has its "Merrie England," a season of innocence, a dew-bright morning of the world. Shakespeare sings of that lost Maytime in many of his plays, and Falstaff—that pot-ridden old rogue—is its perfect embodiment. All the roguery and the tavern wit and the liar and bluff is simply a turn of his—it's a little song he sings for his supper. It isn't really what he's about.[7]

While delineating the lovability of Falstaff, as Shakespeare also does, Welles shapes the five plays he is adapting for the screen to show, more pointedly than does Shakespeare, how Falstaff's fixation on the past prevents him from living in the present. When Hal becomes the king, Falstaff is carried away by his memory of the jolly times they used to have. Even in the midst of them, however, Hal's soliloquy about his coming reformation of himself had prepared us for his repudiating Falstaff's foolishness at the end. Falstaff is totally unready for that. In the coronation sequence, he disgraces himself because he assumes that his relation to Hal is still as it was, and he pays the emotional price of this ridiculous assumption.

Welles spends less time on the description of Falstaff's death than Olivier had in his transposed scenes about it in *Henry V*. As usual, Welles was avoiding sentimentality as much as possible, but also he had already reached the climax of his tale about the evanescent goodness of the past and its devastating effect on anyone who thinks he or she can keep it alive in the present. Welles goes beyond Shakespeare in making this perspective the dramatic focus of the myth that guides and permeates his entire film.

In reaction to a critic's having compared him to John Ford, whose work he much admired, Welles states that they are hooked on different myths and that Ford is one of the myth-*makers*, whereas he himself is really interested in examining "the myth of the past, *as* a myth."[8] This alone explains Welles's denial that his work is autobiographical. Though he talks about ways in which his own past corresponds to details in each narrative, and though he recognizes how greatly his vision of the world is idiosyncratic to himself, he maintains that critics who interpret the contents of that vision by reference to his life are fabricating something of their own invention.

Bogdanovich tells us that when he said that French auteur theorists "believe there *are* no works, only authors," Welles heatedly answered: "Well, I disagree. . . . I believe there are only *works*."[9] More than once, Bogdanovich tries to identify Kane's mother with the one that Welles had and lost in his childhood. When she died, he immediately stopped developing the musical talents she had nourished in him, and Bogdanovich wonders whether she might not have been the key to the Rosebud motif of the movie.

Every time the suggestion comes up, however, Welles vehemently rejects this mode of reasoning. He points out that his mother was totally different from Kane's mother, and he denies that there are any Rosebuds in his youthful memories of her. He does admit that after she died his life with his free-living father was for him a kind of Rosebud in the town of Grand Detour, Illinois, where his father bought an old hotel and used it as a shelter for his show business friends: "Grand Detour was one of those lost worlds, one of those Edens that you get thrown out of. It really was kind of invented by my father. He's the one who kept out the cars and the electric lights. It was one of the 'Merrie Englands'. . . . It's a theme that interests me. A nostalgia for the garden—it's a recurring theme in all our civilization."[10]

A little later Bogdanovich tries to explain this theme in terms of Welles's sensitivity to grace, to gallantry, and to chivalry in general: "Isn't *Ambersons* as much a story of the end of chivalry—the end of gallantry—as *Chimes at Midnight*?" To which Welles retorts: "Peter, what interests me is the *idea* of these dated old virtues. And why they still seem to speak to us when, by all logic, they're so hopelessly irrelevant." He then says that is why his *Don Quijote* film (which remained unfinished at his death) was taking him so long to complete. Even when Cervantes was writing the novel, he adds, Don Quijote was anachronistic. "I've simply translated the anachronism. My film demonstrates that he [Quijote] and Sancho Panza are eternal."[11]

As a rebuttal of an extreme and somewhat simplistic version of the auteur theory, Welles's comments seem to me very telling. They must be taken as ancillary to any discussion about how the cinematographer, the lighting expert, the editor, and all the others who participate in the making of a film collaborate with the director who is given credit for it. The Wellesean concern about the myth of the past, or any other myth, pertains to something else. It is an ideational element that differs from any technical or specialized contributions to this art form, even though it pervasively unifies them all. It is the dimension that reveals the personal and typically human stratum without which the communal product could not have much aesthetic value. An astute director has a great deal of control over all that.

This component of filmmaking creates a meaningfulness that transcends any single time or spatial location. It is something that people of almost every type can respond to in their own way. Fictional characters like Don Quijote and Sancho Panza are thereby rendered universal. Though they exist within the limits of their story, and emanate from the finite imaginations of both the artist who conceives them and the audience that is able to appreciate their truthfulness, they may indeed be called "immortal" or even "eternal," as Welles suggests. They belong to the realm of spirit, as all great art does. In being offshoots of the aesthetic, they exemplify our human ability to exceed nature while also living in it. The genius of Orson Welles consisted in his ability to exploit that fact of our reality. Insofar as he imprinted his personal mode of artistic exploitation upon all the films he made, it seems appropriate to call him their auteur.

In trying to understand what Welles means by the myth of the past, and how that myth operates within the structure of his films, it will be useful to begin by placing his efforts alongside the work of his friend John Huston. Welles acted in several of Huston's productions—most notably as Father Mapple in *Moby Dick*—and Huston collaborated on the script of *The Stranger* and performed in *The Other Side of the Wind,* Welles's unfinished opus about an old director. *The Dead,* the last movie Huston made, is especially a propos in studying Welles's ideas about the past. It too is largely focused on the past, but it deals with that reality in ways that differ from the Wellesean perspective.

Huston's version of James Joyce's long short story incorporates a conception of time—its nature and phenomenology—that deviates from what Joyce himself believed. Though Welles never filmed anything by Joyce, his ideas about past and present are much closer to Joyce's than are Huston's.

To defend that assertion, I need several pages to analyze Huston's *Dead* in itself and in its relation to the thinking of Joyce. Huston warrants this attention not only because of his affinity to Welles but also because his mode of filmmaking prepares us for Welles's alternate achievement at a contemporaneous moment in the history of American cinema. The discussion of Huston and of Joyce that follows will provide a context for what I say hereafter about Welles's use of the past as a mythological element in his films.

Throughout the Huston movie there is a lacquered touch of sentimental coziness, sustained by the folksy Irish music played on a Gaelic harp as background for the opening credits and then recurrently. Welles deliberately avoids such effects in his films, or rather he transforms them by narrative ambiguities and complicated technical virtuosity that I will consider later. There is a poignancy in the past as Welles portrays it, but only because its being dead precludes any possibility of our reliving the vital freshness it may have had. Speaking about himself as a human being who happens to be a director, Welles reports: "When I shoot on location, I sense and see the place in such a violent way that now—when I look at those places again—they're like tombs, completely dead. There are spots in the world that to my eyes are cadavers; because I have already shot there—for me, they are completely finished."[12] As the kind of writer that he was, Joyce could have said the same. It may in fact be a reason why he left cadaverous Dublin and would write about it but never live there again.

More than one reviewer has said that John Huston's terminal film looks like the work of a man who was himself close to death. I am not sure that I know what this means, since not all people who think they are dying react to that circumstance in a similar manner. It is true that during the making of *The Dead* Huston needed an oxygen tank in order to breathe, but he could and did direct as he normally would have. His filming of Joyce's long short story, which was adapted for the screen by his son Tony Huston, can therefore be studied apart from his knowledge of his own imminent demise. For one thing the movie positions itself at the outset as a representation of the past and not the present or the future. An introductory card reads "Dublin 1904." That was more or less the year that Joyce wrote this novella about his city as he saw it at the time he was writing. The manuscript was completed in 1907 and was added on to earlier stories of *Dubliners*, which had been published in 1904. As Joyce intended them, all the entries were not about the past but about present-day life in Dublin.

Can there be a "myth" about the present? We may occasionally think of it in rosy terms, as speculators did recently during the time of the dot-com bubble, and yet that is not the same. For an experience or an epoque to take on mythic proportions, it usually needs the reverberating perspective of cherished memories that we may have about departed possibilities. Whatever it really was before, the past always remains amenable to that employment, much as a gilded frame does in helping us to see a historical painting as an aesthetic object. For a literary realist such as Joyce, who wished to depict the sensory texture of thought and feeling that constitutes a human life, whatever is depicted must be shown in its own current actuality. The past as Joyce envisaged it can be evoked as a persistent and even powerful residue in what is now present; but it will not be idealized or mythically glamorized. In *Ulysses*, Stephen Dedalus, his autobiographical character, says that history is the nightmare from which he is trying to awake. Though characters in "The Dead" may be prone to nostalgia, a common response in men and women, the story is not. Being a consummate realist, Joyce reports what he observes and then nonchalantly pares his fingernails, as Stephen suggests in the speculative remarks at the end of *A Portrait of the Artist as a Young Man*.

In that novel and in its earlier draft entitled *Stephen Hero*, Joyce formulates the principle of what he calls "epiphany." It is a showing forth. In the mystical traditions the whole of reality is said to be that through which divinity shows itself. From the very beginnings of cinema, many film theorists have asserted that their chosen art is inherently epiphanous, more so indeed than any of the other media. These theorists believe that the photographic image, above all in motion pictures, is uniquely revelatory. And surely it does project what is real in a reproduction unlike that of any other art form. Whether they record common appearances, as in the movies of Lumière, or are freely fanciful, as in those of Méliès, films have the power to make us apprehend reality beyond any literary description or theatrical representation. The concomitant artificiality of cinema may impose an unreal filter upon the ordinary, but through that filter the world can be seen to reveal itself with beguiling immediacy.

Though we are always part of some reality, we are usually unable to appreciate or retain its visual and sonic aspects. They are forever transient and overly rich for our meager capacity of assimilation. Goethe's Faust drops dead when his questing spirit envisions an actual moment of true beauty and he wills it to *"Verweile doch, du bist so schön"* (Stay then, thou art so fair). As T. S. Eliot said, humankind cannot bear very much reality—whether or not it is beautiful. In cinematic media, this all-too-human frailty is somewhat overcome. The real and beautiful is renewed in a lively simulacrum through which its enduring properties can shine forth without losing their own essential quality.

Even the unrealistic tricks that occur in Méliès's films—or in the animation and special effects that are familiar to us nowadays—are readily accepted because they instigate a feeling of something that we know as factual and available to direct perception. Far from defeating or curtailing our sense of reality, the formalistic elements in film enable us to watch and to understand a great deal that would otherwise elude us as our consciousness moves in whatever trajectory it may follow from day to day.

The realist ontology or aesthetics defended by thinkers like André Bazin, Siegfried Kracauer, and others is therefore very plausible within its limits. These writers, and those who interpret the nature of film as they do, recognize the role of epiphany in the creation and enjoyment of film. In elaborating their philosophical vision, they use varied terminology; but it generally remains fairly uniform with respect to the notion of a showing forth by means of cinematic art which they deem definitive to it. The Joycean concept is thus attuned to the realism of film as well as literature. Though Joyce was primarily concerned with the latter, he treats it as itself analogous to what occurs in photography and motion pictures.

His spokesman Stephen defines epiphany as "a sudden spiritual manifestation, whether in the vulgarity of speech or of gesture or in a memorable phase of the mind itself . . . the most delicate and evanescent of moments." To make his point, Stephen mentions the clock of the Ballast Office: "I will pass it time after time, allude to it, refer to it, catch a glimpse of it. It is only an item in the catalogue of Dublin's street furniture. Then all at once I see it and I know at once what it is: epiphany."[13]

In this place Joyce describes epiphany as "the gropings of a spiritual eye" that seeks "an esthetic apprehension" of what appears before it. He invokes the ideas of Thomas Aquinas about what is requisite for beauty to exist, and in particular his emphasis upon the "claritas" (radiance) of an object which is a showing forth that enables us to "recognize *that* it is that thing which it is." When this happens, Joyce tells us, "its soul, its whatness, leaps to us from the vestment of its appearance. . . . The object achieves its epiphany."[14]

Joyce's remarks about aesthetic experience of the diverse whatness in all things runs parallel to George Santayana's doctrine of essences and our intuition of them through a contemplative fixation upon their formal being. More thoroughly than Santayana in his one novel *The Last Puritan*, or his other fictional work, Joyce applied this view to the underlying design of *Ulysses*, *A Portrait of the Artist as a Young Man*, and above all *Dubliners*. Each of the short stories in *Dubliners* concludes with a showing that manifests the integrity and indivisible nature of some momentary "triviality," as Joyce calls it. For him, as for Santayana, such occasions are spiritual without being transcendental. They are not revelations of a reality beyond the realm of mundane experience, as Aquinas and the religious traditions believed, but only indications of the whatness in human existence as we all encounter it daily. Joyce's recourse to the concept of epiphany is entirely compatible with both his metaphysical naturalism and his aesthetic realism. As we shall see, the same applies to the overall vision of Orson Welles.

In "The Dead" Joyce depicts a festive gathering that happens each year when the Catholic celebration of the Epiphany occurs, eleven days after Christmas. For the two main characters, Gabriel and Gretta, the evening ends with a new realization about their marriage and the kind of marital attachment that has developed in them throughout the years. This is an amorphous epiphany, less precise though more inclusive than those in the earlier stories. The reality it shows forth exceeds our immersion in a single event or encounter with an object like the clock of the Ballast Office. The party at the Morkans', where the guests discuss topics of musical and local interest, and then the subsequent return by Gabriel and Gretta to their hotel, are realistic preparation for the all-embracing epiphany at the end.

In the film the original structure is radically changed by the insertion of subsidiary epiphanies that lead to the final one like lower steps in a ladder. Watching *The Dead* after having read "The Dead," one is continually conscious of how much the story line in Huston's version is more than just a transference to the screen of what Joyce had written. The film is a running interpretation, a feat of literary criticism, that issues into the numerous and consecutive embellishments introduced by either the scriptwriter or the director. Their innovations serve as cinematic arrows that guide us through the accompanying realism and establish a meaningful continuum in which there are more epiphanies than Joyce employed.

On his arrival in the Morkan house Mr. Browne in the movie, but not in the short story, brings flowers that he likens to the gifts of the Magi and hence suitable for a feast of the Epiphany. It is a joyous occasion allowing even the members of the audience to participate, albeit vicariously as observers. When the dancing subsides, Mr. Grace (who has been invented as an added personage) elicits the first of the epiphanies in the movie by reading Lady Gregory's poem about the girl whose life is ruined by her passionate love for a man who promised her impossible things—among others, gloves of the skin of a fish—but then abandoned her to a sense of total alienation from God as well as him. Some of the younger women at the party comment about the sad yet beautiful character of the poem and how much they are moved by the romantic sentiment it expresses. Though Gretta says nothing, the camera lingers on her bemused countenance as she listens to the recitation and responds inwardly to it. None of this exists in Joyce. Not only is there not a Mr. Grace, but also no one reads that poem or any other.

This first, preliminary, epiphany does not disclose, or even denote, the secret memory that has begun to arise from Gretta's past. But it makes us wonder about the poem's effect upon her, and that leads to the next epiphany. This one occurs at the dinner table when the company has been discussing the condition of operatic singing in Dublin. After the guests have reminisced about the many great tenors of former years, and lamented that there are few who are like them nowadays, Aunt Kate mentions one she heard in her youth whose name was Parkinson. Hardly anyone else remembers him. Her face flushes and tears start to glisten in her eyes as she thinks about his soft and lovely voice. The camera gives us a close-up of her features, and we know that something of importance has

surfaced in her at this moment. It derives from the ability of the
lyric art to embody affective attitudes we may have toward
others, and even toward tenors or comparable artists who
express our deepest feelings through that art. But we learn
nothing much about these elusive realities that matter so
greatly to Aunt Kate. In Joyce there is little of this discussion
about singing. Parkinson is named, and Aunt Kate speaks of
him with "enthusiasm," but she shows none of the emotional
intensity that is so pronounced in the film.

Aunt Kate's reaction functions as a signpost that becomes
obvious when Bartell D'Arcy, the operatic tenor, sings offstage
"The Lass of Aughrim." The song is heard as an isolated aria,
Gretta listening to it in a trance while she pauses on a landing
under a semi-circular stained glass partition that makes her
look like a consecrated saint or even the Virgin Mary. There is
no background noise, no talking or sounds of laughter, as there
is in the novella. In the film this sequence stands out from the
rest of the narrative, as "Vissi d'arte" does in Puccini's *Tosca*. In
Joyce, Gabriel can barely hear or follow the singing that has
captivated his wife: "The song seemed to be in the old Irish
tonality and the singer seemed uncertain both of his words and
of his voice." Gabriel does perceive, however, that the words
were "expressing grief."[15]

In the movie the song is sung with much beauty and
accurate feeling by Frank Patterson, the great Irish tenor who
also acts the role of Bartell D'Arcy. Listening to his singing, we
can see why Gretta, or any music lover, would be entranced by
this music. The film does not tell us, as Joyce does, that Gabriel
thinks that an artist could create a painting of his wife at that
moment and call it *Distant Music*. But though this suggests
how little Gabriel understands his wife's rapt attention, we do

not need to know that in this sequence. We hear the exquisite sounds as she does, and we observe her contemplative and quasi-religious profile under the stained glass as she concentrates on what the music awakens in her.

In Joyce this interlude prepares the reader for the scene in which Gretta later informs Gabriel about Michael Furey, who used to sing "The Lass of Aughrim" to her, just before he died when they were both teenagers. In the film the song is itself an epiphany, and a major one, since Gretta has never revealed to Gabriel its enormous significance for her. The cinematography is somewhat marred because the camera does not quite know what to make of Gabriel himself as he stands at the foot of the stairs looking up at his wife while they listen to the song together and yet separated from each other by their individual line of sight and physical location. The mixture of long shots and close-ups seems to be trying to say something to the audience, but it is difficult for us to decipher what that might be without any Joycean narration to aid our comprehension. What could have been dynamic cinematically ends up being static, visually inert except for the montages of Gretta in her meditative state on the landing.

In Huston's rendition, as in the text, the climactic epiphany occurs when Gretta tells Gabriel about Michael Furey and the crucial period in her past. That happens as husband and wife are about to go to bed in their room at the hotel. At this juncture the movie and the short story are similar, though seeing Gretta (played by Angelica Huston) suck her thumb when she sobbingly falls asleep after airing her remembrance creates a further dimension in the film. Nevertheless, the context of the massive epiphany has been altered. In the story Gabriel had felt a sexual urge toward his wife in the cab as they traveled through the snow-covered streets. She was oblivious to his "more than tender" gesture at the time, but his reluctant renewal of it in the bedroom seems to have elicited her willingness after all the years of silence to admit him into levels of herself that she had always kept hidden.

In the film none of this exists, and even the ride in the cab has been turned into a setting for Gabriel's story about Jonny, his grandfather's horse. (The anecdote shows how an animal's natural instincts can be demolished through enforced submission to civilized restraint, and that may be why Gabriel's self-reflexive account is meaningful to him.) In Joyce, Gabriel tells the story at the Morkans' house, while waiting nervously for Gretta to come downstairs. In her abstracted mood Huston's Gretta attends only slightly to Gabriel's anecdote, and there is nothing equivalent to the erotic rebuff that Joyce presented as transitional to the last epiphany.

Near the end of the story, Joyce describes the effect of Gretta's words upon Gabriel. In the film his face appears in close-up and we hear his own voice speaking the mental impressions that are going through his head. The close-ups of Gabriel are interlaced with his imaginings about Aunt Julia's coming death and about snow falling across Ireland, covering the living and the dead, including those who are buried in cemeteries like the one in which Michael Furey lies. Apart from the banality of the images, this termination destroys the forcefulness of what Joyce had been constructing from the beginning. He had pictured an evening of routine merriment, engaging in some regards but as bland as a Dutch interior, out of which emerges a highly dramatic and emotionally intricate revelation about the nature of the married couple's life together. Though the data are provided by Gretta, the increased awareness occurs in Gabriel. From start to finish the story is an unfolding of his personal rite of passage, his pilgrimage toward the truth about the past and present he has shared with this woman.

In the film the succession of minor epiphanies that I have cited yields a series of linking episodes that succeed within their own partial domain. Nor is anything lost by focusing more than Joyce does upon Gretta and her experience at the party as well as afterward. What is sacrificed, and what lessens the achievement of the film to that extent, is the complexity of ultimate insight toward which Joyce had carefully directed everything. This occurs in the welter of feelings that swirl within Gabriel after Gretta has fallen asleep, feelings he cannot fully digest or adequately turn into language—as a poet might—even by talking to himself.

In Joyce, but not in the film, Gabriel is clearly a considerate and loving husband. That is foundational in the story's comprehensive epiphany. It involves much more than the fact that Gretta may have felt love for Michael, doubtless as a young person who did not consummate her ardent inclinations in any physical behavior. It signifies her never having had with Gabriel himself a strong and compelling romantic love of the kind that Western culture has idealized for centuries in song and legend.

Delineating Gabriel's assessment of what he has now heard, Joyce states: "He thought of how she who lay beside him had locked in her heart for so many years that image of her lover's eyes when he had told her that he did not wish to live." In his love for his wife, Gabriel accepts this as "the full glory of some passion." Responsive to that thought, "generous tears filled Gabriel's eyes. He had never felt like that himself toward any woman but he knew that such a feeling must be love. The tears gathered more thickly in his eyes and in the partial darkness he imagined he saw the form of a young man standing under a dripping tree. Other forms were near. His soul had approached that region where dwell the vast hosts of the dead."[16]

At no point does Gabriel question the goodness of his marriage. He resonates instead to the "full glory" of the love that Gretta once found in relation to someone else. He weeps for himself, as an excluded male, but his tears are primarily a venting of sincere and compassionate feelings about his wife's devastating loss of vibrant impulses swallowed up in the distant past. The dead are buried in that primordial quicksand. Though we who live differ from them in having active yearnings, such as the tender ones that Gabriel felt in the cab and in the bedroom, any sexual or amatory frustration we undergo becomes a foreshadowing of the death that pervades everything in the past. All that we can salvage in the present is the memory, like Gretta's, of moments or events that are inevitably irretrievable. Though Gabriel has been excluded from this segment of her being, his love for Gretta elucidates for him the mythic plenitude that is epiphanized through what has erupted in her.

To some extent Huston's cinematography augments the Joycean vision. In the outdoor shots of snow-covered streets at night, and most notably in the closing scene of Gabriel looking at the descending snowflakes from within his unlighted room, Huston's photography articulates an opposition of black and white. That alone reminds us that life itself, as Joyce would say, and everything of brightest value in it, depends upon material facticities that sooner or later coldly push all reality into the darkened deadliness of the past. Huston provides a pictorial enrichment to this, and in other ways as well the film version makes commendable supplements to the text.

I briefly list a few: the extended conversation not only about past singers but also about everyday matters in the life of Dublin; the enlarged role of Bartell D'Arcy, who dances, chatters with the ladies, and offers opinions about other performers (including songbirds), as well as letting us hear the aria that Joyce can only describe; the many new lines given to Mr. Browne, to Freddy Malins and his mother, and even to the cabbie who takes them home; the identification of Miss Ivors as a political stalwart who leaves the party in order to go to a republican meeting, which amplifies her anti–West Briton taunts that are in the original but never clarified there.

These are all valid additions in the screenplay, but others are sometimes very damaging. For instance, consider what Joyce says about Aunt Julia's singing of the Bellini aria "Arrayed for the Bridal": "Her voice, clear and strong in tone, attacked with great spirit the runs which embellish the air and though she sang very rapidly she did not miss even the smallest of the grace notes. To follow the voice, without looking at the singer's face, was to feel and share the excitement of swift and secure flight."[17] Joyce implies that if one looked at the singer's face one might be surprised by her aged appearance. Huston does show us how old Aunt Julia is, but he has chosen to make her singing match her physiognomic decay.

The voice we hear is so cracked and unpleasant that even the cameraman leaves the room. While the painful singing recedes into the background, he takes us on a tour of the Morkan house and zooms in on relics of the past, mementoes of long since deceased family members who lived there. Having completed this dreary attempt to touch our hearts, he then goes back to the party, where the screenwriter unconscionably turns Freddy Malins's praise for the singing—entirely justified in view of what Joyce has said—into the comically asinine utterances of a man who is three-quarters stewed.

These shortcomings might have been corrected if Huston had lived long enough to spend more time in the cutting room. And, for all we know, the same may be true of the nostalgia that leaves its mark on almost everything in the film. Even so, I think one can rightly believe that, in this movie and at his best, Huston resembles what Welles said about John Ford. Both were makers of a myth about the past, whereas Welles wanted to *examine* that kind of myth in order to learn how something that was once flourishing and wonderful, perhaps, can now be lifeless and often tragically dead. Those who no longer exist have only the past, though the human spirit in them may live on. It survives through expressive arts that preserve it in the present and in whatever future that present can fashion for it. To see the world this way is to see reality as both Joyce and Welles did. They explicitly reject pure sentimentality or nostalgia, and that is why their work—in contrast to Huston's *Dead*—has so little of either. But then, one might say, *they* are not mythmakers.

❀

Though Welles sometimes alludes only obliquely to it, he often mentions his desire to study the nature of some mythic past. He says that what intrigued him in *The Heart of Darkness*, Conrad's novel that he could never manage to film, was a theme that *Citizen Kane* also had—"the search for the key to something." He calls this "a thing I like very much in pictures."[18] At the same time, he expresses doubt about the search for Rosebud that motivates the entire development in *Citizen Kane*. The idea came first from Herman J. Mankiewicz, who collaborated with Welles on the screenplay, and whose name precedes his in the credits. Having denied that he himself had Rosebuds in his past, Welles says that he had formerly wanted a *Rashomon* kind of approach for *Citizen Kane*. In it a person would be shown as seeming to be very different, depending on which people said what about him. That "gimmick," as Welles calls it, remains but is secondary while the Rosebud notion somehow worked even though he felt uneasy about it. In order to minimize the importance of Rosebud, Welles has the reporter at the end claim that his not finding what he sought doesn't really matter because "Kane was a man who got everything he wanted, and then lost it. Maybe Rosebud was something he couldn't get or something he lost."

The camera, which knows more than any reporter can discover, then zooms in on the sled we have formerly seen being covered by snow, except that now it is being burned in a pile of junk. But we miss the point of that if we sigh sympathetically and say: "Ah yes, the fleeting days of happy childhood, never to last for long in any of us." It is the *past* that is being incinerated, for Kane as for everyone. That is the meaning of Rosebud in this film, and of the smoke that rises from a chimney in the final sequence. Time cannot be regained. The past—like existence as a whole—turns into darkened dust. Those who think they can grasp its ephemeral being in anyone's life will be thwarted. The film begins with a shot of a large No Trespassing sign, and then repeats it at the very end as if to underscore the menacing and forbidden nature of the reporter's prying, and ours, into the reality that is hermetically hidden in a person's life.

In *Citizen Kane* we are introduced to this search for a key to the past by the opening newsreel, which is a parody of the popular feature *The March of Time*. In the film it is called *News on the March*. The ebullience and assertiveness of that title as well as the rapid pace in each episode of the newsreel makes the past seem like something we can always count on to enliven our daily existence, something that marches on with us as we bravely face the tribulations of the present and the future. The flashbacks that follow in the narrative are also fast moving, and sharply etched, in almost every segment. In their totality as a kaleidoscopic biography, they relate the story of someone who collects objects that are dead, as all art is, someone who remains throughout a man who never learns how to bring them into any aesthetic experience of his. He collects the past without being able to restore it to the condition of meaningful enjoyability that made it valuable for the flourishing civilizations in which it once existed.

When Kane first meets Susan, he is on his way to the warehouse that stores the belongings of his dead mother. Having been deflected from that, he instinctively tries to turn Susan into an art object that he can possess like the other ones he has wrenched out of the past. In forcing her to be a professional artist, an opera singer, he relegates her to the same condition as everything else he has acquired but cannot truly enjoy.

The myth of the past is equally engrained in *The Magnificent Ambersons*. The film opens with a series of voiceover montages that document life in Middle America during the last years of the nineteenth century. In a wry and semi-comical way, we are regaled with vignettes of men's fashions as modeled by Joseph Cotton, glimpses of upper- and middle-class decorum, and illustrations of how the pace of life in that period still deferred to the needs of ordinary people. We see a housewife keep a streetcar waiting while, still indoors, she dons her outer clothing and then goes forth to mount the vehicle in a leisurely manner. Even to spectators in the 1940s, this must all have seemed like something out of a bygone era. There is a slight touch of nostalgia in Welles's narration, telling us that people then had time for everything. But what follows in the film uses this bit of cultural history as a temporal baseline for considering social and personal problems that have afflicted Americans ever since, noticeably at the beginning of the twentieth century, and increasingly in all later years.

Welles wanted his film to depict the decline and fall of a prominent family, at first wealthy and outstanding in their small city but then reduced to poverty and the misery that accompanies it. By excising forty-five minutes despite Welles's objections, the studio executives all but ruined his intention, because—as he bitterly points out—the portrayal of desolation that descends upon each member of the Amberson family was largely eliminated. Through the depiction of cumulative dehumanization, Welles had sought to show the harmfulness of present-day society in comparison to what there was before. The footage that ended up on the studio's cutting room floor was designed to display past magnificence being wrecked by technological advances on which we now rely so much.

It is significant that the movie industry that committed this mutilation of Welles's masterpiece was itself a product of the modern commercial juggernaut he wished to analyze in his movie. The truthfulness of this film in relation to themselves was more than these moguls could tolerate, though they may have been right in thinking that the audiences on whom their immediate revenues depended would also be averse.

Despite Welles's reluctance to acknowledge the presence of autobiographical details in his movies, he does admit that his father was the kind of person that Joseph Cotton enacts as Eugene Morgan, the independent and wholly likable manufacturer of automobiles. The happy period of Welles's boyhood life in Grand Detour was made possible by the financial success of a headlight that his father invented. Moreover, though Welles does not say this, it must be more than merely coincidental that the spoiled rich boy in *The Magnificent Ambersons* who suffers because he has no place in a modern world that neither condones nor properly recognizes the values of his favored upbringing bears the same first name as Welles himself. The tortured and even tragic career of George Amberson is reborn in aristocratic George Orson Welles. Unlike the former, the latter could turn what he learned about himself, and about others, into a creative resource. This did not keep him from relative failure as a working director in Hollywood, but it enabled him to survive the massive, though partial, destruction of his film.

In Welles's original conception *The Magnificent Ambersons* was entirely oriented toward the myth of the past, its splendor when it existed and the inexorable forces that proceeded to bury it. The problem of the past is most fully expressed in the dining room scene when Eugene admits that automobiles such as his will change all future life in America. George then insults him by archly calling automobiles a nuisance that should never have been invented. Earlier, in the excitement of the Ambersons' last great ball, the theme had been adumbrated by Eugene's response to a suggestion that his homecoming brought back "the good old times." As he puts it: "There aren't any old times. When times are gone, they're not old, they're dead. There aren't any times but new times." As it devolves, the plot sadly vindicates this judgment. George refuses to accept the authenticity of Eugene's past love for Isabel, and he diabolically prevents it from reestablishing itself in their present lives.

Discussing how the studio version butchered what he had shot, the important forty-five minutes having been not only cut but also burned (in all likelihood), as if to hide incriminating evidence of greatness, Welles tells us: "You see, the basic intention was to portray a golden world—almost one of memory—and then show what it turns into. Having set up this dream town of the 'good old days,' the whole point was to show the automobile wrecking it—not only the family but the town. All this is out. What's left is only the first six reels."[19] Within the bifurcated design that Welles had in mind, the line of demarcation between the goodness of the past and its relentless annihilation in later years is established by the iris-out (the closing circle of light that ends a scene) after all the main characters have had a happy day driving through the snow and George kisses Lucy when they roll down a small embankment.

In silent movies the iris was often used to convey a sense of gentle melancholy in something. In François Truffaut's *The Wild Child* (1979), it occurs repeatedly as a marker of time that has elapsed within the narrative. In the framework of *The Magnificent Ambersons* it alerts us to the fragility of this short-lived consummation that the protagonists have experienced on that day. Amplifying a brief reference in the Booth Tarkington novel he was adapting, Welles has the group sing joyously over and over again the refrain from the popular hit about "the man who broke the bank at Monte Carlo." They are chugging along in Eugene's early-vintage automobile. As it recedes into the depths of the closing iris we intuit that this bit of joyfulness will soon be swallowed up into the past and its merciless finality.

The demolition of what Welles created is especially evident in the last moments of the movie as it now exists. Instead of his conclusion, we are forced to see a mawkish and foolishly romanticized scene in which Eugene and Aunt Fanny (Agnes Moorehead) walk toward the camera in a narrow hospital corridor. Eugene relates that he and George have been reconciled during this visit, that he feels that George's dead mother was in the sick room watching over them, that through him she had brought her son under shelter again, and that he himself was "true at last" to his "true love." The faces of Cotton and Moorehead glow with a look of spiritual uplift and unison between them that is supposed to make the audience feel all's right with the world and they can go home without the sadness that Welles's ending might have induced.

Welles had terminated the film with Eugene visiting Fanny in the lower-class rooming house where she finally had to live: "There's just nothing left between them at all," Welles tells Bogdanovich. "Everything is over—her feelings and her world and his world; everything is buried under the parking lots and the cars. That's what it was all about—the deterioration of personality, the way people diminish with age, and particularly with impecunious old age."[20] Watching a rerun on television, decades after the making and undoing of *The Magnificent Ambersons,* Welles smoldered still with unexpressible impotence and anger: "Don't you see? It's because it's the past—it's over."[21]

In Tarkington's book the final scene takes place in the hospital room itself, and the last paragraph describes Eugene's feelings in words that are the same as those that Cotton utters in the released version of the movie. Even Welles's script

included the same words, though transposed to the gloomy setting of Fanny's boardinghouse. In the remake that Alfonso
Arau directed for television in 2001, Eugene uses similar
language but only later, after he has returned to his house. In a
close-up he talks into the television camera while addressing
Isabel, the dead woman, whose smiling face flashes on the
monitor in recognition of the happy ending. Welles would
doubtless have hated this closing as much as the one that the
studio forced upon him, even though Arau's is less saccharine.

The remake announces in its credits that it is "based on a
screenplay by Orson Welles." It does in fact reinstate much,
though not all, of the material that was excised from Welles's
movie. What is lacking, however, is the general conception that
inspired Welles throughout. Shooting in brilliant color, Arau
makes the Ambersons appear visually more magnificent than
before, but without the eventual degradation that Welles had in
mind, and with very little sense of the social or political
implications that Welles emphasized. In the sequence toward
the end, for instance, we see Eugene visiting Fanny in her
boardinghouse. Now, however, it is a middle-class establish-
ment instead of being shabby and rundown. Fanny herself
dresses with the same expensive taste that she had in earlier
parts of the film, and unlike Agnes Moorehead at this stage in
the original she does not look worn or aged.

Having relinquished Welles's mythic conflict between past
and present, the remake also alters the nature of the drama. The
basic theme remains the same—the mother who loves her son
not wisely but too well, the father whose daughter cannot
marry the man she loves because he is not like her father, the

son whose arrogance and possessiveness causes him to interfere tyrannically with his mother's love life. What is lost in the
process of reverting partly to Welles's script, but without the
brilliance of his cinematic imagination, is the high intensity and
visual excitement that he imparted to every scene. In that
respect the remake is closer to Tarkington than either the
original or the released version of the Welles film. In a way that
may be more suitable for television, the remake is a simplified
presentation of the novel rather than a work that entrances us
with the artfulness of its cinematography.

The dramatic effects are therefore different, though possibly equally valid in their own context. Only occasionally does
Arau allow the camera to do anything more than tell the story.
But perhaps that is just as well if one does not want to dazzle
an armchair audience at home with too much technical inventiveness. Enlarged scenes of group dancing at the Amberson
mansion, and shots of its palatial exterior shown more often
than in the Welles version, may be all that is needed to retain
the spectator's attentiveness. At the same time, one pays a price
in courting the favor of viewers who are encouraged to be
passive recipients of the plot rather than being actively aware
of stylistic innovations—as in the filming of the kitchen scene—
that Welles regularly provides. The price consists in a coarsen-
ing that seeps into the finished product and may well affect
each actor's characterization of his or her part.

The most glaring example of this is the role of George. He
must be presented as both a devil and an angel, a devil in his
overweening pride and an angel in the eyes of his doting
mother. In some degree he must appear to be pathological, and
commentators have assigned the notion of the Oedipus complex to his character with great alacrity. In Tarkington and in

Welles, something of that sort is implied but not given weight. They both wished to bring out George's normal humanity instead of making him into a case history. For them he is a spoiled brat who grows up to be an egocentric male in need of what Tarkington calls his "come-upance." In the Arau version the Oedipal suggestions are magnified unduly. George and his mother kiss on the lips, dance together suggestively, and embrace erotically. George even ends up on top of Aunt Fanny in one impassioned scene.

As if to accentuate this rabid sexuality in George's character, his animosity to Eugene as a competitive male is increasingly shown to be mean-spirited viciousness. The George in Arau's version (played by Jonathan Rhys Meyers) is not just a devil but also a monster. It is relevant that Arau does not include a description of George that appears in Welles's screenplay. Having been asked by George's uncle what he thinks of his nephew, Eugene, who has just met George for the first time, says: "All I see is a remarkably good-looking young fool-boy with the pride of Satan and a set of nice drawing-room manners."[22] This in fact is how Tim Holt, who is George in the Welles movie, portrays him. He enacts George as not only boyish but graceful and even sensitive while also being a prig and a selfish autocrat. In each of the versions, the rehabilitated George—once he gets his comeuppance—seems suitably transformed; but the change that occurs in the Wellesean original is more convincing than in Arau's remake, if only because it is less implausible than in the latter.

The Magnificent Ambersons' ambivalent treatment of the past reverberates throughout Welles's imagination as a whole.[23] It shows itself in his belief that there is no such thing as "film culture" that one inherits from the history of past cinema and to which one must adhere. There are just films, he claims, and one becomes a good filmmaker not by swimming in a mainstream of what other people have achieved but only by a personal and "innocent" response to it. For Welles the innocence needed for original work results from being cognizant of the value in some previous output without trying to repeat it in one's attitude toward the present. In his artistic life, he continually evinces and refashions that belief.

❁

The past operates in different ways in the varied films that Welles made. He saw *Macbeth* as a struggle between two religious systems, the Druidical and the Christian. The Witches are presented as relics of the pagan past that the new order of things wants to extirpate. They are not just "forces of evil" but also remnants of the old religion, which is being warded off by all the Celtic crosses that fill the screen.[24] *Mr. Arkadin* is a story about a man who has everything in life except the ability to control the past, and so he obsessively tries to erase every possible memory of it. In order to keep his loving daughter from learning about the crimes and even murders he has committed unknown to her, he hires a patsy to track down those who know about his former life. Arkadin then arranges to have these remnants of his past killed in turn. His plans go awry because the patsy falls in love with his daughter and tells her the truth about her father. Unable to face that, Mr. Arkadin kills himself.

In *The Third Man* the past appears in still another guise. Carol Reed directed this film, and the screenplay was done by Graham Greene, but Reed allowed Welles to write the lines of Harry Lime, the character he plays. Welles interprets him as a charming gangster whose superior, though corrupt and morally twisted, intellect sparkles in his famous speech about the past glories of Italian culture: "In Italy for 30 years under the Borgias they had warfare, terror, murder, bloodshed—they produced Michelangelo, Leonardo da Vinci, and the Renaissance. In Switzerland they had brotherly love, 500 years of democracy and peace, and what did that produce? [pause] The cuckoo clock."

Harry Lime, like Charles Foster Kane, Gregory Arkadin, George Amberson, and others, is a man who intrigues us by his aristocratic, but selfish, assurance of innate superiority over lesser human beings. These characters are Romantic and even flamboyant in the nineteenth-century mode, like Mr. Rochester in *Jane Eyre* and the many similar roles Welles performed with his customary flair. They generally live in opposition to, or at least unmindful of, the mandates and ethical restraints that prevail in most societies. This is especially true of Welles's depiction of Macbeth and Othello, and to a lesser extent Falstaff and King Lear. They all lend themselves to Welles's view of life and art since they, too, must get a comeuppance. In each case the drama issues from the conflict between their personal grandeur and their moral debility.

❋

Now that *Touch of Evil* has been restored in keeping with the fifty-eight-page letter that Welles wrote to complain about cuts the studio made without his authorization, we can best discern the ideational pattern in his woven carpet. Though Hank Quinlan, the corrupt protagonist, is (like Othello) a dedicated servant of the state, his judgment as a law officer has been distorted by an inability to liberate himself from the past. His wife was murdered by a criminal he knew and suspected of killing her, but whom he could not bring to trial. As Quinlan tells his deputy Pete Menzies, she died by strangulation, which makes it exceptionally hard to get evidence about the murderer. This prepares us for Quinlan's strangling of Uncle Joe Grandi, after which he illegally fabricates evidence as he often has in order to prosecute people whose guilt he is sure he knows with certainty. Quinlan admits that all he thinks about in life is the death of his wife and the necessities of his official duties. These are hopelessly entangled in his imagination. At the end Schwartz, one of the two spectators of his demise, remarks that he was a good detective. To which Tania, the other witness to the drama, adds: "But a lousy cop."

After Quinlan's death we learn that he was right in naming Sanchez as the perpetrator of the violent event with which the film begins and in relation to which Quinlan plants evidence needed to indict him. As a motif that runs throughout the film, we are told, several times, that Quinlan has uncanny powers of "intuition." He himself ascribes them to his game leg, which is important in the plot because it causes him to use a cane, and the cane incriminates him when he leaves it by accident at the scene of Grandi's murder. The injury in Quinlan's leg resulted from a time in the past when he stopped a bullet that was intended for Menzies, who later kills Quinlan after being shot by him. In her brief appearance at the end, Tania corrects Schwartz's mistaken assumption that she had loved Quinlan. She tells Schwartz it was Menzies who did. In shooting Menzies, Quinlan murders the only person who could duplicate, in some respect, the love he formerly got from his dead wife. Tania had rightly said his future was "all used up."

I mention these details because in their totality they signify the mythic nature of the protagonist that Welles creates in his screenplay and himself enacts with great aplomb. Quinlan lives in the past, not only with his thoughts about his wife and how she died but also with his memories of Tania's affection before he lost his capacity as a philanderer. In contrast, his antagonist Vargas (Charlton Heston) is a much younger man, and newly wed, whose sense of duty keeps forcing him to postpone his matrimonial delights in the present. Even guilty Sanchez shares a current love with the daughter of the man he has murdered.

The movie has all the ingredients of a B-film noir— the conflicting black and white photography, the use of shadow and light, the frightening circumstances that threaten the voluptuous bride as played by Janet Leigh two years before her appearance in *Psycho*, the frequency of suspenseful intercutting and realistically overlapping conversation, the horror of Grandi's open eyes after he has been strangled, and the action scenes in which acid is thrown at Vargas and in which he beats up the young men who may know about his wife's whereabouts. But the film transcends all that. In gravitating around the character of a flawed official still living in the past, Welles's movie— like *Othello*—becomes a tragedy of lost potentialities that once existed, and that everyone who knew Quinlan intimately seems to have recognized.

Tania, played to perfection by Marlene Dietrich, sums up the meaning of Quinlan's life with the famous line "He was some kind of a man." Her voice is flat and matter-of-fact, but her words are tantalizing. Is she saying, based on her large experience with men, that some of them are similar to Quinlan—that there is a kind of man that he exemplified? Or is she saying that he shows us what it is to *be* a human being, a particular type of man no doubt yet also one who represents in some remarkable degree what all people are? I think the second interpretation suits the film best and probably indicates what Welles was trying to express. In their limited pretensions, movies wholly circumscribed within the genre of film noir do not approximate anything comparable to what Welles achieved.

❁

Touch of Evil was the last film that any major studio would allow Welles to direct. With it the industry had learned its lesson: he was a man who placed his artistic aspirations above the financial goals to which he may have paid lip service but did not really care about as he was expected to. In a modern world that no longer honored highly talented but erratic creators, his productions were—as Jean Renoir said of them—"aristocratic works."[25] Nevertheless the moral and political message of *Touch of Evil* was quite acceptable to the executives at Universal and to the audiences they hoped to please. The message is obvious in the occupational as well as personal differences between Vargas and Quinlan. Though he vehemently denies that he plants evidence, Quinlan prides himself on bringing the guilty to justice, while Vargas insists that in a democracy—as opposed to a police state—everyone must be assumed innocent until proved otherwise. What was felt to be irritating in Welles's use of this idea is the constant and even loving care that he brings to the portrayal of Quinlan as a tragic figure.

In some respects Quinlan is a realization of all the Wellesean characters who are simultaneously weak and strong, depraved though worthy of our attention, driven by lofty ideals perhaps but thoroughly guilt-ridden. He is a completion of Welles's preoccupation with the ethical failure and propensity for evil in Othello and Lear as well as Macbeth, Arkadin,

Kane, George Amberson, the Nazi murderer in *The Stranger*, and also K in *The Trial* and Mr. Clay in *The Immortal Story*. Anthony Perkins mentions that Welles directed him to play K as a guilty man, and that, when Perkins protested that Kafka himself implies the opposite, Welles merely roared in reply: "He's as guilty as *hell*."[26]

After attending a rerun of *The Trial* in the company of Welles, who kept laughing at various scenes, Bogdanovich tells us that he finally grasped the film's meaning: "[It is] a kind of tragic satire on the power of the Law to play on people's innate sense of guilt, even though often unnamable."[27] On another occasion, Welles states that while Kafka does hate the law, he himself hates only the abuses of it.[28] Talking about *The Trial*, Welles asserts that in it K may or may not be innocent, but that he has a *feeling* of being guilty. In the same conversation Welles reports: "I've had recurring nightmares of guilt all my life: I'm in prison and I don't know why—going to be tried and I don't know why . . . it's the most autobiographical movie that I've ever made, the *only* one that's really close to me."[30] When Bogdanovich says that he's always found the movie hard to enjoy, Welles insists that it is not intended as entertainment per se but rather as a "study of the various changing attitudes toward guilt" and must be experienced as a horrible dream— not as a reproduction of one, but as the expression of what a nightmare of that sort feels like."[31]

The guilt of magnificent George Amberson is central to the story that Welles received from Tarkington's novel. George's arrogance issues into the terrible wrong he does his mother and the man who loves her; it incurs the social and even financial decline of the entire family as well as his rejection by the girl he loves. But after he has been thoroughly punished, he is given a

second chance in life. The ending of *Touch of Evil* is less simplistic than that. There Welles has no doubt about the guilt of
the character whose role he plays. Nevertheless he admits that
he has to like Quinlan, because he acts "in the name of the law,"
though he does so through behavior that is totally unlawful.
Quinlan "stands against the law, against civilization." Welles
stresses that, however much he may sympathize with Quinlan
and the others like him, what they represent is itself
"detestable."[32]

I believe that Quinlan is the greatest character Welles created as a filmmaker. He is a synthesis of Falstaff, whom Welles
loves dearly, and Charles Foster Kane, toward whom he shows
only minimal sympathy. Unlike Quinlan, Kane is a man who
"doesn't believe in anything. He's a damned man, you know.
He's one of those damned people that I like to play and make
movies about."[33] Though Quinlan is one of them too, Welles
sculpted him with greater feeling and with greater understanding of his sheer humanity. Quinlan is a nightmare of what
Welles might have been had he ever become a self-corrupted
official. At a time when he was already much overweight,
Welles adds eighty pounds of padding to Quinlan's revolting
corpus and has Tania chide him for eating candy bars. It is as if
Welles were alerting the universe to his own presence within
this hideous person.

❀

When he discusses the tragic characters in Shakespeare, Welles
says that they are all "sometimes detestable—compelled by
their own nature."[34] This provides a clue to what he takes to be
the guilt of his protagonists as well as his variable compassion
toward them. In their search for the innocence and goodness

that may have once existed in the past, they generate dramatic situations that involve an evil strand in their nature that lies beyond their self-control. Welles elucidates what he means by "nature" of this sort in the anecdote about a scorpion and a frog that he tells in his own voice in *Mr. Arkadin*:

This scorpion wanted to cross a river, so he asked the frog to carry him. "No," said the frog. "No thank you. If I let you on my back, you may sting me, and the sting of the scorpion is death." "Now where," asked the scorpion, "is the logic of that?" (For scorpions always try to be logical.) "If I sting you, you will die and I will drown." So the frog was convinced and allowed the scorpion on his back. But just in the middle of the river he felt a terrible pain and realized that, after all, the scorpion *had* stung him. "Logic!" cried the dying frog as he started under, bearing the scorpion down with him. "There is no logic in this!" "I know," said the scorpion, "but I can't help it—it's my character." Let's *drink* to character.

The anecdote is appropriate for the story of this film. In it Arkadin is hoist with his own petard. Both he and Stanton, the palsy I mentioned earlier, fail in their duplicitous relation to each other. They are thwarted by unforeseeable events, but also by their individual character—different in each—as it pulls them down. Of equal interest is the last line of the recital. It transcends the schematic and moralistic homily of the anecdote. In drinking to character as the human phenomenon that causes people like Stanton, Arkadin, and his troubled daughter as well to act as they do, Welles proclaims his own aesthetic credo as an artist whose creative powers bring these figments of his imagination into being. He drinks to their goodness as persons whose vitality he can represent and augment through the contrivances of his art.[35] In *F for Fake*, his visual essay in documentary make-believe, Welles in close-up enlarges upon this credo: "Everything must finally . . . wear away into the ultimate and universal ash. The triumphs and the frauds, the treasures and the fakes, are a fact of life: we're going to die. 'Be of good heart,' cry the dead artists out of the living past. 'Our songs will all be silenced. But what of it! Go on singing.' "

❀

Together with these quasi-philosophical remarks, Welles formulates specific ideas about his craft that are worth examining. What he calls his "profoundest conviction in this whole business of moviemaking" takes us to the heart of his aesthetics. Bogdanovich had wondered whether the camera is a lie detector that shows when the emotions expressed by a film actor are false. Welles replies with a short but carefully shaped statement to the effect that the camera does serve as a kind of litmus paper, but only about the presence or absence of feeling. Beyond that, and capable of being totally altered in the cutting room, he suggests, is the quality and veracity of an emotion that occurs on screen. To make this point, Welles contrasts stage acting with acting in the movies: "*Emotional force* can charge up a living theatre, but on the screen there's often trouble keeping it in focus. Strong feelings can get very messy. What the camera does, and does uniquely, is to *photograph thought.*"[35]

Welles amplifies his notion by stating that the camera is more like a "Geiger counter of mental energy" than a lie detector. What it strongly registers is something the naked eye can perceive only vaguely. That something is thought itself, the act of thinking on the part of the actor—not the actor self-consciously thinking about the lines he has to speak, but rather the actor as one who shows forth the human ability to think, in other words, the actor as a thinking person. "Every time an actor *thinks*, it goes right on the film."[36]

This "profoundest conviction" seems to me helpful in several ways. For one thing it shows why so many hostile critics have misunderstood the nature of Welles's own acting in almost all the roles he performed in movies. If one glances at a book like *The Complete Films of Orson Welles*, which faithfully records the responses of different reviewers throughout his career, one is struck by the frequency with which he is condemned for being overly emotional and even bombastic in his delivery.[37] The critics fail to recognize how often he modifies the affective assertiveness of even the most melodramatic personages he projects. In his rendition, Macbeth, Othello, Falstaff, Lear, Quinlan, Harry Lime, Mr. Rochester, and many of the others he enacts—some of them in relatively minor roles—come through as more than just the ranting embodiments of pain, suffering, and one or another contortion of the human soul. They are also presented as men whose thoughtfulness, whose mere capacity to think, is an essential ingredient of their agony and mortal frailty.

Welles imparts to those characters a deliberative and inwardly meditative manner that we do not always find in even Gielgud or Olivier. At telling moments in his acting, Welles slows and carefully measures the tempo of his characters' words in a way that makes their utterances more than just the emoting of powerful feelings. While hamming up a personage, as sometimes happens, he makes him into a pensive ham. And, as Welles maintains, the cinema is especially adept at registering and graphically retaining this effect. It does so most obviously through close-ups, which fill the entire screen and thus serve as an imaginative counterweight to whatever emotionality is being simultaneously augmented.

Welles's insight about the importance of thought in film acting is relevant to the question of realism. Defenders of that approach to cinematic art have often claimed that the essence of this medium consists in the camera's remarkable ability to capture "the surface of things." Far from being a kind of X-ray machine that can penetrate beneath the skin, the camera is thought to concentrate upon the sheer appearance of reality.[38] More judicious realists may recognize that the camera can often do something else as well. It can present the visual world in a manner that empowers the viewer to make correct inferences about the underlying nature of reality. But the actor as a thinker, as one who expresses the process of thinking, is usually not included within the roster of what counts as the realism to which a camera has legitimate access. Welles makes up that deficiency in realist theory by insisting—as any formalist would—that good cinematography does indeed possess this wondrous capacity.

The formalist implications of what Welles believes are equally present in his proclaiming that he wants "to use the motion picture camera as an instrument of poetry."[39] He holds that all art, whether in poetry or on the screen, surpasses reality, and in the case of film even becomes "another reality."[40] This comports with his attempt in *The Trial* to evoke in the audience the feeling of a nightmare without his trying to represent or copy one. From within the new reality created by the art form, spectators were to have an experience compounded of uneasiness and trepidation similar to what real nightmares cause. These nocturnal occurrences are not presented symbolically, since that would mean that the filmmaker is purveying information, albeit in some metaphorical or hidden format. Instead the camera must be envisaged as a poetic instrument that engenders in the audience a radically imaginative immersion that only its type of artfulness can instigate.

Since Welles himself was a magician, a *professional* one (he tells us) because he was paid to do his feats of magic on stage and none of his friends would allow him to do them privately at home, one might have expected him to enlarge upon the analogy between film and magic. Ingmar Bergman does so occasionally in comments about his own movies, such as *Fanny and Alexander* or *The Magician*; and his autobiographical book *The Magic Lantern* describes how his childhood obsession with magic led him naturally into his career as a filmmaker. But Welles sees magic differently, perhaps *because* he was professional in his practice of it. He claims that the art of magic is inherently foreign to both theater and cinema. It is primarily directed to men, he says, since women dismiss it as just trickery. It succeeds, if and when it does, by getting adult males to return momentarily to their gullible childhood. "Magic begins and ends with the figure of the magician who asks the audience, for a moment, to believe that the lady is floating in the air. In other words, be eight years old for a minute. And that has no connection with movies or the theatre, I think."[41]

In *F for Fake* Welles plays himself in the role of a magician. He even performs before an audience consisting of a single wide-eyed boy who might very well be eight years old. The film deals with fakery in the form of art forgery and false claims of authorship. But Welles nowhere implies that the fictionality of fictional movies, or the resemblance of their photographic images to the world as we usually see it, should be taken as fakery. He shows himself being filmed in all his makeup and, later, chatting with friends, or alone in his cutting room, with no makeup on. None of that is fake, nor is the investigation into fakery to which this essayistic fiction devotes itself.

At a pivotal juncture in *F for Fake*, Welles does confess that though he spoke the truth for an hour, as he promised, that hour was up some time earlier and he has been "lying [his] head off" since then. His use of the word *lying* is not entirely correct, of course, since he made no claims to literal truthfulness in the statements he would be uttering as narrator beyond the specified time. He was, however, tricking us in not reporting beforehand that what would follow after the first hour is all make-believe. This trickery was the sleight of hand of a magician. Welles may be right in denying that the inventiveness of stage or screen is the same as in the art of magic, but he resorts to some of the *psychology* of magic in *F for Fake* and, I believe, in all his other films.

What Welles liked most of all about magic shows was the performance of the magician luring people to suspend disbelief. He approvingly quotes Robert Houdin's quip that a magician is a "great actor playing the part of a magician."[42] Though Welles denies any connection between magic and film or theater, the fundamental technique that characterizes his work in both those media consists in artful tricks designed to captivate the audience. When he describes his use of overlapping speech by different characters in several of his movies, he says it adds a bit of realism. This may be true, and yet the device heightens tension in the drama while also submerging irrelevant details of a conversation. That is evident, and wonderfully successful, throughout *The Magnificent Ambersons*. The many low-angle shots in *Citizen Kane*, and the rapid dissolves back and forth in that film, are effective because they imaginatively activate our perception in keeping with the director's structural intentions. We do not need to justify them, as Welles implies, by saying that in the real world we sometimes look up and see the ceiling of a room, or that different but related events often occur simultaneously.

Welles himself is cognizant of how greatly he draws upon purely formal contrivances. Asked why the cuckatoo shrieks after Susan walks out on Kane, he answers: "Wake 'em up. . . . Getting late in the evening, you know—time to brighten up anybody who might be nodding off."[43] Reminiscing years later about that first film of his, Welles criticizes it as too obviously the work of someone who is trying to show everyone that he has learned how to use the camera in startling ways. In relation to the famous opening crane shot in *Touch of Evil*, he admits to feeling uncertain about it because "it's one of those shots that *shows* the director making 'a great shot.' " As if in opposition to the recent fashion of revealing technique, he mentions that "the directors I admire the most are the least technical ones—the ones freest of this very thing I'm strongly accused of being."[44] He cites Ford, Renoir, and Pagnol as exemplars in this respect. To the extent that Welles's self-criticism is accurate (though he himself insists that the crane shot does further the plot in *Touch of Evil*), I think we should take his comment as the judgment of someone who was more than just a magician. He was, at the least, a realist among cinematic magicians.

❀

Several of those who have written about Welles believe that his greatest contributions were mainly to the art of radio rather than to the art of film. Talking about innovations in his movies, he himself says: "I *did* invent, but my big inventions were in

radio and the theatre. Much more than in movies."[45] Even if
this is true, one must note how greatly Welles used his radio
techniques, and also those of the theater, in the films he made.
In *The Magnificent Ambersons* we hear but do not see him: he is
the recurrent host as on a radio show, the voiceover speaker
who presents and occasionally interprets the plot for us. In the
closing credits, during which the actors are named by him
while they appear in film clips that identify them with the roles
they played, only a microphone is shown when his own turn
comes up. His voice establishes him as the unseen narrator: "I
wrote the script and directed it. My name is Orson Welles."
This is much as it would háve been when he produced and
acted in his Mercury Theatre of the Air, and on countless other
programs. Moreover, it serves to remind the audience of
Welles's worldwide celebrity, at age twenty-three, as the radio-
phonic perpetrator of the Martian invasion scare.

In *The Magnificent Ambersons*, Welles presents the views of
the townspeople by having them stand clustered in a group
like a Greek chorus on the stage. As in the classical plays,
members of this cinematic chorus give information and intone
platitudes that convey public opinion relevant to the action.
Together with his brief narration and the series of sharply
dramatic scenes, that device enables Welles to strip away
Tarkington's discursive descriptions of the town, the influence
upon it of industrial progress, and the subsequent changes in
social mores.

Watching Welles's films based on Shakespearean plays,
including his unsatisfying version of *Macbeth*, I always regret
never having seen his theatrical productions of them. He
staged *Macbeth* three different times, and the *Voodoo Macbeth* of
1936, with an all-black cast, was an enormous success. In a way

that is common among stage directors but not filmmakers, he says: "I think words are terribly important in talking pictures."[46] He means that movies must be heard and experienced much as they would be on radio and in the theater. Elsewhere he says that in a difficult acting scene he tends to rely on the sound to tell him how a shot will look: "If it sounds right, it's gotta look right."[47] Welles would seem to have had little of the adulation of silent films that Hitchcock manifests in calling them the true embodiment of "pure cinema."

Keeping in mind Welles's early career as one who wrote for radio and acted in it, we can readily see its effect upon the thematic content as well as the formal pattern in most of his films. *The Lady from Shanghai* could very well have been aired as a radio adaptation of the dime novel that Welles turned into a movie. Spectacular scenes like the shattering of the mirrors at the end would have been lost, but most of the plot develops as it might have in a Mercury Theatre venture. Welles even provides a voiceover continuity throughout while enacting a leading role himself, as he often did in productions for the microphone. But also events in the shallow story unravel as they would have in radio dramas of the 1930s. Among the various other possibilities for cinematic treatment that Welles proposed, but usually could not fund, many were explicit transformations of what he had already done on radio (and/or on the stage).

In this connection it is interesting to note that the latter-day advent of television did not elicit either the artistic talents of Welles or his wholehearted approval. Though television combines the cultural effects of both cinema and radio, he criticized it as an aesthetic decline in modern civilization. During his final years he did appear in various television commercials, for

which critics reviled him without recognizing that he hero-
ically applied his large fees to the making of films for which he
could not otherwise raise the money they required. But to him
this was just a practical necessity. He considered television dis-
tinctly inferior as an artistic medium. In a 1983 interview on
French TV he expresses this idea as follows:

[Television] demands less from the public than any other medium.
And the strongest mediums are those which ask the most from the
public. When we had only black-and-white in the cinema, we
demanded something from them. When we had no sound we
demanded something. The closer we got to the approximation of life,
the less was asked of the public, and therefore the less impact it had
upon the public. That's why the theatre has a stronger impact than
the cinema—because the audience must pretend that they aren't an
audience. It is already part of the performance. In French you say
"assister," [which] we do not say in English. It is a wonderful verb for
being at a performance: you assist the performance by being there.
You don't assist television; it's just on.[48]

These opinions about television are shared by Ingmar
Bergman, who bitterly complained that the performers in it are
denied access to the moment-by-moment direction and
response that they would get from stage productions or screen
rehearsals.[49] But Welles does not tell us exactly what he means
by "impact," or why it is aesthetically as important as he
implies, or what we should infer from the fact that the theater
has an impact that is even greater in degree than the impact of
cinema.

Moreover, *The Immortal Story,* and other films that Welles
made for television, are virtually indistinguishable from those
he made for the large screen. Is it the different setting to which

he takes exception, watching something casually at home and peering at a small box rather than being at a performance as one among many others who have likewise come to see the play or movie? Even so, we could say, members of a stage or film audience are not really part of the performance they observe, or, if they are, it is only indirectly and as appreciative spectators. The performance to which they do contribute is the one that consists in their demonstration of interest that is elicited by the particular work of art being offered them. But then, might we not believe that television also includes a comparable potentiality? Just think of the communal watching of football games on the tube.

In any event, at another juncture Welles is quoted as having praised television for its "frugality": "On television, you can say ten times as much in one tenth of the time taken in a movie, because you're only addressing two or three people. And above all, you're addressing the ear . . . Television is nothing but illustrated radio."[30]

❋

When Welles said that he thinks of cinema as a form of poetry, he was employing the loaded term in its broadest reference— as when (using poetic license) we talk about the "poetry" of life in a great city. For Welles, as for Hitchcock, it is actually music that is most analogous to the art of directing. Unlike Hitchcock, Welles was born with a considerable gift for music. He was on his way to becoming a child prodigy on the piano and violin until his mother's death put an end to all that. In *Citizen Kane* it was he who suggested to Bernard Herrmann the phony or parodistic *Salammbo* sequence that portrays Susan's disastrous debut as an opera star. He himself wrote the tune "Oh Mr.

Kane" in the party scene where Kane celebrates his theft of the *Chronicle's* editorial staff.

Of equal importance, however, is the fact that Welles, similar to Hitchcock in this regard, likened the director's function in filmmaking to the role of an orchestra conductor. Welles nevertheless approached his art form in a way that is totally different from Hitchcock's normal method. Instead of trying very hard to remain faithful to a script or storyboard, as Hitchcock did, or any other prior plan of direction, Welles treated his initial ideas and sketches as exercises to be discarded in the actual shooting. For him filmmaking was an improvised craft that was always at the mercy of unforeseeable forces: "An actor reaches out a hand, the sun is there, a cloud moves, and the whole story is changed."[51]

From this it follows that the "innocence" Welles sought, and the nature of the inventiveness he could attain, had to consist in an exploratory, free-ranging attitude that refuses to limit either the filming or the cutting of a movie to the fixed and even egocentrically rigid constraints that Hitchcock regularly imposed. In saying this, I realize how greatly Hitchcock experimented on the set with special effects and other techniques that enabled the camera to work its quasi-realistic magic. As I remarked in the chapter on Hitchcock, he relished the imaginative contrivances that he and the crew deployed in shooting films like *Rope* or *Lifeboat* or *Foreign Correspondent*. In the latter, for example, the camera moves in one sequence from the exterior of an airplane in flight to its inside and then, further on, seamlessly shows the ocean engulfing the whole interior. Welles too seemed to enjoy the playful inventiveness needed to overcome the difficulties of production. But for him such feats required constant improvisation and readjustment that must occur in each aspect of filmmaking. Compared to Hitchcock's self-assured demand that the finished storyboard determine everything else, the Wellesean methodology may seem chaotic and amateurish—until one sees how fruitful it can be in his application of it.

Describing his working habits, Welles states that he makes "the damnedest, most elaborately detailed plans you ever saw, and then I throw them all away."[52] He explains that the plans exist only to prepare him for improvisation in view of what is offered to him by the actors. His approach makes sense only in relation to the conceptual stance that I have described and that is basic to it. Welles's ideas about the myth of the evasive past and the ambiguities in human character operate as a fertile resource for him because they elicit the need to improvise different modes of expressing his ambivalent feelings about life and about the protagonists in his films.

More is involved than just the fact that Welles believes that "*most* heavies *should* be played for sympathy" and then adds that "all the good ones in the theatre are."[53] This way of thinking establishes a perspective that scarcely applies to Hitchcock's films. The suspense that Hitchcock cultivated rarely exists in relation to someone's character. On the contrary, it is because we immediately perceive the innocence and (most often) friendliness of some ordinary person in his movies that we are lured into feeling concerned about what might happen to him or her. Welles does not aim for that kind of audience involvement. Most of the personages he creates or presents are intrinsically and dramatically isolated in themselves. They are extremely ambitious as well as being highly damaged or, at least, imperiled morally and in need of human assistance that no one can really give them. From the very beginning they are clothed in the shroud of the exceptional but doomed outsider. As an actor or director or screenwriter who tells their story, Welles represents them with greater compassion than they may possibly deserve.

In this act of bestowal Welles often manifests a loving attitude toward those who are indeed guilty as hell, and even thoroughly evil. The same could not be said of Hitchcock, though on occasion he too appears somewhat sympathetic toward erring humanity. There is no one in the Hitchcock films who is comparable to Quinlan or Kane, but an *almost* Wellesean approach does cause us to experience some minimal sympathy for the drummer man in *Young and Innocent* or the cat woman in *To Catch a Thief* or the pathological murderer in *Frenzy* or the Herbert Marshall, James Mason, and Robert Young characters in the movies in which they play the role of culprit. The failings in the Welles protagonists are cinematically more enlarged and thrust upon us in greater detail, and their charm is imbued with a texture of intellectual turpitude that Hitchcock does not exploit as fully. For that reason, the semi-compassionate responses that Welles elicits, as Shakespeare also does, have only a secondary or even tertiary place in Hitchcock's cinema.

This difference between the two filmmakers may be related to the fact that Welles was himself an actor of a special kind. In explaining his performances on the stage as well as in films, he reminds us that in the Comédie Française there is always someone known as a "king actor." He is not necessarily the best actor in the group, and he does not always have the most important part; but he is the one who plays the monarch and other remarkable characters of that type. Welles says that his own voice and stature put him in this category, and that critics who say he overacts or complain about his kind of delivery fail to understand the nature of whatever dramatic gifts he does have.[54]

Both as a filmmaker who wrote many of his own screenplays, and as one who frequently took the leading role for himself, Welles thus had a mentality that was divided into two contrasting modes. He sought to imprint upon the sensorium of the audience a bravura presentation of some doomed or tragic character, although he himself—as the progenitor of this character—remained faithful to a strictly ethical code that condemns the evil acts while also expressing humanitarian feeling for anyone who brings them into being.

This complexity of sentiment as it defines the art of Orson Welles shows itself in the diversity of techniques that he employed. The reliance upon deep-focus shots, which Welles did not originate but used with great insight, was successful in *Citizen Kane* because it alone conveyed a sense of ambiguity. The spectators had to decide which portion of the frame they would attend to, while being aware that they were thereby relegating the rest to some other visual or mental plane. In that degree, at least, Welles repudiated the desire of an Eisenstein or a Hitchcock to manipulate audience response in accordance with the predetermined effects that these directors chose for reasons of their own.

In a similar fashion, the sharp and sometimes frenzied cutting in *Othello* and other Welles movies institutes a counterpoint that is quite different from Hitchcock's. In Welles it is an interaction between systems of thought, between antagonistic views of the world, rather than between people who are caught in a situation of engaged suspense. This difference shows itself not only in the details of the plot but also in the meanings and instrumental techniques that go into the making of each contrapuntal movie. Hitchcock would have considered the Wellesean film far too "aesthetic" for an ordinary moviegoer, and therefore too uncommercial. In that respect, alas, he was more or less right.

※

Depicting his general orientation, Welles gives us a further clue when he distinguishes between the real and the true.[55] Since films are the artifacts of a poetic medium that resembles music to some extent while displaying the vicissitudes of human existence more directly than music can, Welles maintains that even the most realistic films exceed the boundaries of theoretical realism. Cinema is unreal by its very nature, he would say, if only because the filmmaker is always free to use his artificial techniques in any manner that succeeds. Filmic authenticity consists in giving the audience a visual and sonic experience that has relevance to the real world as we know it but does not, cannot, duplicate it. For the experience to ring true, and for movies to *be* true in themselves, the final cut must show not only the ambiguities of life but also the ambivalences of the filmmaker. This dialectical goal, paradoxical as it may sometimes seem, is present in everything Welles did as a director or actor or scriptwriter for film, theater, and radio. It is the key to his enormous talent, much of which we are beginning to recognize only now.

Welles revered the work of Jean Renoir. More than once he spoke of him as "the greatest of all directors."[56] He and Renoir are alike in several respects, above all two that are fundamental throughout their entire work and that I will return to in the chapter on Renoir. The first of these is their sense of communality in the actual making of films; the second is their conception of the actor's primacy in each scene.

Welles tells us that on the set he used to play records of jazz music while production was going on. Possibly he felt that it encouraged or increased his own sense of improvisation. But mainly, as I understand his motive, he wanted to have an informal setting in which he and his coworkers could relax while also carrying out their different professional activities. Time and again, Welles asserts that the job of the director and, even more so, the producer is much overrated. The success of a film, he claims, can result from almost any one of the department heads—the cinematographer, the art or music director, the person who is in charge of the lighting, and so on. Unlike some filmmakers, Welles encouraged all members of the crew to offer suggestions about whatever aspect of the film they were working on as a team. He would make the final decision, of course, but he tells us that some of the best things in his movies originated with others on the job.

One may detect in this a democratic attitude that was quite remote from Hitchcock's ironhanded control over each element of his filmmaking. In general, Welles speaks as a follower of Franklin Delano Roosevelt, for whom he campaigned and some of whose public speeches he wrote. While Welles's movies are not polemical, they have more political savoir-faire than Hitchcock's. The first word in the title *Citizen Kane* prepares us for the connivance of the story's multimillionaire publisher to grab power by getting elected on a populist platform. He is defeated by Gettys, the party boss who trumps him by enlisting social mores about sex and marriage which mattered to most of the electorate. But the plot also turns upon Jeb Leland's ultimate conclusion that his former buddy, on whose behalf he had himself harangued the populace, was not truly a friend of the people but rather an egoist who wanted only to acquire for himself everyone else's love.

Lurking behind these themes there resides an implied commitment to liberal democracy. It merges with the creation of characters through whom we are able to see what Welles himself believed in. This, however, is never allowed to become tendentious or propagandistic. In *Touch of Evil* Vargas is obviously speaking for Welles when he rejects Quinlan's view of law enforcement. Even before we know the ugly depths of Quinlan's criminality, we are encouraged to recoil from his autocratic pursuit of what he considers justice. But though Welles's sympathetic depiction of Quinlan makes him the main character, that paradoxically prevents the film from being overly didactic.

There is no reason to think, as some commentators have, that *Touch of Evil* is an "autobiographical" attempt by Welles to do penance for his own guilt—presumably analogous to Quinlan's—as a domineering maker of films. For that to be tenable, one would have to think that Welles was a director who did manipulate the actors or the crew as ruthlessly as Quinlan planted evidence and slaughtered whoever got in his way. But there is much to be adduced against any such idea. Various actors have testified to the time, effort, and corroborative assistance that Welles put into helping them perform at their best without losing sight of the panoramic goals he had chosen for their film. An occasional workman has complained that Welles did not treat members of the crew as if they were equal in importance to the actors. Even if this is true, it may, or may not, have been a limitation in Welles. In any event, it can hardly be considered a source of guilt.

❋

Many of the themes I have been discussing come together in *The Immortal Story*, a little-known masterpiece of Welles that he derived from Isak Dinesen's novella with the same title. Welles directed, wrote the script, did the meager narration that it needed, and played the central role of Mr. Clay. It was the last movie Welles finished apart from *F for Fake*. The film, fifty-five minutes in length, was commissioned and performed as a presentation on French television. Welles hoped it would be the beginning of an anthology of Dinesen tales that he would put on screen. The funds for that never materialized.

The "immortal" story that is a unifying component in the plot is itself a myth of the past. Its meaningfulness for Welles issues from the ambiguity in the word *myth*. In colloquial usage a myth is something false, though often widely taken as true. That is how Levinsky, Mr. Clay's agent, interprets the story that Mr. Clay remembers hearing in his youth. It is a fanciful tale about a sailor whom a rich old man hires to beget a child for him, and whom he pays for this service five guineas in gold. To Levinsky the account is just a make-believe that sailors like to repeat—a fictional wish fulfillment and even a ritualistic mantra, which explains why the payment of five guineas in gold always remains the same. But in the alembic of Mr. Clay's imagination, the story becomes mythic in another sense. Whether true or false, it serves to embody an ideal culmination to his life. By actualizing it in the present, in his house and under his own direction, it comprises something profoundly meaningful in relation to himself.

In the story the woman who is to bear the sailor's offspring is the wife of the rich old man. Though she is young, she has not been able to give him a child. Mr. Clay has never married, however, and in his devotion to business he has armored himself against all sexual or amatory attachments. He therefore thinks of the boy or girl who may issue from his scheme as mainly a product of his will and productive thought. Though Mr. Clay tells the sailor that he wishes to defeat the hopes of remote relatives whom he hates, and who expect to acquire his wealth, this motive is only peripheral. By instantiating the original story, while altering it since he has had no wife, he intends to fulfill in his old age the creative will to power that has governed his entire existence. The event, as Mr. Clay conceives of it, will match his achievement in having amassed a fortune through his ruthless cunning as a businessman. His design can be carried out with any woman, not just a spouse, and regardless of who inherits what he leaves behind. The story thus becomes a myth that is neither true nor false but instead an artwork that expresses a deep and recurrent pattern in all of life.

Mr. Clay's plan and what follows from it constitute a myth of the past in two respects. First, his memory of the sailor story dates back to when he arrived in China as a young man almost fifty years earlier. It projects an image of one's youth that old men often savor as a time when sexual adventures of various kinds seemed always possible. The fact that Mr. Clay eshewed every occurence of what he calls "fellowship, friendship or love" is congruent with this trope. Now that death is close, he wishes to regain past time by imposing upon reality a surrogate of what he might have done when he was young but did not want to then. Asserting himself in this fashion, he would validate his avoidance of human intimacy. He would also be fulfilling his character, as in Arkadin's anecdote.

Something similar applies to Virginie, the woman who agrees to play the female part in Mr. Clay's "comedy," as Levinsky calls it. She is a French courtesan-type who has become weary of her life as a plaything of foreigners in China. At first she refuses to have any dealings with Mr. Clay, whom she blames for the suicide of her father many years before. Her father had been Mr. Clay's business partner, almost a friend, but was ultimately the victim of a scheme that brought about his ruin. Just prior to his death, he ordered Virginie never again to look at Mr. Clay's face or enter the family mansion that he has taken from them. Having lost their home to the marauding partner, Virginie's father destroyed all its lavish furnishings except for the mirrors. They were to stay as a proof to Mr. Clay that what he sees reflected in them is the visage of a cruel and evil man. In Welles's cinematography, the images in the mirrors next to which Clay sits at dinner or while conversing with Levinsky reverberate inwardly and forever, as the open door-ways seem to do in *Citizen Kane* after Susan has walked out on her despotic husband.

Though she accepts her role in Mr. Clay's reenactment of the immortal story, Virginie describes it as a further reverbera-tion of the continuing decline that began when her father died and left her impoverished. She tells Levinsky that she had been reared in France as a lady in the court of Louis Napoleon. The family motto being *"pourquoi pas?"* (why not?), she has survived since then by resorting to affiliations with men she would have disdained as a younger woman. In the film she is played by Jeanne Moreau, who beautifully embodies her proud but defeated willingness to do what she must do in exchange for the large sum of money that she exacts from Mr. Clay. Virginie is living still in the myth of her past as a socially select and proper girl, but also it is in *her* character to seek a way of outdoing the man who caused her father's ruination. She is motivated by the possibility that in his weakened condition the old man's yearning to force his comedy upon the world will culminate in his death. And even though the gesture she must make occurs in the house filled with memories and forbidden to her by her father, she reasons that her degradation there will serve as a further example of the evil in Mr. Clay.

What actually happens in Virginie's encounter with the sailor is something neither she nor Clay had anticipated. While they are engaging in copulation, he speaks of them as "jumping-jacks," young creatures filled with reproductive juices that no longer exist in himself but are subject to his command. As he rightly asserts, their behavior is just a consequence of his manipulation. They are merely puppets he dangles on a string for the sake of staging the act he is paying them to carry out for him. Dying during the conjugal performance, he never learns that in the process they have experienced an authentic attachment that transcends their subjugation to him. While this love is being achieved, he remains outside the bedroom and cannot observe it. He has no comprehension of what it is or how it enables them to attain an ideality that negates his intention and triumphs over it. He does, however, see the pair at a distance in a farewell embrace as the dawn comes up, and Welles uses that long shot to suggest that this observation of oneness may have then brought on Clay's fatal stroke.

As a person who plies the trade of lovemaking without normally feeling much herself, Virginie had not expected to experience love of any sort. Having heard that the sailor is very young, she looks at herself in the mirror and recoils with a painful sense that he will see how old she is. What we, the film audience, see is the face of a woman in her middle thirties, perhaps, a woman who is not old but slightly worn by the beginning ravages of middle age. Yet the sailor perceives nothing like that. His first glance of Virginie, lying naked in their connubial bed, leads him to say with perfect honesty that she is the most beautiful girl in the world. When he asks her whether she is seventeen years old, as he is, she answers yes and he believes her. At the end of their night together, when he must leave to join his ship, he calls her "my girl."

In montages of Moreau that Welles shows at this moment, Virginie says nothing. She regards the lover who will soon be gone with a rapt expression of devoted resignation superimposed upon her hidden agony of imminent loss. She looks as if she might well be a seventeen-year-old girl, and even one who has bestowed her virginity as a testament of pure affection. Assuming it ever did make sense, Mr. Clay's plan about contrived procreation that amounts to nothing more is now emptied of its original meaning. From the mythic point of view, his dying signifies the utter failure of his enterprise. Love has conquered it entirely.

Nevertheless it is a failed love, and would be a tragic one if the lovers died—as in the legend of Tristan and Iseult—instead of Clay. Like the medieval lovers, Virginie and the sailor, whose name is Paul, cannot surmount the pressures of society represented by their need for money. As Virginie reminds him, Paul has accepted the five guineas with the understanding that he would leave after having performed the deed of fornication. And though the large sum of money she has received as the price of her participation can buy unprecedented freedom for them both, she knows that Paul's character as a seaman whose father lived and died at sea prohibits his taking her along. In adapting Dinesen's novella, Welles ends it by having Virginie watch Paul's departure from the porch on which Mr. Clay has suddenly expired. Long after Paul is out of sight, she stands silently looking in that direction as if she will always be waiting for his possible return.

We surmise, however, that she knows he will never come back. In his innocence, this having been his first experience of sex, he may not have noticed how much older she is, and how thoroughly her features have been frayed by her previous life. His realization of that might well occur to him once he has reached his ship, and it would surely awaken him to the reality of the situation if he were ever to return. Virginie knows this, to her sorrow, because she has great wisdom about human feeling. Paul may someday acquire it but as yet he is still a beginner. In this connection, the names that Dinesen has given these two lovers resonate with irony that must have been more than fortuitous. *Paul et Virginie* is the title of the eighteenth-century bestseller by Bernardin de Saint-Pierre that recounts the amatory adventures of the childlike and wholly innocent couple who enact their indelible oneness in the American wilderness to which they have fled. The young man and the woman in *The Immortal Story* are not like that. They bear the scars of nineteenth- and twentieth-century sophistication.

Even so, the bond between these two lies beyond the imagination of the gentle and compliant Levinsky as well as Mr. Clay. In Welles's portrayal of Paul's departure, Levinsky stands at the landing above the stairway on which Paul is descending. At the beginning of the film we had watched Levinsky walk down those stairs, only to be summoned back by Clay on the flight above him. Now at the end, Levinsky has carried out his mission and can appear as himself an icon of interpersonal power. He tells Paul that he is probably the only sailor who can relate "the story" truthfully. In his heavy-hearted condition, Paul asks what that story might be. Levinsky repeats the details, including the payment of five guineas. But Paul rejects the suggestion that the love he has discovered can be vulgarized or reduced to a merely sexual encounter, as Levinsky assumes. That story, Paul insists, "is not in the least what happened to me. . . . To whom would I tell it? Who in the world would believe it if I told it?" And then: "I would not tell it for a hundred times five guineas."

From the very outset, encapsulated in Welles's abbreviated voiceover narration, the character of Levinsky has been presented to us as a vestige of the oppression and indignity he had undergone throughout his life. He is a man who has lost all ambition and any hope of attaining significant relationships with other people, but after Paul's parting declaration he feels toward him—as Dinesen puts it—"the same strange kind of sympathy and compassion as all his life he had felt toward women and birds."[57]

Levinsky elicits our own sympathy because he submits so mildly to the suffering he has endured. He is a man deprived of the connective impulses that issue from a native family or clan or country or familial religion. His people having been killed or scattered by a pogrom in Poland, he moved across the globe from one land to another without being at home anywhere, without learning Hebrew or Yiddish like most Jews even though he picked up several other languages. To entertain Mr. Clay, Levinsky reads some words of the prophet Isaiah from a little scroll that a kindly gentleman gave him in the course of his travels. Levinsky does not know who Isaiah was or even that he lived more than a thousand years before. The scroll foretells a time of peace and joy and great abundance of goodness that God will bestow upon the chosen race.

Mr. Clay ridicules this, like all other prophetic utterances. He cares only for accounts of what has existed in the past, or what does so now in the present. He believes in the actuality of facts, not poetic dreaming. But Levinsky, despite his complete alienation from the realities of life, has a vague and inescapable sense that something of importance has been denied to him. However ignorant he may be about the origin or meaning of Isaiah's words, he carries the scroll in his pocket as if it were a talisman.

After Paul has gone off and Virginie stands helplessly on the verandah, Levinsky picks up an ocean shell that Paul left behind. In Dinesen's account, he leaves it with Levinsky and asks him to give it to Virginie because it is so rare and smooth and when you hold it to your ear "there is a sound in it, a song." In Welles's film, Paul puts the shell on Clay's lap, not realizing that he is dead, and Levinsky discovers it after it has fallen off and rocked back and forth on the floor. This yields a visual effect beyond the novella. By fixating our attention upon the rhythmically repeated movement of the shell, it foreshadows Levinsky's poignant words in the text as well as the film: "I have heard it before, long ago. Long, long ago. But where?"

This "where" is also a "when." It is temporal as well as spatial. Like the shell itself, it reverberates with the muffled noise of some primordial ocean of Levinsky's being from which he has been cast out and about which the myth of the past enlightens us. For that matter, all of the main characters are creatures of alienation. In the novella the action takes place in Canton, which Welles changes to "Portuguese Macao" but also refers to as China. Virginie and her parents are French, Paul is Danish, and Mr. Clay is English (changed to American by Welles). While not as totally rootless as Levinsky, they each live in an alien land of Chinese servants and laborers whom they take for granted, though Welles's camera does not.

In one of her earlier conversations with Levinsky, Virginie remarks that when he came into her room she thought at first that he was just a small rat out of a warehouse owned by Mr. Clay but that now she can see that he is the *Juif Errant*. In the myth of the Wandering Jew, the protagonist has sinned against the devil and is condemned to flee unceasingly from country to country without ever being at home in any of them. In some versions the tormented man is a sea captain who sails from port to port with a phantom ship and a crew of ghosts. He is the Flying Dutchman, as in Wagner's Romantic opera, who can be liberated from his guilt only by a pure-hearted woman willing to die out of love for him.

The combination of mythic guilt and painful separation from a legendary past is more than just an element in the cinematic philosophy of Orson Welles. It also informs his interpretation of a tragedy like *King Lear*. Though he directed and produced that play on stage more than once, taking the leading role himself, as he did in a televised version directed by Peter Brook, Welles could never find the financial backing that he needed for a film of it that he fervently wished to make. On one occasion he tried to raise funds with the following description of his conception:

[What is truly important in *King Lear*] is not that the tragic hero is an old king, but that he's an old man. . . . *King Lear* is about death and the approach of death, and about power and the loss of power, and about love. . . . Of all the aches of the elderly, the loss of power is the most terrible to bear. The strong old man, the leader of the tribe—the city, the church, the state, the political party, or corporation—demands love as a tyrant demands tribute.[58]

In another context, Welles says that Lear has no knowledge of women and has not lived with them: "Obviously, the play couldn't happen if there were a Mrs. Lear. He hasn't any idea of what makes women work—he's a man who lives with his knights. He's that all-male man whom Shakespeare—who was clearly very feminine in many ways—regarded as a natural-born loser in a tragic situation."[59]

Given the variations in the fictitious circumstances, these words apply to the willful Mr. Clay as well as Lear. Like the maker of a pornographic movie, Clay directs a performance of sexual intimacy without any awareness of, or personal acquaintance with, the love that can sometimes arise in it. He is as much of a natural-born loser as Lear, and as guilty as the Flying Dutchman. Welles may have gravitated toward that aspect of humanity because he feared that he might have a similar character himself. But unlike the personages he presented, he also knew that through the magic fire of his art he could cleanse some, if not all, of the characterological impurities embodied in the myth.

❀

This brings us to a moral and social aspect of Welles's poetic view of cinema which links him most overtly to Jean Renoir. In words that Renoir would have relished, Welles offers the following as his concluding statement to filmmakers of the future: "What the student movie director should be taught is as much of our whole culture as we are capable of synthesizing. Synthesizing, not specializing. To make a film for today's world, we should strive to comprehend as much as possible of the human accomplishment in these last twenty thousand years."[60]

Asked what is needed to teach others how to direct movies, Welles then replied:

Hold a mirror up to nature—that's Shakespeare's message to the actor. How much more does that apply, and how much more is it true, to the creator of a film? If you don't know something about the nature to which you're holding up your mirror, how limited your work must be! The more film people pay homage to each other, and to films rather than to life, the more they are approximating the last scene of *The Lady from Shanghai*—a series of mirrors reflecting each other. A movie is a reflection of the entire culture of the man who makes it—his education, human knowledge, his breadth of understanding—all this is what informs a picture. . . . [The mechanics of making a film] can be taught over the weekend by any intelligent person. . . . The rest of it is what you have to bring to the machinery. . . . The *angle* at which you hold that mirror. What's finally interesting is not the romantic tilt or spastic quirk at which you hold it—but what the mirror has to show back to you. . . . Which is determined by moral, aesthetic, and ideological orientation. We know to what an extraordinary extent everything depends on that angle. A mirror is just what it is.[61]

If Renoir feels that [his films] are all the same and the manifestations of a single continuity, it is because he perceives in them the evolution of thought and sensibility which constitutes his own idiosyncratic existence as an artist living when he did. They reveal the sheer humanity in himself as the person that he was in the world he knew directly.

Jean Renoir

In his writings on his career in film, Renoir makes many far-reaching statements about his movies, about art, and about life. These statements often seem to be independent of each other, but actually they are highly integrated among themselves. They emanate from a unified and more or less coherent view of the world. They all prefigure a search for various forms of harmonization. What that means in terms of Renoir's overall perspective will preoccupy us throughout this chapter.

"I've basically shot one film," Renoir states. "I've continued to shoot one film, ever since I began, and it's always the same film."[1] He says this in reply to a question about whether *Grand Illusion* is his best movie. He refuses to make any judgment about that because he sees a continuity that is fundamental in all his works. From their beginning, he says, they all seek to establish a "conversation" with some audience, however limited that audience might be, that takes an interest in his kind of cinematic art. He claims not to know, or really care, whether the conversation gets better or worse from one film to the next. Most essential, he thinks, is the need for it to proceed, to go on progressively.

In relation to the work of Hitchcock or Welles, or most other filmmakers, this notion of conversation makes little sense. Recognizable genres—types of thrillers, for instance—recur in Hitchcock productions, and his public responds to them (and to his self-expression through them) with remarkable consistency. There is also the particular pattern in many of Welles's films which I have been trying to elucidate. But it would be difficult to treat these uniformities as the basis for a cinematic *conversation* with the respective viewers. That mode of approaching Renoir's movies is therefore relevant to his filmmaking in a way that does not truly apply to either Hitchcock or Welles. One might call this predominant orientation in Renoir a philosophical point of view, and indeed it issues into his many insights about crucial and largely theoretical matters that interested him.

The suggestion that he has been making only a single film is itself significant. The thirty-five or so movies that he directed, wrote, and sometimes acted in are often disparate among themselves. Some are adaptations from stories or novels, some are projects to which he was assigned and could alter only through subtle modifications, and some are known to us only as a final entity that others edited without his approval. If Renoir feels that they are all the same and the manifestations of a single continuity, it is because he perceives in them the evolution of thought and sensibility which constitutes his own idiosyncratic development as an artist living when he did. They reveal the sheer humanity in himself as the person that he was in the world he knew directly.

Ambiguous though Renoir's films may have been in various respects, they nevertheless display the ongoing—and predominantly personal—intentionality that defined his identity throughout their making. Each artistic effort of his was a step toward ever increasing engagement with other people and their situation in life, as well as his.

❀

One might, however, question whether the notion of a conversation is an accurate portrayal of what may occur between any filmmaker and his or her audience. Conversations are fundamentally linguistic or quasi-linguistic exchanges. In them people reciprocally impart ideas and attitudes through symbolic systems of discourse they have acquired. Since film audiences are expected to be silent, though receptive, the analogy seems somewhat inappropriate for cinema as well as other art forms. In *The Rules of the Game* Renoir varies his interactive concept in a way that makes it more plausible. In that movie the character Octave, who organizes everything and is played by Renoir himself, laments having failed throughout his life to achieve a "contact with the public." Octave says this to Christine, whose father was a famous orchestra conductor who had greatly succeeded in making contact with his public. The same was true of Renoir's father, Pierre Auguste Renoir. A comparable attempt through the art of film remained as a determining motivation in the son's cinematic activity.

To make contact with the public implies a saying, doing, creating of something that others can appreciate as clearly relevant to their experience, to their own immediate feelings, aspirations, conflicts, and daily problems. In order to attain this result, the artist must be willing to disclose *his* own reality, his place in nature and his social involvement as one among other men and women striving to find meaning in life. It is very tempting for a filmmaker to try to hide his or her personhood by means of the mechanically projected images that robotically appear on screen. Renoir resists that temptation. The conception of the artist as someone who remains "beyond or above his handiwork, invisible, refined out of existence, indifferent," as Joyce's Stephen Dedalus says in *A Portrait of the Artist as a Young Man,* does not hold for Renoir.[2]

As we saw, Welles claimed to reject the idea of an auteur, of a creative person whose autotelic being defined the ingredient meanings of his art. There are only the works, Welles insisted, even though everything he did was recognizably his in its characteristic cinematography, narrative style, and deliberate point of view. In a Hitchcock film as well there is always the manifest presence of the master's all-pervasive control. We are aware of it even though Hitchcock, like Welles, would seem to deny any overt desire to impose his personality upon the spectators he is nevertheless seeking to mesmerize. Renoir differs from both Welles and Hitchcock in taking his role as director/producer/screenwriter to be a showing forth of himself, the human being he was, in a gesture of solidarity with those for whom he made his cinematic efforts. This populist self-identification appears in all his films.

While trying to establish the "contact" that he wanted, Renoir fully understood the egocentric dimensions of what he sought. It resulted from his existence through time, but was also a demonstration of the sheer persistence of his personal aspiration. "I feel that sometimes voluntarily, often involuntarily, I've been following the same line ever since I began making films."[3] The "conversation" might or might not get better, he remarks, but what matters most is the generative process itself. One may think of this as a kind of paternal love on Renoir's part for all of his offspring, each of them eliciting from him an unremitting bestowal of value. But Renoir means more than that alone. He is also calling attention to the fact that everything he creates has a special niche, a unique tincture and raison d'être that it possesses within his life at the moment of its birth and in conformity with his current manner of self-presentation.

One might also think that Renoir is stating something similar to what Welles subsequently suggested in claiming that a true artist creates for himself alone, rather than succumbing to other people's standards. But this also falls short of what Renoir meant, though he would have agreed that undue concern about commercial success will throttle one's originality. Beyond all that, Renoir was emphasizing the fact that an *authentic* contact can occur only if the filmmaker is wholly cognizant of how greatly the self he expresses in his art will always change, and at best develop, through time and the variable character of the political and cultural environment in which he lives.

Renoir claims that he is not deterred by the realization that only a small number of people will be interested in his attempt to make contact with them. Throughout the course of his uneven career he suffered, as Welles did, from the exigencies of an art form that demands public acceptance directly geared to financial viability. Though not as fortunate as Hitchcock in meeting this constraint, Renoir managed to endure quite well over a period of forty-five years in the profession. He did so by maintaining his ability to *continue* in his work, that being more essential than the critical and commercial failures or successes he might encounter along the way.

⊛

Renoir contrasts his attitude with the view "shared by many people, by the majority of people, whether it's the public, critics, film people, producers, or directors—that the important thing in art is perfection."[4] He insists that the desire to make a perfect movie has less importance than simply the *making* of a movie, as one could also speak about the making of a table or a meal. His idea is that one establishes contact in and by means of the process itself. An artist must create his conversation and build his bridge to other people through a succession of inventive acts and without undue concern about the fact that they may be aesthetically good, bad, or of middling value. Renoir cites the technical deficiencies in Chaplin's work. Though lovers of perfection have been harsh in criticizing the Chaplin films, Renoir asserts that they were masterpieces. While academic productions, as in official paintings for instance, can be perfect in many details, those are boring, *because* of their perfections.

This notion of aesthetic excellence may seem paradoxical. It is as if Renoir were saying that trying to do a good job in a film or painting or other venture makes it harder for one to succeed in actually doing a good job and thus fulfilling one's promise as an artist. But to the extent that a filmmaker throttles his or her desire to attain an outcome that is excellent in every respect, or as good as possible, will this not result in a slovenly, inferior, outcome? That seems to me like a plausible response to Renoir's suggestion, and the kind that may rightly be offered by theorists who refuse to separate the achievement of artists from their capacity to become the creators they want to be through their unrelenting self-criticism of whatever they have done. If Renoir is to be defended at this point, it can happen only by moving the analysis to another, and more revealing, level.

In fact, Renoir does that immediately after having uttered the statements I have been discussing. He maintains that in life itself the establishing of human contact is preferable to any search for perfection: "The most important thing in life, after all, is love; and I don't think that one is attracted to a woman because she's pretty."[5] Renoir does not tell us why it is that human contact outranks prettiness or beauty in a relationship of love. Nor does he tell us much about what is involved in the "contact" that is so pertinent to the goodness of love between human beings. But the direction of his thought is fairly clear, and extremely helpful for understanding his conception of film art as well as the kind of outlook that permeates his own movies.

It was Plato who first awakened Western consciousness to the search for perfection that is basic not only in human ideals but also, he thought, in the structure of reality. Plato explained love in all its varieties as a longing for the possession of goodness that exists in some person or object or other possibility in the world. Since we are programmed to want what is best, as Plato believed, the highest and most fertile type of love was the love for goodness in itself, for the idea or form of the good. Only it could indicate the nature of ultimate perfection that we and everything else pursue. Since the gods are themselves perfect, they would have no need to love. It was not part of their character.

In his critique of Plato's philosophy, Aristotle rejects this line of inference. He argues that since the gods are perfect they must have access to everything that is good, including love. An ability to experience perfect love, which is itself the greatest perfection, must therefore belong to them as gods. Over a period of centuries, Christianity then transmuted Aristotle's doctrine into the belief that God *is* love: in his very nature he radiates the cosmic perfection that all human beings wish to emulate through their overt or latent love of divinity.

If we read Renoir's statement in the context of this controversy within the orthodox tradition, we see at once the significance and the brilliance of his idea. In the universal order of things, he asserts, neither perfection nor the search for it would seem to be the kind of constant envisaged by Plato, Aristotle, Christianity, and the idealist approach in general. Even in relations of love, as I myself have held, a striving for perfection in the object of one's interest can actually preclude the occurrence of love. We may appreciate or want to possess the apparent goodness we perceive in someone else, but to love the other person we need to bestow upon him or her the additional goodness of our own attachment and concern. Merely admiring the other's degree of perfection is not enough. Indeed, if he or she were perfect in some appraisive sense, we might find it difficult to invoke any amatory feeling—or even any desire to please or benefit or protect. A disposition to love that we might feel would appear to be unneeded by someone who is already perfectly replete with goodness.

❀

This naturalistic position underlies all of Renoir's thinking about his art and its philosophical import. Time and again he glories in the sheer wonderment of nature despite, and in fact because of, its inescapable imperfections. As a way of bracketing Renoir's naturalism, we need only note the similarities between his 1936 film *A Day in the Country* (*Une Partie de Campagne*) and his *Picnic on the Grass* (*Le Déjeuner sur l'herbe*) twenty-three years later.

The former is a bittersweet rendition of nascent but unconsummated love between two young people who seem well matched; the latter is a comedy about unforeseen but eventually florescent love between a highly cerebral scientist of middle age and a blossoming country girl with few inhibitions and virtually no formal education. Renoir adapted *A Day in the Country* from a short story by Guy de Maupassant. In it we see the beginnings of an attachment between the man and the woman, but we get no evidence to indicate whether or not their relationship is sexually complete. In *Picnic on the Grass*, which Renoir wrote himself, it is essential to the narrative that the couple have biologically fecund intercourse. Nevertheless both films contain scenes of climactic intimacy that are the same in one respect: they include a visually symbolic interval during which the camera revels in the panorama of flowing water, open skies that are sometimes sunny and sometimes darkened by clouds threatening rain, woodland views, close-ups of trees and plants and various insects on them that are living out their instinctual mode of being.

These natural settings are not presented as perfections. They are not always or especially beautiful, and the gnarled, sprawling, and irregular trees in the landscape of Provence that provides the locale for *Picnic on the Grass* seem rather ugly in the vivid coloration of this film. In both movies the portrayed aspects of nature are designed to remind us of elements in our reality that do not depend upon human acculturation. It is not a question of their being better or worse. They are shown as brute phenomena that we must understand and accept for what they are in their primal actuality. The scientist in *Picnic on the Grass* manifests throughout a great facility in formulating biological truths, but he comes to realize—and then transcend—the meaning of what he has been saying about libidinal urgency only after he experiences it himself. This happens in his vitalizing encounter with the fertile peasant girl, who represents the sex goddess whose ancient temple stands ruined in that part of the forest.

In other Renoir films, locations in nature have a similar role. For instance, in *Boudu Saved from Drowning* (*Boudu sauvé des eaux*) (1932), Boudu escapes his impending wedding and its dangers of middle-class respectability by drifting down a river that functions as a reminder of, and means to reenter, the vagabond life he had previously enjoyed. It is not perfection that is being sought, but rather oneness with internal as well as external nature of any sort that human beings crave. And here too, as with *A Day in the Country*, the landscape in which Boudu gleefully returns to his former condition is not at all beautiful.

Boudu himself is a twentieth-century version of Molière's Tartuffe, though without his religious hypocrisy. Boudu even outdoes Tartuffe in captivating the affections of the paterfamilias while seducing his wife and daughter. He then puts himself in a position to inherit the family's wealth by marrying the girl. He is as much of a selfish scoundrel as Tartuffe, and yet, as played by Michel Simon, he changes into a lovable creature. Why? Because Boudu lives in nature more directly than anyone else. At the end he flutters away from civilization much as the two liberated jailbirds do in René Clair's *À Nous la Liberté* (*Freedom Is Ours*), made about the same time, after they also conclude that bourgeois society exacts too high a price for whatever material goods it may provide.

Renoir's naturalism exists on various levels. To begin, his faith in process rather than perfection recurs throughout his role as screenwriter as well as director. He tells us that, unlike some authors, he finds it hard to be sincere in starting his work if he has to be all alone with it. Even at the earliest stages, he needed the contact with others. But this continued to be the case once he arrived in the studio. Having constructed a plan of action, and possibly the last of several versions of a script, he would regularly discard it and rely on moment-by-moment improvisation. Not only did he encourage suggestions from the actors and others on the set, but also his ideas about the project grew in relation to what the actors presented to him merely in being the persons that they were. As individual examples of nature, they too showed forth the reality to which he must attend. Each improvisation would then constitute a slightly different redirection, thus requiring further changes in order to accommodate the novel circumstance.

Comparing his method to Mack Sennett's, Renoir laments the fact that he could never improvise as completely as Sennett did. As much as he would have liked to, Renoir found it impossible to sit around with the actors and the crew and decide with them what they would shoot that day. He says he always has to come in with a definite idea of the work the company will be doing. But then he adds: "What I wind up shooting may be different . . . never different as far as the props, the set, and the general feeling of the scene go—only the form changes."[6]

One senses that as a rule Hitchcock could not have proceeded in this manner, and largely because of a basic belief he may have had in the possibility of perfection. Renouncing that shibboleth entirely, Renoir would freely resort to whatever improvisations might arise out of the great variety in persons and places that nature afforded at any moment. The weather having changed from sunny to rainy, he abandoned his initial script for *A Day in the Country* and introduced corresponding alterations in the shooting. His adaptation of Maupassant ended up considerably changed.

The art of film, as Renoir understood it, generally demands an improvisatory attitude more than other arts. He thought of filmmaking as largely dependent upon the discoveries that result from technical obstacles inherent to it: "You discover the content of a film as you're shooting it. You obviously start with guiding principles that are as firm as possible, but when the subject is worthwhile, each step is a discovery, and this discovery brings others. . . . [The] battle with technical obstacles forces you—more than in any other medium—to discover and to rediscover."[7]

Apart from these technical hurdles that elicit new ideas that a filmmaker can turn to his creative advantage, the characters themselves also contribute to the requisite improvisation. Discussing his work on *The Rules of the Game* (*La Règle du jeu*), Renoir points out that he could not follow the shooting script he had written because "I made many discoveries through the characters. The characters came alive and confirmed their need to move and to speak in a way that I hadn't foreseen."[8]

Authors and playwrights often make comments of this sort, and a similar concept was immortalized in Pirandello's *Six Characters in Search of an Author*. But what such artists have in mind must always be significantly different from what Renoir is alluding to. The characters who enter a writer's imagination as real persons are not the same in film productions as they are in novels or even plays. Stage directors are not permitted to revise the details and general scope of a dramatic vehicle in accordance with some actor's presentation of a character. In film that is, at every moment, a valid possibility.

Playwrights can, of course, rewrite their working text in the manner that a filmmaker like Renoir continually altered his. But eventually they must end up with a finished play that is frozen in the mold of some theatrical production they have had access to. Later productions may, and always will, be somewhat different. By putting a definitive version on screen, once and for all, cinema precludes the many transformations that plays go through as companies inevitably reinterpret them on every subsequent occasion. The mere capacity for such transformations gives theater its excitement as a living art, an art in which live people are acting before an audience in the temporally determined parameters of each performance. Though filmmaking is unable to duplicate that aesthetic virtue, it allows a more intrusive richness of transformational changes in the narrative and technical details that precede the final wrap. With greater awareness of this disparity than most cineastes have had, Renoir was totally adjusted to the innovative possibilities that *only* the limitations of film require and make available.

Since Renoir's habitual improvisation occurs as an agency of his attempt to establish contact with an audience, it is not surprising that he thinks of *each* audience as a cocreator of his films. When *The Rules of the Game* was being continually booed during its premiere showings in Paris, Renoir in the projectionist's booth kept snipping the celluloid in order to remove the offending footage. His stratagem failed, and by the time the film was withdrawn he had merely shortened it disastrously. On that occasion his faith in the audience as a collaborator in his work led him astray. But his desire to arouse responses in the spectators, which would then serve an important function in the actual making of his art, normally served him very well. If the contact was genuine and profound, it had to include more than just a superficial relation with the viewers. They too had to participate in an exchange that contributes to the vitality of the project.

In articulating this idea, Renoir uses stronger language than I have employed in my formulation of it. He says one *cannot* make an artwork without the active involvement of the audience. He claims that this is a "necessity" nowadays when so many people lead lives of regimented alienation. Film is needed as a technological force that liberates its clients from the perils of technology as a whole by engaging them in the meaningfulness of one or another cinematic effort. Each member of the audience makes his or her contribution through the cumulative interpretation of what is seen and heard. It follows that a film is not a single, unitary entity but rather a multitude as diverse as all the responses that interact within its plenitude. Renoir voices this pluralistic belief as follows:

It's impossible to have a work of art without the spectator's participation, without his collaboration. A film must be completed by the audience. . . . I think that one of the ingredients for success is to have a lot to say, to have too much to say, so that you do say it, but you don't say it all. There are certain parts that you cannot manage to formulate, that you forget, or for which you simply can't find the words, the terms, the camera movements, the lighting, or the right expressions for the actor to express it. The audience compensates for it. What's interesting is that each person in the audience, each viewer, compensates in his own manner.[9]

From this, Renoir infers that "a film is as many films as it has viewers. If there are a thousand viewers, you have a thousand films, if it's a good film. If it isn't a good film, it's precise, and it's the same film for each viewer."[10] By a "precise" film Renoir means one that aspires to perfection in every detail. That misguided search, he says, causes the dismal uniformity of contemporary life that separates each of us from other people instead of uniting us with them. By refusing to care about perfection, true art is "one of the ways of fighting against modern boredom. . . . Art is a little bridge that you erect. The director of a film, if he has a little talent, sometimes succeeds in creating a little bridge between the screen and the audience, and then we're all together, and we create together, we build the film together."[11]

❋

Within Renoir's aesthetics of building bridges together, there resides a differentiation of function and significance among the contributors. Helpful as it was for him to have collaborators in the writing of his scripts and thereafter among the many people in the crew, he thought of the film medium as supremely pivoted upon the reality that each actor presents in revealing what he or she is as a person who is also a professional. Renoir's films do not ordinarily portray the lives of performing artists, though *The Golden Coach* (*Le Carrosse d'or*) and *French Cancan* are exceptions to this rule. The theatricals that he makes so prominent in several other movies illustrate his disdain for perfectionism and his love of amateurish improvisation by people who share a sense of communal oneness. But more relevant is the emotional rapport that he cultivated and deeply felt toward the actors who convey not only what their characters are but also what they themselves are in merely being people whose individual talents give an audience access to those characters. The bridge from the screenwriter or director to the actors as human beings like any others is, for Renoir, the primordial type of contact to be constructed in the making of films.

This is one of the principles that Welles learned from Renoir and, in vastly admiring him, sought to emulate. Like Welles, Renoir acted in several of his own movies. But unlike Welles he always took secondary or minor parts, and sometimes as a mere ne'er-do-well or failure in life. In *A Day in the Country* he has the slight role of the innkeeper on the river, the effusive *patron* (boss) as Renoir himself was nicknamed by his associates in later productions, who proposes to the young men the erotic philosophy of love 'em and leave 'em. In *The Human Beast* (*La Bête humaine*) he is the homeless bum who protests his innocence but to no avail. In *The Rules of the Game*, the role of Octave that he takes for himself is a depiction of mismanagement and ineptitude. Though Octave has a major part, he often appears on camera as someone who swells the scene while performing side by side with the really important actors. Renoir does not try to take center stage, like Welles, or even imitate Hitchcock, whose cameo vignettes provided a casual amusement that viewers could look for from film to film as a brief distraction from the business of each narrative.

In justifying his deliberate effort to improvise, Renoir emphasizes how much the contact with actors controlled what he did: "The actors are also the directors of a film, and when you're with them, they have reactions you hadn't foreseen."[12] Renoir did not resent this situation, unlike Hitchcock and many other directors. He repeatedly expresses his joy in being among actors, knowing them personally and observing how their personalities wonderfully affect their presentation of the characters they represent. He says that he always has a good time on the set or as a director on the stage, and that he would not have stayed in the profession otherwise. His appreciative disposition undoubtedly bolstered the performers in ways that elicited what he was hoping to get from them.

The word that Renoir chooses to describe the input he wanted actors to yield is *sincerity*. He means by that not a venting of the actor's own personality or subjective and possibly unfathomable existence, but rather his or her immersion in the role. "The true character is the acted character, not the actor. We couldn't care less about the actor in real life."[13] In living as they do in "real life," actors are liable to cognitive distortions, to the copying of other people's judgments and other actors' techniques, or else what Renoir calls "acting out the moment." Having to show involvement in some event, Renoir remarks, an inferior actor will revert to some derived generalization about how a person might respond at such a time. For the acting to be effective and sincere, it must arise out of another kind of experience. The actor must *absorb* his role, allowing himself to respond in a manner that neither he nor the director may have thought about in advance. When that happens, the actor does not behave as he would off camera, but rather he expresses the being of his character, who is fictional and therefore exceeds any neat or foreseeable codification of his reality.

In relation to filmmaking, this idea about what an actor can offer as a co-contributor has several ramifications. For one thing, it affected Renoir's presentation of a character to an actor's imagination. Instead of spelling out the role by giving the actor information about some character's mind and personality type, he used "the Italian method." In the course of many rehearsals the actors recited their lines at first without either enunciating them fully or trying to formulate theories about their meaning. The import of what they would eventually portray had to suggest itself after a considerable period of simply repeating the same words. Only when the newly generated ideas about the meaningfulness of their lines took hold in the actors' consciousness intuitively, spontaneously, could they experiment with gestures that might be appropriate to each scene. "I don't ask them to try to act naturally," Renoir reports, "but to act in such a way that the discovery of exterior elements comes after the discovery of interior elements, and not vice versa."[14]

Renoir demands this ordering because he believes that acting out the gestures first can cause an actor to depict the superficialities of the character instead of imbuing it with a sense of what the words being used signify about him or her as a human being. That takes time and familiarity with the dramatic role, and it cannot be instilled from without. It must come slowly from within an actor's unreflective powers of imagination. When Renoir contrasts his kind of directing with the practice of directors who perform the scene for the actors and then tell them to do the same, one thinks of how Charlie Chaplin proceeded. He did exactly that, the very opposite of Renoir's approach. As several of Chaplin's actors attested, he was so great an actor himself they could not conceive of anyone finding gestures that would be better than the ones he proscribed for them. To this, Renoir might have replied that possibly they could not realize how much their imagination, and hence their capacity as performing artists, was being curtailed by Chaplin's invasive methodology.

As a director who not only cared about actors as collaborators in the directing of a film but also tried to further the creative potentialities of their inner being, Renoir can be compared with others who have had a similar goal. In lines that are reminiscent of Carl Theodor Dreyer, Renoir mentions that what particularly fascinates him is the actor's face. Like Dreyer, and unlike Welles, Renoir saw it not as an expression of thought but rather as a manifestation of generic humanity. Dreyer believed that he could capture the personhood and even the soul of a character by a series of short takes, montages, of the performer's face. In *The Passion of Saint Joan*, he used this cinematography to good effect. Renoir rejects any such attempt, for the simple reason that "shooting shot by shot" means frequent cutting and therefore a pattern of interruptions that he finds harmful for making contact with the actor-as-character.

In relation to physical as well as psychological determinants, Renoir wished to give the actor space within which he or she could move around. He preferred shooting on location, especially outdoors, because that allows the actor to find an appropriate place in nature rather than being limited by a prearranged marking on the set. The actor could thus make contact with the material world in a personalized fashion that is meaningful to him or her as a human being who has always lived in it. This then augments the essential sense of feeling at home within some natural and recognizable context that an actor must convey to a spectator.

George Cukor is famous for having mastered a comparable rapport with the actors he directed on film. In the chapter on Cukor in Peter Bogdanovich's book *Who The Devil Made It*, we see a photo that shows him rehearsing Katharine Hepburn for a scene in *The Philadelphia Story*. Cukor's face is glowing with hypnotic delight as his features and parted lips simulate what is present in Hepburn's face, while his body strains forward isomorphically with hers. He seems to be mouthing the same words that she does and projecting a mirror image of the same sentiments that she expresses.[15] This is precisely the kind of attunement that Renoir recommended for a director to help his actors find the affective region out of which their fictional characters can truthfully emerge.

❀

Renoir's efforts in this endeavor blended harmoniously with his naturalism and his realism, as I have suggested, but also with his attempt to reach poetic goals beyond them both. Before examining the technical aspects of this harmonization, I want to consider how his faith in the primacy of the actor informs the thematic structure of several of his movies.

Talking about *The Golden Coach*, Renoir tells us that he wanted to make an "Italian film" that would summon up a pre-Romantic period in Italian culture. But *The Golden Coach* does not take place in Italy, and most of its characters are not Italian. The setting is a Latin American colony of Spain in the eighteenth century. The music that flows, or rather bounces, throughout is by the great Venetian composer Antonio Vivaldi, who died in 1741. Renoir dedicates the film to him, and in various interviews proclaims that he was his associate in the writing of the script. In Renoir's imagination, Vivaldi's music served as the embodiment of commedia dell'arte, which is central to this movie and distinctively Italian.

The story of *The Golden Coach* is simple, even simple-minded. A troupe of Italian commedia dell'arte players—

mountebanks, as their eventual impresario calls them—arrives in the colony after a long voyage across the Atlantic. On the same boat there traveled a magnificent coach that glistens in all its glory in Renoir's technicolor. During the trip Camilla, the company's leading lady, played by Anna Magnani, sleeps in the coach together with the young aristocrat who loves her and wants to marry her. Having arrived in the capital city of the colony, the actors meet all the challenges of their precarious condition. They rebuild the barn-like theater; they succeed in getting the town's greatly worshiped bullfighter to attend their performances and thereby bring in paying customers; they perform for the Spanish governor-general and gain his support as well, though not the approval of the disdainful noblemen on his council and their wives. The comedy revolves around the frantic skirmishing by the three lovers that Camilla has now collected—the young aristocrat, the bullfighter, and the governor-general, whom the scandalized councilmen seek to overthrow. At the end she rejects all three of them, despite her successive love for each, and returns to her principal dedication as an artist on the stage.

The golden coach figures in the narrative because the governor-general precipitates a constitutional crisis when he gives it to Camilla. She resolves the problem by donating the coach to the church for its exclusive use in charitable activities. She then departs with the rest of the company on a tour of other cities. Reverting to her life in the theater, Camilla learns from her misadventure that art is the only reality to which she truly belongs. At the same time, she perceives, as Renoir's spokesman explains to her, that the men who love her are themselves real only as members of an audience that watches her sing and dance. We too have been observing her performances on stage and in the amatory excursions that the plot depicts. Being commedia dell'arte, both types of play-acting are largely improvisational, as if to illustrate Renoir's ideal aspirations in his making of any movie. For him as well as Camilla, this mode of creativity is always guided and restrained by a professional commitment that becomes the meaning and the justification of their existence in one or another society. Having attained that elevated state, neither Camilla nor Renoir need fret unduly about the worldly goods they have lost or relinquished.

To impart this message with as great immediacy as he can, Renoir knows that he must entrance his audience by entertaining it. He does so in the frivolous clowning of the commedia dell'arte sequences, in the vivacity of the musical score (written by other composers as well as Vivaldi), and in the rapid cutting as well as the farcical character of everything related to Camilla's flighty affairs. But in addition, Renoir delights us with the sheer presence of Anna Magnani in this role. In an interview he remarks that she would arrive on set looking haggard and worn, possibly from spending the previous night in bars. But after repeatedly rehearsing in the "Italian method," as he requested, she was completely transfigured: "At the fourth and fifth rehearsals, Anna looked exactly like a young girl. I like to tell this story, because that's what characterizes a *great* actor or a *great* actress. The art is stronger than the physical self, the power of the spirit overcomes the body."[16]

※

In saying this, and in emphasizing how much he admires Anna Magnani as a human being he is happy to know and to work with, Renoir testifies to his faith in the goodness of the professionalistic approach to life. In order to make aesthetic contact with the person of the actor, one had to touch and bring forth his or her reality as a professional. As creatures in the world, actors and actresses are relatively uninteresting, like most other people. It is only through their successful immersion in their profession that they can transmit the humanity of characters who then enter into the aesthetic community Renoir wished to achieve.

This theme of professionalism as the key to the meaning of film (as well as other art forms) is equally evident, and even more pervasive, in *French Cancan*. What we see there, as its narrative motif, is the life that goes into the *creation* of an artistic profession. As if it were a historical documentary, the movie depicts the beginnings of the type of populist theatrical dancing, typified by the cancan, that had become a flourishing institution in Paris by the time that Renoir wrote his script. In his fictional simplification, Renoir focuses upon the Moulin Rouge as a theater that his audience would know or, at least, have heard about. The protagonist, played by Jean Gabin in his late middle age, is the impresario who finally manages to make this raucous entertainment a staple of show business in Montmartre during the Belle Epoque at the turn of the twentieth century and thereafter.

Celebrating that much-glorified decade, *French Cancan* recapitulates something Renoir said in relation to *A Day in the Country*. He remarked that he dated the earlier film as he did because he was starting to agree with René Clair's idea that there should be a "cinematic period," specifically localized in the last half of the nineteenth century: "This is an idea that I approve of one hundred percent: Get rid of realism entirely, and do all our films with costumes from a period that would be the film period. It's the opposite of cinéma vérité."[17]

Renoir admits that he is influenced in this judgment by the fact that his father worked in that period, and so did the other painters he himself knew as a little boy growing up in their world. Of equal relevance, I think, is the importance that his father bestowed upon the beauty of female flesh and the natural goodness of masculine pursuit of that beauty. It was a time of wealth and relative stability in French society, a time when many people felt entirely at ease in their leisurely existence as cultivated sybarites.

Though *A Day in the Country* deals with emotional stultification in a middle-class family, it documents this human failure—more graphically than Maupassant's schematic story could—by contrasting it with that visual setting of trees, open skies, and flowing water which promised the kind of liberation through nature that Renoir's father and the other painters of his generation had idealized in their works of art. By harking back to this period twenty years after he shot *A Day in the Country*, and by treating it again as the exemplary cinematic era, Renoir attests to his continuing regret that the world has lost the effusive gaiety and erotic sensibility of the Belle Epoque.

The plot itself, apart from this background and the use of costumes, deals with two other themes that often intersect in Renoir's work. One is the necessity for any artist, and above all an entrepeneur who wishes to invent a new kind of theater, to surmount great monetary impediments. Much of the film consists in showing how the Gabin character, whose name is Danglard, imaginatively evades one after another financial hazard. The second theme is sexual love, not an uncommon theme in world cinema but one that has a special configuration in Renoir's work. Though Gabin was by then overweight, with graying hair mingled in the black, and much less alluring than he had been, he still retained the vestiges of his former charm. If only by stirring the audience's remembrance of the attractive idol he once was on screen, he could and did radiate the sex appeal that Danglard has in the eyes of the women he directs professionally and personally enthralls.

In this film Renoir treats the commercial problems as simply hurdles that interfere with an artistic life that exists on a higher plane. In themselves they are not worthy of much attention; they are neither sociologically interesting nor especially challenging to humanity's quest for the good and beautiful. They mainly matter as motors that drive the characters into their choice of whom to love and how to reach their goals as performing artists. Danglard's financial entanglements as he fights his way toward the theater of his dreams interweave with his amatory interests in different women, two in particular whose rivalry belongs to the sexual byplay of the plot. One is an older performer who has had successes in the theater that give her access to the money Danglard needs; the other is a young girl whom he discovers and then trains to a level where her talent as a dancer, and vibrancy as a person, leads her into a brilliant career.

The two women are professional competitors as well as ferocious rivals for Danglard's affections. In his usual way, Renoir presents their struggle for love and sex as a biologist might. He has no desire to assess the moral implications of such purely natural occurrences. If anything, he finds it all amusing and even largely farcical. This conflict between an older woman and a younger one, each trying to snare a clever man, he exploits much as Mozart does in *The Marriage of Figaro* when Susanna and Marcelina entertain us with the spectacle of their generational battle by viciously insulting each other.

I do not mean that Renoir has no ideas of his own about love as a value that people can and do and possibly *should* pursue. But the investigation into the nature of affective ideals is scarcely developed in *French Cancan*. These ideals have virtually no place in it, or at best only as secondary considerations that must be subordinated for the greater glory of one's art form. The pursuit of art, his own above all, is what motivates Danglard's behavior throughout the film. He has not only a love of dancing but also an absolute attachment to the professional expression of this love. That commitment underlies the romantic elements in the film much as Proust's love of art—the only love he truly understands—structures the social and erotic themes in his great novel.

Renoir's film is a tribute to the way in which professionalism such as Danglard's can bring people together as creative beings who must bravely suffer through prolonged mental as well as physical training, and who must learn how to resist interpersonal, or other, inclinations that can distract them from their work. In the end the struggle succeeds—for the movie is a romanesque fable in which the protagonists are idealized devotees of art and its human oneness as we in the audience may also be. The tribulations that attend the all-important culminating performance are overcome with sparkling brightness and panache before a discriminating public that finds the dancers supremely meritorious in their noble profession.

The last portion of the film, in which the splendor of this artistic effort shows itself to the fullest, contains a lengthy presentation of the cancan. The word itself is noteworthy in relation to Renoir's intention. In Parisian slang it means not only the dance form we associate with Montmartre and the

Moulin Rouge but also, as a derivation from the verb *cancanner*, frivolous gossip or trivial chatter. By putting this ambiguity into his title, Renoir assures us in advance that nothing ponderous will be found in the movie. In the subtitle he promises a "musical comedy." He keeps that promise, while availing himself of this opportunity to impart a message about art as meaningful as Proust's, and as affirmative and optimistic as anything Proust believed in.

In Renoir's film *Nana* (1929) the dancing of the cancan expresses the protagonist's wildly orgiastic, even depraved, attempt to escape a sense of failure in her life. Nana leaps into the group of dancers performing it after she becomes hopelessly inebriated, no long capable of facing the fact that she has caused the death of the two men who loved her. The later film puts the cancan to a very different use. It is now a triumphant acceptance of the carnal aspects of our natural state.

In *French Cancan*, the most striking declaration about the role of professionalism as a life-sustaining bridge that connects us to our human condition occurs just before the company goes out to perform the cancan. In a fit of jealousy, Nini has suddenly decided to leave the troupe. She is the young girl whom Danglard picked up after meeting her in a lower-class dance hall where he and his friends were slumming. After getting the permission of her mother, Danglard adopts Nini as a protegée. He puts her into the dancing school that elicits her talent and makes her into a fledgling professional.

In conformity with Romantic ideology about the role of sex in the development of artistic creativity, the story follows Nini's teenage introduction to the pleasures of physical lovemaking with a baker's apprentice. She is well matched socially with him, and he wants to marry her. We then see how her nascent career stifles that possibility, while increasing her attachment to Danglard, whom she treats as the Pygmalion who has made her what she now wants to be. Having become his mistress, she wrangles with the older dancer he slept with previously. When she catches him cavorting with still another protegée, she refuses to go on stage at the grand opening of Danglard's new theater unless she can have him for herself alone.

In a vehement attempt to liberate Nini from misconceptions about the nature of his feelings for her, Danglard bursts into a tirade backstage and before the entire company, though addressed to Nini, that serves as the thematic resolution of the film. He tells her that if she wants a lover or a husband, or both, she must find them not in him but somewhere else. He shouts at her:

Only one thing matters to me: What I create. And what do I create? You! Her! [the older woman] Her! [the new rival] There've been others, there'll be others. In the end, does it matter what *we* want? All that counts is what *they* want [pointing toward the audience beyond the stage]; we're at the service of the public. It breaks my heart to see you go; not because they'll wreck the place . . . but because the profession's losing a good trouper. If you're not one of us, then *get the hell out*.

After brooding for a while, Nini yields to her desire to belong. She joins the other dancers and exuberantly throws herself into the finale. In the exhilaration of his victory, Danglard hits upon still another young woman, a member of the audience, and enlists her into his professionalistic cause.

❀

While recognizing that all of *The Golden Coach* aspires to the condition of commedia dell'arte and all of *French Cancan* is a glorification of art that defines itself as a professional enterprise devoted to creative unity among performers who then make contact with their viewers, we must also emphasize Renoir's great preoccupation with the uniqueness of each artist. His own professional love for Anna Magnani and Jean Gabin as actors predates his using them as representations of the arresting characters who energize their respective surroundings. Without Camilla or Danglard, none of the human bridges could have occurred; but without the charisma of Magnani or Gabin, the characters that Renoir presents would not have been the same. Being grounded in these actors, the characters they enact are systematically different from their counterparts in Welles's films. Unlike Welles's protagonists, Renoir's are not isolated individuals trying to cope with a hostile world. They are, instead, the remarkable though wholly human creators of mankind's social and cultural growth.

Renoir's mature thinking about the professionalistic attitude arose after 1945. Like many others who were excited by the prospect of there being "one world" that would now come into existence, he predicted a gradual but persistent decay of nationalism in Europe. Professions do not have to recognize the boundaries that separate one sovereign state from another. In his writings and interviews Renoir points out that in the Middle Ages people identified themselves with their training and their craft rather than with the nations in which they lived, even though those were more numerous than in the twentieth century. Speaking of the earlier period, he says that "divisions among nations were much weaker than the division by interest, by profession, or by intellectual tendency. For example, a medieval clerk—a man whose profession it was to be educated, to try to learn—was not specifically an Italian or a

French intellectual but, rather, an intellectual who belonged to the great Western civilization."[18]

Renoir immediately applies this insight to the state of his art form after the end of World War II. Foreseeing what we nowadays call globalization, he expected that filmmaking would turn into a profession that extends beyond all national limitations by joining men and women throughout the world either as film artists or as lovers of cinematic achievements. He saw in this new occurrence an opportunity for people like himself to share in great cultures that arise out of countries that are not their own.

This facet of Renoir's thinking was already present, though not fully developed and largely ignored by most commentators, in *Grand Illusion*. On more than one occasion, Renoir himself expressed surprise that this film of his should have had the immediate acceptance that it received when first released in 1938, and ever since. He brushed off its success, saying that of course everyone likes an escape movie with a happy ending. That may be true, but also *Grand Illusion (La Grande Illusion)* is meaningful as an emphatic statement about the making of bridges by various means, including one's profession. What unites de Boeldieu, played by Pierre Fresnay, and von Rauffenstein, played by Erich von Stroheim, is more than just the fact that they are both aristocrats rather than lower-class enlistees who have risen in rank. Unlike Maréchal (Jean Gabin) and Rosenthal (Marcel Dalio), or the others, they are *professional* officers. They are military men who have devoted their lives to the rigorous rules and ideals of their profession. De Boeldieu says it is in the nature of his commitment as an officer that he should want to escape, as in playing tennis one plays to win, without needing any other reason.

Von Rauffenstein feels the same way, and that is the basis of his friendliness toward de Boeldieu. Though von Rauffenstein will be outwitted by the French prisoners, and by his own illusions about his tenuous relationship with de Boeldieu, he speaks for Renoir himself by enunciating the basic issue in the film. In the scenes that consist of his conversations with de Boeldieu, von Rauffenstein urges the belief that as members of their professional caste they are more deeply united than either of them is to his fortuitous nationality.

Though the entire movie maps out the limitations of this view, von Rauffenstein's conception mimics Renoir's faith in the subordinating of nationalistic allegiances to the oneness people share just in belonging to the same profession. Even so, this emphasis upon professionalistic goals is muted in *Grand Illusion*. Throughout the film our sympathies are primarily directed toward the French escapees. The music swells when Maréchal and Rosenthal lower themselves out of the German fortress on their way to freedom. Listening to the words of von Rauffenstein, we detect the arrogance of a class-ridden, even feudal, social order. Despite his personal coolness and military correctness, de Boeldieu seems heroic in his willingness to risk his life to help the more plebeian Maréchal and Rosenthal. He acts out of professional dedication, but also as a fellow Frenchman.

Furthermore, in its dramatic impact *Grand Illusion* counters the nationalistic viewpoint with a sweeping humanitarian sentiment that exceeds mere professionalism. Much of Renoir's work in the 1930s comprised the inspection and artful exploitation of this broader outlook and its possible consequences. To understand the profundity of *Grand Illusion* and its message about the unity of mankind, we need to consider its place within the cycle of films that Renoir made throughout that period.

※

The movies Renoir finished in the years just before World War II were largely concerned with social problems of the time. As I mentioned earlier, Hitchcock chafed under the necessity of producing only commercial films and wished he could do some that were politically relevant and quasi-documentary. He eventually found a way of introducing realistic portrayals of settings he had known in his own life—Covent Garden, for example. But at no time was he able to concentrate at length upon the everyday existence of ordinary people, or extend to it the care and comprehension that appear in the 1930s Renoir films. The cause is obvious. Hitchcock's perspective was not truly political or populist although it dealt with feelings and situations that persons of any socioeconomic class might conceivably experience. For him it sufficed that this alone could be used to induce the suspension of disbelief that his thrillers generated.

Renoir approached his films from the opposite extreme. They might occasionally include elements of suspense and thrilling melodrama, but they sprang from a desire to explore how people do and can relate to each other, to nature, and, as we shall see, to the technologies that might or might not improve their condition as human beings.

Toni, the movie he made in 1934, is a convenient starting point. Coming a couple of years after *Boudu* and films such as *La Chienne*, it is even more proletarian than they were. Whereas *Boudu* is a human comedy that pokes fun at the false values of the bourgeoisie, and *La Chienne* digs into the dirt of sexual self-deceit and exposes faults within the legal system, *Toni* focuses on a specific section of contemporary workers. It deals with a migrant group of Italian laborers in Southern France, almost self-contained but also interacting with the local population. In some respects it anticipates the neorealism that arose in Italy some twelve years later.

At the beginning of *Toni* we see a trainload of foreigners arriving in the hope of finding jobs; at the end another trainload of the same kind serves to indicate that the socioeconomic situation remains as it was before. In between these points of reference, we follow the emotional mishaps of a good-hearted man whose capacity for love leads to one sorrow after another and finally to his legal death in relation to a murder he did not commit. A similar miscarriage of justice occurs in *La Chienne*, and *Toni* also duplicates that film's preoccupation with the violent failures of sexual love and hate-filled marriage. But *Toni* nevertheless marks an advance toward Renoir's later and more positive ideas about the nature of viable connections between human beings, and how such goodness might be brought about by political change.

The fruit of this vein of thought appeared the following year. In *Le Crime de Monsieur Lange* Renoir chooses a small community of men and women working together in a publishing house in Paris. The vicissitudes of sex and love are presented as a part of their lives, but now these realities occur as normal and potentially wholesome aspects of human society. Though they can be dangerously passionate and the cause of suffering, they are generally subsidiary to the necessities of earning a living in the company of people who work together within a common enterprise.

Batala, the head of the firm flamboyantly played by Jules Berry, is an egocentric and fraudulent cheat who seduces his female employees without remorse. At a troublesome moment he flees the city in order to avoid his creditors, leaving the publishing house to flounder at the edge of bankruptcy. Monsieur Lange saves the day. He is a mild-mannered, utterly scrupulous and honest man, a cartoonist whose contributions to the firm's magazine consist of serials that depict the Wild West adventures of a character called Arizona Jim. Lange creates Jim as an expression of his own keen but unfulfilled longing for erotic and moral heroism. After the worthless Batala has left, and then is reported dead, Lange organizes his fellow workers into a business organization based on purely democratic principles.

When Batala returns and seeks to appropriate for his own benefit the assets that have been accumulated by the commune, Lange kills him. He does so without premeditation, almost mindlessly and with little awareness of what he is doing. Killing the bad guy in a routine fashion, if the killing is legitimate, is the way that Arizona Jim would have handled things. Batala resembles Boudu in being a grandiose and selfish scoundrel, but he differs from him in seeking to subjugate the entire community to his own dictatorial ends. Boudu separates himself from society; Batala is eradicated from it.

We see all that in a lengthy flashback. Lange and his girlfriend have escaped to the border, but before they can reach safety in the neighboring country they are apprehended by the local townspeople in a bar. The woman recounts the preceding events in an attempt to get this ad hoc jury to recognize that Lange has committed not murder but justifiable homicide. They so decide, and the lovers are allowed to continue on their way to freedom. We knew all along that there would be a happy ending because so much of the film is romantic, light-hearted, and even comic. After he has snatched the newborn commune out of the jaws of bankruptcy, their somewhat zany benefactor offers to finance a series of filmed episodes based on the Arizona Jim stories. Lange and the others feel at first that this lies beyond their capabilities, but the benefactor cheerfully insists in words (self-referential in Renoir's case) that duplicate what Hitchcock used to say to his actors: "But it's *only* a movie!"

Le Crime de Monsieur Lange is not as directly political as the propagandistic film *La Vie est à nous* (*People of France*), which Renoir made for the Communist Party in 1936, or even *This Land Is Mine* and *Salute to France*, which he directed in America during the war. *Le Crime* is much more interesting as a work of art than those movies are. It tells a fascinating story, albeit one that is as fanciful as the comic book personage who becomes the model that Lange wants to emulate. Out of this fantasy Renior constructs an archetypal representation of communal unity not dissimilar to what he must have found in Rousseau's philosophy. Lange kills without authority but is exonerated in the eyes of the people. Why? Because no one like Batala should be allowed to impede the life-enhancing conversation among members of the human race. That is so great a virtue, and so thoroughly embedded in Renoir as both a person and a filmmaker, that it represents a natural culmination—an elemental component of nature itself—and becomes an aesthetic imperative as well as a moral obligation. Though the political implications are not elaborated, and in the context of this fable need not be, they establish their own kind of contact with the appropriate imagination of an enlightened public.

Written and produced shortly afterward, *La Marseillaise* continues in the same humanistic, even anarchistic, voice as *Le Crime de Monsieur Lange*. The title itself tells us that this film is a cinematic glorification of the popular song that became the revolutionary anthem in the 1790s. Despite this national importance, the movie is not especially nationalistic. The French Revolution is not treated as the effort of patriots. The narrative evolves from the perspective of peasants and working men and women, mainly lower-class southerners who travel to Paris and join forces against the monarchy as if they were participating in a cheerful lark and grand excursion. The shifts of power within the political turmoil, the details of divergent social theories, the morality of the loyal aristocrats as well as the conscientious revolutionaries who oppose them— little of this enters into the scope of the film. Instead Renoir concentrates on the individuality of a few persons, fairly younger ones, who carry their commitment forward in a jaunty fashion that solidifies just before the major Battle of Valmy.

Not only does *La Marseillaise* reject the illusion that the French Revolution was a unitary event or one that is properly emblazoned in some image of the guillotine, but also it emphasizes the primal humanity of King Louis XVI. He is presented as an unprepossessing supernumerary and a rather pleasant person, like most of his entourage with the exception of Marie Antoinette. Far from being an unscrupulous ruler, he is an ordinary man caught up in historic forces he cannot understand. There is nothing that can be taken as blatantly class-ridden in his thinking or demeanor, any more than in the people who finally dethrone him. The revolution is thus portrayed as a mass movement resulting from a rudimentary and unforeseeable unison within the populace at that moment in time. In his own benighted way, the king himself has a role in this variation on the theme of contact with a comprehensive public.

The film ends in shots of the determined marching of the revolutionary troops, no longer a ragtag conglomeration of ill-equipped stragglers but now a trained army joined in an idealistic cause. They are about to engage in warfare against the emigrés and their foreign supporters. They fight at Valmy as equal and fraternal Frenchmen devoted to the ideal of liberty that binds them all. But the sentence we see on screen before the final fade-out implies a residual and more universal meaningfulness for the lives of people everywhere. The words are translated from Goethe's firsthand account of this pivotal event. The English version reads: "In this place and on this day a new epoque in the history of the world began."

Though *La Marseillaise* undoubtedly adds to the sense of national grandeur that the French may have needed during the year or two before the onset of World War II, it proclaims a humanitarian outlook that is similar to the one in *Grand Illusion*. That was made about the same time as *La Marseillaise*, though released eight months earlier. Both films express humanitarian attitudes that rise above the boundaries of any single country. While recounting its story about French officers imprisoned by their German adversaries in World War I, *Grand Illusion* gives a view of the conflict that bypasses the fighting and the killing on both sides.

Grand Illusion was vilified at first by French critics who complained that it was a distorted representation of what their men underwent for so long in the trenches and in the prisoner of war camps. De Boeldieu, Maréchal, Rosenthal, and the others receive ample food packages from their families back home and enjoy comfortable quarters denied to any noncommissioned soldiers. Moreover, they are officers in the French air force, which thought of itself as an elite outfit that competed, as if in sport, with German aviators who belonged to a comparable club that was also select and largely aristocratic. What the critics did not realize or appreciate was the extent to which Renoir's film was an accurate portrait of the life he knew himself as an air force officer who was also shot down and briefly imprisoned during the war. As such, he could understand the mentality of the German as well as the French aviators, and that insight strengthened his ability to delineate the communality among people of different countries despite the nationalistic interests that had led them into warfare with each other.

As a movie about escape from imprisonment, *Grand Illusion* was akin to the overarching struggle for liberty that permeates *La Marseillaise.* Not only is this theme applicable to the feelings in everyone, but also the various types of Germans in *Grand Illusion* are never shown in a pejorative way. They too are prisoners of their own wartime condition.

When von Rauffenstein first appears in the film, it is as one who has just shot down the plane that carried de Boeldieu and Maréchal. He graciously invites them to share the dinner he and his fellow German officers enjoy together. Maréchal's arm having been broken, the German next to him at the table kindly cuts his meat for him. Toward the end of the meal, an orderly brings in a large wreath with words on it that memorialize a gallant French aviator who has been killed in aerial combat and will now be buried by the Germans. Later in the film we see German soldiers marching in the street outside one of the prison camps to which the French have been consigned. Old peasant women watch their young German soldiers pass, and one remarks: "Oh, the poor boys." We are given no reason to feel differently, to hate Germans because their mission now is to kill or capture Frenchmen. We are not encouraged to see the Germans as a breed apart. The problem is how to make contact with them and establish a sense of mutual humanity.

❄

As always, Renoir's solution consists in advocating the return to nature. At the end of *Grand Illusion*, Maréchal and Rosenthal reach the Swiss frontier in the mountains. The ground is covered by snow and one of them wonders where exactly the border is. The other replies that nature doesn't concern itself with borders. And neither should we, Renoir implies. At first the German patrol that guards the frontier fires at the two men who are crossing into Switzerland. But the Germans too do not know where the border is and soon relent. In doing so, they accept the authority of nature as an indiscriminate home for all human beings.

Previously we had seen this accommodating attitude on the part of the German guards in the fortress where the French officers are imprisoned. Arthur, the guard who is the principal liaison with the Frenchmen, is particularly sympathetic toward them, but to a lesser degree so are the other guards. At one point the French internees put on an amateur theatrical that the German officers attend. During it, after news of a French victory has been announced, Maréchal leads the prisoners in a triumphant singing of the *Marseillaise*. In solitary confinement, to which he is then subjected, he all but goes out of his mind. The old man who guards his cell treats him with great compassion, and even restores his will to live by affectionately giving him a harmonica. Though he had wildly complained that he cannot live without hearing French spoken, Maréchal survives as a result of the transcending goodness in whatever music he can now experience, thanks to the guard's loving-kindness.

Oneness with nature as the basis of a wholesome contact with people regardless of their nationality is also the dominant motif in Maréchal's relationship with the German widow who befriends him and Rosenthal during their stay on her isolated farm. Maréchal falls in love with her because there are no barriers in this rural countryside. They are drawn to each other as a man and a woman who find that they can communicate harmoniously and as suitable sexual partners. This goes beyond the friendship that Maréchal and Rosenthal attain once they surmount the mutual hatred that erupts during the hardships of their escape. Earlier Maréchal had tried, unsuccessfully, to reach the soul of de Boeldieu, whose superior airs were upsetting to him. De Boeldieu rejects Maréchal's well-intentioned overtures for reasons of his own personality and not because of the social differences between them. Refusing to use the familiar pronoun *tu* (thou, in archaic English) instead of the more distanced *vous*, de Boeldieu explains to Maréchal: "Je dis *vous* à ma mère et à ma femme" (I say *vous* to my mother and to my wife).

That attitude does not prevent de Boeldieu from giving his life in order to help Maréchal escape and find the freedom they both want. Through his self-sacrifice, not through any effusion of feeling but in acting as a professional would, de Boeldieu makes contact and expresses solidarity with Maréchal (and Rosenthal as well). The question that remains at the end of the film is whether contact between Maréchal and the German woman he loves at that moment will hold fast in the weeks and months until the war ends and he can return to live with her in this idyllic setting, this bit of nature that has been hospitable to them as a well-matched pair regardless of their national origins.

Unlike the pessimistic ending of the first draft of his script, Renoir's final version offers hope of a happy outcome. While still suggesting that the universalist solution that he espoused may be illusory, Renoir leaves the matter open as a reaffirmation of the great importance that he himself attaches to this ideal.

❋

Le Caporal épinglé (*The Elusive Corporal*) was a 1962 reconception of *Grand Illusion*, transferred from World War I to World War II. Though we see few, if any, officers in the later film, it traces the experiences of French prisoners of war who finally escape their confinement by the Germans. Instrumental to their successful attempt is the assistance of a German girl who is emotionally attached to the French soldier whose adventures we are following. Once he reaches Alsace, still occupied by the German forces, he receives aid from a French farmer who has stayed there and is happily married to a German woman. These intimations of a future state of affairs in which national boundaries will lose their former significance in a more homogeneous Europe are tempered in *The Elusive Corporal*, as they were in *Grand Illusion*, by the fact that the escaping Frenchman finds his way back to Paris in order to continue the country's war effort. Renoir retains that much of nationalism as a basic premise. It is, for him, an expression of piety and identification with his own people, his own personal origin.

In Renoir's creative imagination this fidelity to one's nation fuses with his adoration not only of nature, but also of the ordinary people who live on the land, especially people who come from Provence and the south of France, as he did. Although his father had a studio in Paris, both he and Jean thought of themselves as southerners. In a much neglected film entitled *The Southerner*, made in English and in the United States at the end of World War II, Renoir presents with almost documentary detail the drama of a dirt farmer in the American South who has to fight against the enormous difficulties of living close to his hostile soil. When he finally succeeds, though barely, we have the feeling that he has learned how to converse with nature by overcoming its negative aspects as well as the animosity that exists in other farmers who are less in touch with its reality than he is.

As in his other work, Renoir is able to examine and portray this mode of conversation and of contact by establishing a relationship with the actors that delves into particularities of their being that make them authentic embodiments of their characters. Renoir's camera, as well as the script he wrote, highlights the physical strength and securely catlike movements of Zachary Scott, who plays the farmer and speaks in local terminology partly supplied by William Faulkner. Renoir reports that he was pleased to have Scott in the role because he "is himself a southerner. . . . He knows their language, he knows their habits, and he contributed a kind of exterior accuracy to the film that I found to be extremely valuable."[19]

Renoir's approach to his first American film, *Swamp Water*, shot in 1941, was similar. Refusing an opportunity to have studio stars, he chose unknown actors with whom he could work from his own point of view without being burdened by audience expectations that accumulate with fame but undermine the naturalness he wanted to achieve. He did use well-known performers like Walter Brennan and Walter Huston in supporting roles of this film, but Dana Andrews in the leading part was still beginning his rise to stardom. Andrews's character is a young trapper who confronts the treacherous Okefenokee Swamp in Georgia, hunting there despite the dangers that frighten off the others in the region. Like the Walter Brennan character, who is hiding out in the swamp, he comes to feel at home in it. The two men have the sensibility, and the cleverness, that is essential for making contact with its vegetative and animal life. At the end they return to the civilized world outside the swamp. They have learned how to effect a harmonization between these two, thereby augmenting rather than diminishing their love of nature. It is a resolution that adumbrates the conclusion of *The Southerner*, where Renoir expresses his underlying belief in the possible harmonization between technology and nature. I turn to that later in this chapter.

❁

In *Le Déjeuner sur l'herbe* (*Picnic on the Grass*) the contact with nature is encased in a whimsical tale with poetic and nonrealistic elements that Renoir also employed in other films. Toward the beginning of his career, *La Petite Marchande d'allumettes* (*The Little Merchant of Matches*) (1928) includes a surrealistic sequence that portrays the delirium of the girl who is dying of cold and starvation in the snow. Without words or music, or sound of any sort, we see her being carried through the skies by a rider on horseback who is both a Prince Charming and an angel of death. These images are juxtaposed, before and after, with realistic shots of the match girl pitifully trying to sell her matches in the busy city and then being found lifeless by unsympathetic passersby.

That short film is adapted from a story by Hans Christian Andersen, and another of his occurs in Renoir's terminal movie *Le Petit Théâtre de Jean Renoir* (*The Little Theater of Jean Renoir*) (1969). This one shows the quasi-marital love of two homeless people on a Parisian quai whose last meal, a sumptuous repast acquired from the vulgar rich at Christmastime, is followed by illusory but jointly experienced images of the earthly happiness they merit merely in loving each other. The next morning they too are found dead in the snow, wrapped in each other's arms. *Le Déjeuner sur l'herbe*, made ten years earlier, is a fantasy of a totally different sort.

The relationship between reality and surreality is not the same in *Le Déjeuner* as in the Andersen adaptations. The latter use reality as a backdrop that caustically illustrates the harshness of things-as-they-are, both in physical nature and in what normally characterizes human society. They leave us with a sense of authentic but displaced beauty that issues from creative imagination, in the filmmaker as well as in the dying characters. It is imagination that must always remain in painful isolation from factual existence. We surmise that the "real" world can only be second-best to the ideality of our heart's desire, which nothing but aesthetic innovation encompasses. This is a testament to art for art's sake, but also a venting of self-pity in view of what artists undergo in the unfeeling modern world. *Le Déjeuner*, however, rises above all that. Fantasy now operates as an appropriate means of depicting facts about the human condition—even biological and other scientific facts. They appear within the context of a richly metaphorical narrative.

The title itself suggests the artistic tradition made famous in the nineteenth century by Manet's painting. It shows the painter himself, or someone who represents him, at a picnic with two models and a friend in some clearing of a dense and leafy forest. In Manet the setting and the human figures are designed with great attention to their realistic exteriors. One striking detail instantly intrigues us: the men are fully clothed as they sit on the grass next to the women, who are naked. How should this be explained? Well, one might say, they have taken a luncheon break on a day when the models were posing in the nude. This can happen outdoors, in the midst of a choice landscape, as it could in the artist's studio. Yet something else is also at play. Manet's painting, like others in its genre, transfers our fondness for the beauty of the grass and welcoming trees to the situation of the human beings who are present there in a relaxed community that is equally natural. The women are unclothed because men, those who are not painters as well as those who are, like to see their naked flesh. Throughout the ages, and for whatever reason, many women have catered to this masculine predilection. By amalgamating the loveliness of the circumvening vegetation with the loveliness of the women who expose themselves, Manet affirms the vital goodness in this sexual—also social and aesthetic—facet of human nature.

In Renoir's film there are no painters and no naked women on the grass having lunch. Instead there is the magic of an old peasant playing his panpipe in an antique shrine of the goddess Diana. He is accompanied by a wise-but-randy-looking goat. They intrude upon the premarital repast of a distinguished couple who may soon become the president of a unified Europe and his consort. The man is a world-renowned biologist who advocates the making of test-tube babies as preferential to how they have always been produced by natural means. His fiancée is an equally advanced person, the head of all the Girl Scouts and a forceful, liberated woman on her own. Once the peasant and his goat evoke the powerful energy of the sirocco through which Diana does her libidinal work, the lives of these two people alter completely. The puritanical scientist gravitates toward the luscious and affectionate girl who originally wanted to have a test-tube baby in order to escape the duplicity of some potential father. Having changed his mind about reproduction and the role of sexuality, the future president marries the earthy lass instead of the straitlaced scout leader.

The fantasy in *Le Déjeuner sur l'herbe* thus arises from reality as the epiphany of an indigenous magic about which we are willing to suspend our disbelief in movies of this type. Farcical as the action of the film may be, it vigorously affirms our existence in nature as well as the possibility of a beneficial conversation between humanity and the rest of life. Placed in the postwar period of France that was seeking to be entirely up-to-date, the movie begins with a sequence on television and later includes shots of factory workers riding into the countryside on their mopeds. Interlarded with these examples of modern technology are jolly scenes of the more primitive farming family (who are mainly idle) to which the young girl belongs. Like the biologist, we watch her swimming in the nude. The country folk and their ease in the rural surroundings of Provence evince the possibility of happiness without unnecessary worldly goods and without anxieties that beset those who are not pleasantly in touch with nature. Renoir's point is unmistakable.

❀

The River, made in 1950, enabled Renoir to extend this naturalistic and humanistic approach to the spiritual dimensions afforded by his trip to India. Collaborating with Rumer Godden on a version of her novel, he wisely chose to balance its setting and local color with the pivotal experience of Westerners who reside in that country. Radha, the girl who returns home after having studied abroad, is given an Anglo-Saxon father and must come to terms with her mixed lineage. Far from distorting Godden's novel, that kind of change allowed Renoir to make the movie an honest reflection of his own involvement as a foreigner in India who shared its predominant attitude toward nature. He saw the film as itself a manifestation of ongoing conversation between West and East, between himself as a Frenchman and the characters who are born in India. The binding thread throughout is the great river, presumably the Ganges, which appears at the beginning, lends its presence to various scenes, and then flows on in the closing shots.

There is no evidence of racial or national conflict in *The River*, and the Westerners are shown as constructive contributors to the native economy. The film, like the novel, is a semi-autobiographical portrait of Harriet, the young English girl, as she grows awkwardly into adolescence. The account is guided occasionally by a voiceover narration by the much older person that Harriet will someday become. Her development, and the life of her family, constitutes most of the plot. But that is only the focus of their immersion in the Indian culture and mode of being that excite Renoir's camera from beginning to end. What inspires him most is the spirituality that he calls Hindu. He considers it fundamental in everything his film portrays.

Discussing what *The River* means to him in this connection, Renoir says that Hinduism is "not exactly" a religion but rather a metaphysics. Its principal notion, he suggests, "is that the

world is one. We're part of it, we're part of the world just as a
tree or your tape recorder is. That doesn't imply an acceptance,
as in the Muslim tradition, which is fatalistic. No, it's an
empowerment. But nonetheless, you can't go back to what has
been done."[20] Renoir does not clarify these remarks, though he
extends them in other comments. At one point, he calls
attention to Radha's telling the wounded and somewhat
troubled American that he must learn how to "consent" to his
predicament. The idea of acceptance of the given, through an
attitude of consenting to things being what they are, pervades
the entire film. Renoir claims to have learned this message from
his year in India working on *The River*. But he also states that
he found the Indian perspective on reality very similar to the
French outlook he already knew.

In being alike in this respect, the two approaches illustrate
Renoir's beliefs about living in nature and attaining a sense of
oneness that human beings can experience in relation to nature.
At the same time, he had no hesitation in painting trees in the
Bengal woodland where he filmed *The River*. Though he
thereby gave the leaves a color of green they did not have but
that suited his purely cinematic conception in several scenes,
he denied any inconsistency between that and either the Indian
or his own belief in accepting nature as it is.

Explaining how he and Rumer Godden adapted her novel,
Renoir states that where Indian culture had been shown to
penetrate the walls of the villa in which the English family live,
they now decided to break down those walls. The lifestyles of
Westerners and of Indians, their approach to nature and to
their own patterns of thought, interpenetrate throughout. At
the end the American moves on, the English and Anglo-Indian
girls who have had a crush on him learn to make do without

his presence, the river of life continues to meander as before. In India, Renoir says, he discovered that everyone has his own reasons. In *The Rules of the Game,* made eleven years earlier, the character Octave laments that everyone insists on having his own reasons. By the time *The River* was made, Renoir would seem to have recognized the spiritual import of treating that as a constant in human nature. I myself think this affirmative view occurs in most of his later work.

Nevertheless, despair recurred at times of stress and temporary defeat. In *The Rules* it contributed to the ambiguities that gave the dark comedy of that film its magnificent amplitude. But even there, the search for responsive conversation at the various levels we have been discussing remains as a major propellant in the narrative. *The Rules* may even be seen as a buddy film, not entirely dissimilar from the comedic masterpieces that René Clair had been making in the same decade, except that in this one the two friends—Octave and André—fail in their ill-fated attempt to make contact with an upper-class society whose reasons are not the same as theirs.

Renoir's enthusiasm for the aspect of Hinduism he appreciates is related to his comparable ideas about the nature of spirituality itself. His work is infused with a radical egalitarianism that he mentions in several places. He contrasts the *material* differences among people, and even events, with the fact that *spiritually* they are all of equal importance. He means that every person and every event has its own ultimate value that must be recognized. "There are no different classes, no gradations, first and foremost, because we are all one."[21] This faith sustains his professional as well as his political beliefs, his methods of filmmaking as well as his views about artistic creation in general. It elucidates his love of improvisation. If one follows a rigid plan that has been laid out in advance, one cannot benefit from the equal right to self-presentation that all people and every moment in time retain indefeasibly.

Since these rights are likely to conflict, they contain within themselves the dramatic tensions that a filmmaker can exploit. His or her work is then "realistic" in a sense that Renoir cares about very much. It hews to what he considers a definitive truth about individuals that is falsified by gradations or quantifications. The death of a ditch-digger is more meaningful for his family, he says, than the death of Einstein. In some domains Einstein is certainly more important, and yet "the one thing we don't know is the importance of these domains."[22] Since Renoir is unwilling to accept any absolute other than equality itself, he ends up with a kind of relativism that may seem counterproductive but is actually fruitful for an artist's work. The inherent ambiguities stimulate imaginative powers that can then elicit responsive acts of imagination in the audience.

In the chapter on *The Rules of the Game* in my book *Reality Transformed*, I examine the panoply of ambiguous effects in that film. I consider how they contribute to its formal structure.[23] Among them is one that Renoir returns to frequently in his writings. It arises from the ambivalence that he felt about technology in relation to human values. Convinced that "one of the artist's roles is to try to recreate the direct contact between man and nature," he is concerned about the extent to which technological developments increasingly alienate us from nature as a whole and from our own particular nature.[24] This problem has dogged Western civilization for more than two hundred years, but Renoir addresses it afresh from his perspective as a filmmaker.

In his receptive way, congruent with his egalitarianism, Renoir makes no attempt to minimize the benefits that have accrued from technology. With a delight equivalent to Hitchcock's, he revels in the aesthetic utility of inventions such as Technicolor and the ever advancing modifications in lenses and the camera itself. He remarks that without nineteenth-century technology, the impressionism of painters like his father might never have come into existence. Previously paints were stored in jars that were too large and heavy to be carried easily. With the manufacture of the little tubes that could be transported in knapsacks and small cases, artists were able to work in nature at any location they chose. By extension, we can nowadays say something similar about the opportunities afforded by handheld cameras and computerized filmmaking. Renoir never questions the degree to which technology of this sort has furthered the evolution of art and of civilization itself.

What troubles him is a mechanistic and reductivistic tendency that seems to be inseparable from modern technology. The search for perfection, as he describes it, augments the problem. Technology lures us into illusory pursuits of that type, he suggests, when people focus it on limited projects that can be carried out with extraordinary, sometimes absolute, success regardless of how little may be achieved in terms of any meaningfulness or human value. As a director, he must always seek ways to overcome this danger. Far from trying to use the latest devices to capture reality, as recommended by those who believe that realism is the uniquely proper approach to filmmaking, he feels instead that he must help his audience *see* better.

"One thing that has happened over the past fifty years," Renoir says in 1954, "is that people have lost the use of their senses. This is due to what we call progress."[25] He ascribes that phenomenon to the baleful seductiveness of technological conveniences whenever they separate us from direct contact with nature. But as an instrument within an art form, the camera can nevertheless serve to *correct* the deleterious effects of technology. Employed with this intention, it restores our ability to see modes of reality to which we have become oblivious.

As a means of comprehending this conception, we should compare it with the ideas that Bazin proffered in essays like "The Myth of Total Cinema" and "The Ontology of the Photographic Image." Bazin argued that technological advances in film and photography are part of the typical human quest for greater control over, though also oneness with, physical reality. He thought that the camera presents us with the very being of any object whose appearance it records. He maintained that technical improvements in the camera's operation will bring humankind that much closer to the ontological ideal it has always pursued.[26] In Renoir's foreword to Bazin's book about his earlier movies, he expresses admiration for the perceptiveness of this film theorist.[27] But in wondering "whether our technical progress isn't simply a sign of total decadence," he separates himself from Bazin's adherence to the myth of total cinema.[28] Reaffirming his own outlook, Renoir does not mention Bazin, but he clearly perceives the difference between the naturalism in his movies and the Bazinian type of realism.

Nevertheless, Renoir is always aware of how much technology can further the search for immediate and sensory contact with nature. He speculates about the possibility that spirit liberates itself from matter through technology, which then becomes a new form of matter that spirit must cope with at a higher level. Though he does not develop this concept, which seems reminiscent of Hegelian dialectics, it bolsters his belief that the artificiality of film alienates us from nature and yet enables a cinematic artist to gain a new unity with it by means of the aesthetic use of his technical contrivances. In this vein Renoir claims that primitive artifacts—Etruscan works of pottery, for instance—are generally beautiful until the relevant techniques are perfected. At that stage the products become ugly (or boring, as he sometimes says), until there arise "artists who have enough genius to master the technique."[29]

❀

These ideas about technology in relation to art reverberate throughout Renoir's creative life, but only toward the end of it does he fit them into the polemical aspects of a film. In *La Cireuse électrique* (*The Electric Waxing Machine*), a section of *Le Petit Théâtre de Jean Renoir,* he offers an outrageous cartoon-like farce about the dangers of everyday technology in the home. It is a comic opera, for which Renoir wrote the libretto and in which the death of a housewife and her yuppie husband is designed to have no emotional effect whatsoever upon the audience. The narrative illustrates how an ordinary woman may become obsessive in her love for a machine that waxes her floor and makes it shine to perfection. When her first husband expires after slipping on the floor and her second husband throws the offending object out the window, she jumps after her beloved machine and dies embracing it.

The *cireuse* may be taken as representing the camera, which can so easily snare us with its perfected trickery, but we also know that the cautionary content of the script applies to all technology. The film relates that message about current civilization in a flow of melodious humor that partly reconciles us to the perils that we face, while sharply imprinting them upon our imagination.

Modulated as it may be, the comedy in *La Cireuse électrique* is sarcastic by and large. As Bergson in his book on laughter might say, it shows the human spirit floundering in its conflict with the materiality it wishes to subjugate. The waxing machine is shown to be a physical object that does more harm than good, and we laugh at the idea that anyone can voluntarily submit to that. But Renoir's thinking about physical objects goes beyond the Bergsonian notion. The *cireuse* differs from the *boules*, the small balls, that have a major role in *Le Roi d'Yvetot*, the last segment of *Le Petit Théâtre*. The balls belong to the popular outdoor game of *pétanque*, which is played in the town square and embodies the communal mentality of all the local inhabitants. Commenting on *Le Roi d'Yvetot*, Renoir says: "The chief actor in this little drama is the game of *pétanque*, which I firmly believe to be an instrument of peace."[30]

In *La Bête humaine* Renoir had expressed, some thirty years earlier, an equally favorable attitude toward technology and the material objects it creates. In his rendition of Zola's novel about passionate sex, adultery, jealous murder, and inherited though intermittent insanity, the only recipient of any enduring love is the locomotive that Lantier (played by Gabin) mounts as its engineer. The film begins with a four-and-a-half-minute sequence in which the camera rides in the cabin with Lantier. When it is not glancing at him as he operates the train, or at his assistant (played by Carette) as he stokes the firebox, the camera observes the panorama of rails and surrounding landscape that the great machine passes through on its way to Le Havre. When it reaches its destination, a slight upsweep in the accompanying music occurs, as if to celebrate this achievement in the cooperation between humanhood and technology.

Before and after its arrival, Lantier attends to the locomotive's needs with loving devotion. He has given it a name, Lison, meaning Big Lisa. He always refers to it with a feminine pronoun, and throughout the film he is shown to be content and wholly alive only in relation to his locomotive. At the end, when complications in his sexual life have become unbearable to him, he commits suicide by jumping off Lison at high speed, in a sudden eruption of madness. Earlier in the movie, images of this and other trains provide a continuity to the dramatic events, and sometimes contribute to them. We are given access to the daily lives of the men who work on the trains or as stationmasters. We see them wash up, take meals together, converse about their lovelife and their families, chatter aimlessly as members of the same profession. Lantier's final decline occurs after his love affair with the wife of a stationmaster. The enraged husband kills an older man who sexually abused her since girlhood. The murder takes place on a train when Lantier happens to be there. In their subsequent relationship, Lantier and the wife skulk around dark corners of the rail yards.

While trains enter into the background significance of many scenes, two occasions of this are especially noteworthy. In one the stationmaster and his unhappy wife have taken a train to Paris, where they are to spend a short vacation in a colleague's apartment at the edge of the Gare Saint Lazare. When the stationmaster returns to their temporary lodging a little before his wife, he instinctively walks to the window and looks out at the rail yards, where a train is just pulling in. So completely is his life an appendage of the railroad, even though he is off duty, he automatically takes out his watch in order to see whether the train is on time. As he steps away from the window, the camera shows us two empty birdcages on the ledge outside. We never learn why they are empty, but their existence overlooking the yards suggests that even the birds who may have once lived there were also captivated by the spectacle of the arrivals and departures. And, of course, the birds would have been locked up in their cages, which is also true of the stationmaster and his wife. As we presently discover, those two are imprisoned not only by their place within the oppressive bureaucracy but also by their marriage, which is an empty cage since there is no love in it.

The other scene I have in mind is equally crucial to the plot. Since Lison is being worked on in Le Havre, Lantier takes a train to a nearby station where his godmother lives in the company of a young girl to whom he is deeply attracted. His love for her, and hers for him, are presented as entirely genuine. But for that reason alone, he feels that he must not inflict upon her his congenital depression and episodes of near insanity. All the same, they embrace and kiss tenderly while lying on the railroad embankment in an open field. After a few moments, a wild expression distorts Lantier's features and he begins to strangle the girl. He is unable to arrest his violent behavior until a train comes roaring down the track, as if to shock him back to his senses.

Lantier regains his self-control and frees the girl he loves. She does not appear again in the film, and we surmise that Lantier cannot face the possibility of harming anyone as amiable as she is. He relinquishes all hope of loving a woman like her. When he gives vent to his sexual feelings toward the seductive wife of the stationmaster, he knows that she is a clever and worldly woman accustomed to lying and adultery. His behavior with her is a desecration of the true love he has now despaired of finding, and his murdering her serves as a quasi-natural retribution for what he has lost in life.

In the course of this display of human beastliness, the one shining object that remains worthy of our affection is Lison, together with her family of trains that tower like cathedrals of speeding efficiency and breathtaking mobility. Only the life that radiates from these artifacts has lasting meaning in the film. They alone are a source of potential beauty. In their thunderous splendor the huge machines both symbolize and manifest the glory of modern technology. Renoir responds massively to this allure. Perhaps that is why he emphasizes the necessity of making sure that none of our wonderful technological creations will ever run over us, or otherwise mangle what matters most in the nature of human beings.

Renoir's insights about technology supplement his devotion to cinematic technique. Particularly when he was starting his career, he experimented with lighting, lenses, and the varied use of the camera as much as anyone did at the time. *La Petite Marchande d'allumettes* reveals a great deal of technical ingenuity. Later in his career, he settled into a pattern of restricting the movements of the camera and letting it quietly observe what the actors were enacting. From start to finish, however, he recognized the primacy of technique while also warning neophytes about the need to subordinate it to the more fundamental forging of intuitive oneness with an audience through authentic feeling that the camera can both portray and express.

In all his work Renoir's film techniques are remarkably consonant with his humanistic views about his art form. Since he wants to make contact through the face and personality of the actors, he instructs the camera to *follow* them, to give them room to move about and improvise the little gestures that we associate with human individuality. Compared with Hitchcock or Welles, Renoir himself—as director or scriptwriter—seems unobtrusive by and large, though always present. Welles's use of the camera is often histrionic, while remaining brilliant in its visual evocation of some dramatic moment. However greatly Welles identified with his fellow actors, his artful cinematography appears less concerned about the performer as a unique embodiment of the character than as a revelation of the filmmaker's inspired ideas about that character and his or her situation. In the case of Hitchcock, the camera is used as a manipulative agency that moves the narrative step by step in accordance with the filmmaker's desire to arouse suspense from within his preestablished pattern. Hitchcock's cinematography relies upon the realistic presentation of the actors but in a way that systematically reduces it to what the director has decided that the audience shall see and experience. Renoir's technique functions on another plane.

With Renoir one usually feels that the camera—its placement, its filters, its panning or dollying or zooming in and out—is not just an implement of reproduction but also a surrogate for the filmmaker as a thoroughly concerned person who is watching what the actors are doing in front of him. The initial shooting, like the subsequent cutting and editing, exists as the vehicle by which the audience can enter into the personal conversation that Renoir has been having with the performers. Without dominating or being a mechanism of self-assertion, the camera could thereby represent his reality just as the actors it was following represent the humanity of the fictional characters they embody.

At the same time, Renoir avails himself of all the tricks of filmmaking. Before deep focus shots were used so well in *Citizen Kane*, he used them to unify foreground and distant fields of vision in *The Rules of the Game*. In his book on Orson Welles, Bazin shows how this creates a provocative acuity in *Citizen Kane* that enlivens the imagination of the spectators, as I have mentioned, by forcing them to decide what is visually most important in the presented scene. The same can be said about the arrival of the guests at the marquis's country estate in *The Rules of the Game*. By keeping in focus the cars that drive up to the chateau's entrance as well as the remote woodlands in which much of the action also takes place—the hunt, for instance—the camera alerts us to what will occur later on. In one shot of *La Bête humaine* we see a close-up of Lison that establishes, early on, her importance in the plot. It is filmed from below in order to make the locomotive loom even larger and more impressively than in life. With great relish, Renoir reports that the images of Lison speeding down the track were sometimes taken by having the cameraman (his nephew Claude) strapped on the outside of the train, entwined with it like a pretzel.

For the most part, however, the masterpieces of Renoir's maturity generally avoided cinematography that might interfere with our ordinary perception of the people or events in nature with which we might commune. He interpreted this predilection as coherent with his evolving interest in film as

theater. By announcing itself, through its title, as *his* theater—
Le Théâtre de Jean Renoir—this movie reminds us of all its
predecessors that either dealt with the life of performing artists
or else included onstage theatricals that furthered the drama in
different ways. If one is filming a play *as* a play, one wants to
convey the sense of being in an audience watching a live
performance. Too much movement of the camera or cleverness
in its intervention would destroy that effect. As Renoir himself
became an author of works for the theater, which he also
directed, he progressively wedded his kind of naturalism to the
position of someone who is both in the theater and at the
cinema. This in turn facilitated identification between the
viewers and the characters who have a theatrical experience
within a film.

A project of that sort requires a great deal of cinematic
expertise. In order to "create this confusion between theater
and life," as he calls it, Renoir encouraged his actors to
exaggerate a bit their enactment of real events. He thought that
would "give life to this theatrical side." Moreover, he
eliminated, as much as possible, the fourth wall in any shot,
thereby duplicating the appearance of a staged performance.
He notes that this is especially evident in *The Rules of the Game*.
In it, and in his subsequent films, there are very few reaction
shots resulting from the camera passing back and forth within
a conversation between the characters. In terms of the overall
composition of a scene, "I never divide [it] into action and
reaction shots, start with a master shot, and then move to closer
shots, and then, in the editing, use all of them."[31]

As an extension of his approach, Renoir usually filmed
chronologically, or almost chronologically, and in the cutting
phase put the pieces of celluloid together in the order in which

they were shot. There are two consequences of this method. First, by having the camera stand in front of a scene and merely shoot it, what appears on film not only reinforces the theatrical sense as something foundational in the cinematography but also creates an identification between the filmmaker and the audience. Both are observing the same occurrence, albeit one looks at people in performance and the other looks only at a consequent reproduction. And second, Renoir's procedure hews closely to the principle that he always considers foremost: "The goal is to tell a story."[32]

He makes that statement in the context of explaining why some subjects are best presented in color while others are optimal in black and white. The nature of the subject and the demands of story telling determine which of the two alternatives should be chosen. To rely unduly on the latest technology, and some perfection in *it*, is to go astray from the very outset.

Similarly Renoir says that after rehearsing the script he never comes on the set with prearranged notions about the camera angle. That depends on the scene as he and the cameraman finally decide to shoot it. As we know from the many occasions on which critics have praised outstanding examples of Renoir's imagery, his self-imposed restrictions did not prevent him from using the camera to express elusive feelings and ideas as only cinema can. In *Le Crime de Monsieur Lange,* the camera stands back in its observant fashion throughout the scene in the courtyard where Lange will kill Batala, but it also swings nervously across it in rhythmic panning shots that embrace this site of communal oneness upon which Batala has tyrannically intruded. In that comprehensive gesture the camera's action contrasts dramatically with

Lange's sudden and unexpected pistol shot. In scenes of *Grand Illusion* in which the French prisoners discuss their plans for escape, Renoir has the camera move in a semicircle within the room as if to register their joint commitment and group involvement despite their inevitable differences. When Gabin ends up in solitary confinement, the famous shot that arcs across his little cell prepares us for the outstretched kindness that the elderly German guard extends to him.

In other films and other sequences, the camera performs in a diversity of ways. In the hunt scene in *The Rules of the Game* it withdraws continuously as the army of beaters marshal the rabbits into the firing range. When the slaughter begins, it offers a succession of montages that are sharply cut and carefully stitched together during editing in order to express the disconcerting horror of what is being shown. In this and all the other examples of outstanding camerawork that one could mention, Renoir intentionally limits the sheer bravura of his technical competence. Too great a display of it would distract us from the narrative story telling and from the ability of the actors to present themselves as manifestations of the characters.[33]

❈

One of the principles that show Renoir's thinking about technique is what he calls "the balancing act." When a story line was strong enough, he would balance it against peripheral side events and even discussions that would add to it without being a deterrent. He states that while the brief conversation about the generosity of Rosenthal, and of other Jews, does not advance the escape plot of *Grand Illusion*, it helps fasten the plot in a larger reality. He mentions this as a procedure that is comparable to propping up a table or other piece of furniture in order to keep it from being unsteady on the floor.

Renoir balanced his stories with related, but unnecessary, incidents or details of character in the hope of making the fiction seem more plausible. In his realistic film *Toni*, he tells us, the manner and action of the people are so ordinary that he felt he should strengthen that fact by balancing it against the natively poetical language of their daily speech. Because *The Rules of the Game* was an original story, he experienced self-doubt that he claims to have been characteristic of himself when he was not writing an adaptation of someone else's text. He says that he balanced this feeling by imparting extensive and repeated ambiguities to the narrative: "I pushed one side and then the other and then set it upright ... You feel as though you're walking a tightrope, with a big stick and your weight. But it's exciting."[34] Though these ambiguities constitute a specific and coherent view of the world, that alone does not fully explain this aspect of Renoir's governing method. Only through *some* technique or other can any kind of meaning-fulness exist. This particular technique issued from Renoir's perception of aesthetic and formalistic dangers, and without that perception he could not have expressed his vision of human nature in this movie.

Something similar in Renoir's approach elucidates his ideas about the role of music in films. He declares himself opposed to the notion that the music should duplicate what is happening on screen. Instead, he suggests, it should "counterbalance" the images and not "repeat the action and sentiments." In Renoir's works one encounters few places where the music tries to elicit an emotional response, as in Herrmann's scores for Hitchcock's thrillers, or even interpret the quality of some event, as often happens in Welles's films. I am not entirely clear about the meaning of the word *counterbalance* in Renoir's statement. It occurs just after he says that he is against "the modern principle that music underlines the images."[35] But surely he does not want to deny that music can enhance and possibly clarify them. What then does he mean?

The two films that may best help us answer this question are *The Golden Coach* and *The River*. In the first of these, Vivaldi's music occasionally occurs as an accompaniment to the commedia dell'arte being simultaneously performed on stage. To that extent it does function as a kind of duplication through another medium of the images that are therefore being underlined. But more essential to the structure of the film is the pervasive sound of Vivaldi's music. It sets the mood for long stretches of the action. Since Renoir wrote the script while listening to Vivaldi recordings that he credits with having assisted him throughout, the entire movie is an attempt to provide the audience with some corresponding experience. Though only as beneficiaries of what appears on screen, we too can share the sonic inspiration that contributed to its beginnings. Without *underlining* every moment or event in the action, the music counterbalances the images by creating a comparable feeling, a spontaneous vivacity and frivolous playfulness definitively characteristic of commedia dell'arte.

In *The River* the presence of Indian music is obviously designed for Western rather than Eastern ears. Indians watching the film from their own perspective, and thus not seeing it as its European or American audience would, might well wonder why they are being regaled with this concert of music whose style is so familiar to them. But in the context of a work that is oriented toward people who have not grown up in

Indian culture, and specifically a movie that deals with
Westerners who live as permanent foreigners in India, the
musical accompaniment yields the type of counteraction that
Renoir wanted. It is a balancing of musical forms and cultural
conventions, presupposing the Western types but deploying on
the soundtrack the different modalities that belong to the
civilization portrayed in the images.

For Renoir there was also another type of counterbalancing
that is pertinent to his Indian experience and his use of it in *The
River*. Discussing the improvisatorial practice that developed in
him as a director—starting each day with a rough idea of what
he wanted but then changing the script and the shooting in
collaboration with the actors and the crew—he describes this
routine habit as itself a counterbalance to the usual studio
process. He speaks of the difference between these alternative
methods as similar to the difference between Indian music and
Western music that has existed since the introduction of the
well-tempered scale: "In Indian music, there is a general theme
. . . and you must follow it. And then there is a general note
given by a string instrument. Before beginning, everyone
comes to an agreement, and the note is repeated constantly, so
as to bring the other instruments back to tonal unity. . . . Aside
from that, everyone is free. I think it's a marvelous system, and
I try to do a bit of that in motion pictures."[36]

Coordinate to this sense of artistic balancing encouraged by
Renoir's method was that belief about everyone having his or
her reasons. In *The Rules of the Game*, Octave/Renoir offers that
opinion in a self-pitying tone. The outcome of the film discloses
Octave's utter inability to deal properly with anything that

matters to him. But as a filmmaker who has managed to overcome the problems in his profession, Renoir shows how he himself succeeds by putting the welter of reasons to good use. Instructing the camera to follow the actors in whatever expressiveness they need for the presentation of their characters, he was able to get their individual reasons to serve as counterbalances against each other. This generates an inner dramatic tension that is structured for the viewer by the patiently attendant cinematography.

In his technical comments about the courtyard scene of *The Crime of Monsieur Lange*, Renoir elaborates upon his preoccupation with counterbalancing and its role in the total composition. "Technically," he says, the sequence is "an attempt at linking the background and the foreground in the same shot. It's an attempt at camera movements uniting both what's happening in life, in the background action, and what's happening in the minds of the actors in the foreground."[37] The counterbalance was introduced to carry out Renoir's usual desire to give the actors aesthetic room to move about without imposing the intervention of unessential cutting. The accomplishment of this formalistic feat, Renoir informs us, required "some incredibly complicated camera movements. Believe me, . . . the cameramen had a hard time."[38]

Though the unity Renoir sought is established by maneuvers of this sort, he is always mindful of the fact that unity itself is not merely a matter of technique. Like many others who know they must also reach a quasi-mystical layer in their audience which resides beyond the pragmatic actualities of life, Renoir strives to instill the "magic" of awakened imagination. Talking about *La Marseillaise*, he says that his act of balancing episodic vignettes in that film was designed to show how personal behavior and social action are both motivated by the historical development of ideas. Through this harmony of meaning and technique, he rightly felt that he could surmount the difficulties of filmmaking that are engrained in the art form.

As a by-product of his reasoning about technique in its interaction with meaning, Renoir is able to resolve his ambiguous conception of technology. When it is an abstract and dehumanized quest for the specific perfections it can attain, technology is a threat to the human spirit. But within an art like cinema, he says, its presence as the basis of needed innovations can be an impediment that actually stimulates further inventiveness. Though the problems of technique are not intrinsically humanistic, they constitute "a good hurdle, one that you have to get over, and getting over it you acquire spiritual wealth that has nothing more to do with technology."[39] The sound and photography in a film may be good or bad technically. That is "not all that important," Renoir insists, and yet dealing with the challenges that technology presents is aesthetically "necessary."[40]

By extension, one might add, the same is true in all of human life and may serve as a guideline in any effort to make life itself a work of art. Renoir does not labor this extrapolation as much as a mere philosopher might. But it resonates within everything he says about his own view of the world.

❋

The inclusive nature of that view becomes evident when we consider what he means by "spiritual wealth" in the passage from which I quoted. Its profundity is hardly indicated, I believe, in films of his like *Le Testament du Dr. Cordelier* (*The*

Testament of Doctor Cordelier), which he freely adapted from Robert Louis Stevenson's *Dr. Jekyll and Mr. Hyde* together with some suggestions of Goethe's *Faust*. In that 1959 film, good and evil are ritualistically opposed to each other in ways that are unoriginal and, worse yet, tedious. The truly Renoir touch only occurs in the almost Chaplinesque treatment of Opale, the chemically created monster who wears the clothes of the staid Dr. Cordelier that are too big for him, and who hobbles along in a kind of contorted dance, reminiscent of Jerry Lewis in his youth, that makes every movement of his seem comical. Opale is described as the embodiment of the evil that comes from submission to our baser instincts. That, at least, is the official message of the film. But seen within the scope of Renoir's vision, Opale comes through as one who enjoys his natural state as many others do in both the earlier and the later films. Using the great versatility he had as a mime, Jean-Louis Barrault plays Opale like a ludicrous character in commedia dell'arte, in contrast to the rigid verticality of the ever upright Dr. Cordelier, whom he also enacts.

By merging in one personage, and one actor, the idealistic surgeon and the lively sport of nature he brings into being, Renoir plays upon the counterbalancing relationship between André and Octave that *The Rules of the Game* borrowed from Musset's *Les Caprices de Marianne*. In Renoir's film, André, the sky-blue man, becomes a sacrificial scapegoat for all the shortcomings of the society that admires his heroic qualities but is nevertheless inadequate in itself. Octave, the natural being who is feckless and parasitic, ends up badly but survives. In *The Testament of Dr. Cordelier*, the two personae are inseparable aspects of a single person and so the death of the evil Opale requires the death of the virtuous Cordelier.

That outcome does not comport with Renoir's usual belief in the possible harmonization between mankind's natural and spiritual inclinations. The narrative is, however, coherent with most of Renoir's work in showing how an authority figure can turn out to be a more dangerous criminal than anyone he or she condemns and feels justified in tracking down. The exposure of the self-induced sinfulness of Dr. Cordelier is, to that extent, a continued statement of Renoir's lifelong faith in anarchistic humanism.

The broadest sweep of Renoir's philosophy is encapsulated in what he said to prove that the search for technical or other perfection is only secondary in either art or sexual attachment. I am referring to his remark, in the passage from which I quoted, that love is the most important thing in life.[41] Renoir makes this statement quite casually, as if all of us would doubtless agree. Be that as it may, his comment emanates from a persistent inquiry that plays a role in almost everything he did in film. His entire oeuvre could be analyzed from this perspective.

Renoir's ideas about love begin their unique unfolding in works like *Nana* and *La Petite Marchande d'allumettes*, and then evolve through all his later adaptations and original screenplays. They reach their culmination in *Le Roi d'Yvetot*. Like *Le Déjeuner sur l'herbe* and many of his other explorations of love and sex, *Le Roi d'Yvetot* takes place in the south of France. The relative heat and the languid pace of life contribute to the erotic atmosphere he wished to celebrate. Renoir's attitude in this short film must be seen in its relation to the earlier fable about the old couple who freeze to death in each other's arms on a Parisian quai. That was a quasi-realistic story about true love that triumphs in its own fashion over modern degradation. As such, it makes a diptych with *La Petite Marchande d'allumettes*, where the girl's dying in the snow, after her fantasy about a knight on horseback who carries her off, is presented as an imagistic version of Liebestod. In its setting in southern France, *Le Roi d'Yvetot* also depicts a victory of love over traditional notions of life and death. But now the tale is comic rather than tragic or melodramatic, and thoroughly luminous in the bright sunshine of Provence. Its plot deals with affirmative adjustments among people in love who are not at all frozen by the hostility of the world but rather capable of living happily ever after in the warm climate of their interpersonal bond.

Le Roi d'Yvetot centers on the experience of an elderly retiree, a former sea captain, who has a robust sense of life and is married to a much younger woman. She has healthy sexual needs that her husband cannot satisfy as he would like. After much soul-searching, and in contrast to her freewheeling maid, who is not married but loosely frolics with a boyfriend of her own age, the wife enters into an affair with a veterinarian who expertly treats her female dog. This *chienne* is a totally different kind of bitch from the one that Renoir portrayed in *La Chienne*, his early drama about love at its worst. Both the wife and her lover care about the feelings of the husband. They greatly regret exposing him to the ridicule of his friends and fellow townspeople. For reasons of honor, he is expected to retaliate, possibly to kill the two who have destroyed his status as dominant male. Instead, in his love for his wife he accepts the realities of their sexual condition and appreciates her legitimate desire to find solace elsewhere. He continues to live his cheerful life close to nature and harmoniously companionate with his neighbors. Eventually he comes to enjoy the enlarged relationship that now includes not only the young woman he loves so much but also the considerate, respectful man whom she loves and who becomes a good friend of his.

In his cameo introduction to *Le Roi d'Yvetot*, Renoir tells us that it is dedicated to an ideal that is much neglected nowadays, the ideal of "tolerance." Renoir does not pause to mention that in the entire history of sexuality in the Western world the pursuit of that ideal was rarely practiced by men. Only women were supposed to tolerate the multiple types of infidelity that their spouses eagerly sought. Renoir repudiates this inherited shibboleth about female sexuality. In opposition to the prevalent view, he recommends social toleration toward women who seek the freedom in sexual matters that men have always arrogated to themselves.

Renoir had originally thought of using the title *C'est la Révolution* for the collection of short stories to which *Le Roi d'Yvetot* belongs. In this segment those words occur when the lover, shocked by the tolerance and magnanimity of the husband, exclaims that their ménage à trois would undermine social conventions. The husband insists that little revolutions of this kind are good for society. This one, reenacted at the end of the 1960s when European and American society was going through a comparable "sexual revolution," continues the thematic mood of *La Marseillaise*. It is through the small but mounting changes in human relations, as Renoir depicts them in his films, that the momentous events of history come into being.

In its formal design this concluding fable about human affect is similar to *Les Caprices de Marianne* except that Musset's

ending, as well as Renoir's use of it in *The Rules of the Game*,
illustrates the failure of love—both marital and extramarital. In
Les Caprices the husband is a tyrannical old magistrate who
hires henchmen to murder his wife's lover. In Renoir's
screenplay for *The Rules*, that important detail is altered. There
is indeed a killing of the rival but not because of any intention
on the husband's part. In Renoir's variation, the likable but
ineffectual husband, the marquis, at first engages in fisticuffs
with the other man but finally manifests the strength of his
own love for the woman by letting her have whatever joy she
can experience through sexual intimacy with his rival. In the
closing shots we see authentic tears in the eyes of the marquis
as he tells his guests about the tragic shooting of their idol,
André the heroic aviator, who had become his friend.

Although *The Rules of the Game* is a masterpiece built out of
the many narrative props that Renoir introduces within his
balancing act, the equivocations they effect do not issue into a
definitive answer to the profound questions that Renoir poses
dramatically. These are questions about the nature and pursuit
of love, about the society in which the characters live at that
troubled moment of French history, about the political
relations between masters and servants, about mankind's
place in nature as a whole, and about the endless vagaries of
erotic feeling. The omission of any facile resolution undoubtedly augmented the public distaste for the movie when it was
first released. Thirty years later, at the terminus of his career
and in a film addressed to a world that was then aspiring to
libertarian ideals more than before, Renoir felt that he could
suggest a domestic arrangement that might harmoniously
settle the urgent sexual issues. In *Le Roi d'Yvetot* nature seems
wholly amenable to the possibility of human consummation,

and here at least the camera displays the landscape at its most beautiful.

In *Le Déjeuner sur l'herbe* Renoir had already glorified the goodness of erotic and romantic fulfillment, but there it occurs only within the parameters of marital and premarital attachment. In that film he considers neither the established condemnation of adultery nor its acceptance under recognizable conditions of love. *Le Roi d'Yvetot* is a pleasant "anecdote," as Renoir calls it, that demonstrates how amatory dalliance can be precious not only in the midst of nature but also in a social order that tolerates and supports interpersonal love of any type through a permissive as well as pluralistic adhesion to the values of natural existence. No one in film, and few artists in other media, has equaled Renoir's consecutive achievement as a bearer of that philosophical banner.

As a pluralist and humanistic philosopher, I revel in the explorations of Renoir. Even at their least successful, his movies have deep meaning for me. But as an American intellectual who is familiar with the sense of alienation, even isolation, that so rare and audacious an artist as Welles experienced in his life, I respond to his vision and to his fate with feelings of protectiveness as well as indignation. For Hitchcock's technical skill I have endless admiration. It's how I feel about the grandeur of modern technology, and about those who produce and comprehend its arcane but godlike achievements. I see no point in grading the three filmmakers as better or worse among themselves.

A Family Portrait

In studying the philosophical dimensions of the three film-makers, I have not hesitated to compare them with one another in various places. I now want to explore some further implications of the differences and similarities among them. By positioning the three artists in a family portrait of this sort, we should be able to resolve some of the issues previously encountered but left in limbo. New lines of inquiry may also arise.

As I have emphasized throughout my reflections about film and other arts, the common distinction between meaning and technique can only have a preliminary, preanalytic, importance. Meaning must always depend on some operative technique; and technique can have its greatest aesthetic value only as the vehicle of meanings that people find relevant to whatever they experience as their reality. Accomplished artists are able to master the potentially infinite outcome of this interaction. Indeed, all three of the filmmakers I have been discussing were supremely preoccupied with both the thematic meaningfulness of their work and the technical maneuvers that were instrumental in the expression of such meaning. Though Hitchcock considered himself a maker of pure cinema, he was entirely aware that his artificial effects had to further a pictorial representation that the audience would accept as more or less true to life. And though Welles and Renoir wished to communicate social and political ideas through their films, they did so by means of cinematic contrivances they adapted to their artistic needs with great inventiveness.

❀

At one point in his interviews with Truffaut, Hitchcock remarks that he is "not concerned with plausibility" and that "if you're going to analyze everything in terms of plausibility or credibility, then no fiction script can stand up to that approach, and you wind up doing a documentary."[1] In a parallel vein, Hitchcock honestly shows his hand when he says that *Spellbound* is "just another manhunt story wrapped up in pseudo-psychoanalysis."[2] But he also states, more than once, that his talent in concocting effects for which he is renowned is based on an ongoing conversation that he establishes with the audience. It is not identical to the contact with the public that Renoir sought in each movie. That occurs through the ideas that he exhibits and communicates as someone who mutually observes, albeit as a director, what the actors and the mise en scène are displaying to the camera. For Hitchcock the interpersonal exchange consists of audience reactions that he anticipates and then defeats or otherwise orients toward narrative ends he is pursuing at every moment.

Talking about the filming of *The Birds*, for instance, Hitchcock glories in his calculated ability to outsmart the audience. People come to the theater, he says, thinking they know what to expect. "So, I have to take up the challenge: 'Oh, you know what's going to happen. Well, we'll just see about that!'"[3] In order to develop the romantic elements of the plot, he delays the scenes in which the flocks of birds are clustering. But since the title is unmistakable and the prior advertising has awakened expectations, he carefully introduces occasional birds in the earlier sequences. "Those references at the end of each scene were my way of saying, 'Just be patient. They're coming soon.' "[4] From within this implicit conversation that he has originated, Hitchcock deploys his highly acute imagination to envisage what each shot will mean to a likely audience that he can reach through his well-constructed plots.

When Truffaut mentions that, beginning with *The Lodger*, almost all of Hitchcock's movies are about a man who is accused of a crime he did not commit, Hitchcock replies: "That's because the theme of the innocent man being accused, I feel, provides the audience with a greater sense of danger. It's easier for them to identify with him than with a guilty man on the run. I always take the audience into account."[5]

One might reply that Welles and Renoir also took their audiences into account. But the relationship is nevertheless different for them. With Renoir one always feels that he is one of us or, in his effort to make contact, would like to be. Particularly when he plays a role himself   as in *The Rules of the Game* or *La Bête humaine* or *A Day in the Country*—he gives the impression that he is not a person who asserts any creative eminence or managerial power. Whether or not he appeared on screen, he disclaimed any authoritative position in the fictional world whose reality he was fabricating. Outsmarting the audience, for whatever reason, was not his intention.

Nor was it Welles's. Except when he serves as the voiceover narrator whose sonorous intonation is recognizable as uniquely his, one rarely feels that Welles seeks a conversation in the manner of either Hitchcock or Renoir. In more than one

place, Welles says that he does not make his films with any
spectators in mind. He argues that movie audiences are so
diverse in age, in native language, in geographical location,
and in taste that a filmmaker can only rely on what seems right
to him or her. In this variation on the concept of art for art's
sake, Welles maintains that he makes movies only for himself,
not merely as a performer who takes the major roles on most
occasions but also as a cinematic creator who pursues aesthetic
principles whether or not they matter to anyone else.
Compared to Welles, Hitchcock would seem to have been a
company man. Welles refused, or was unable, to emulate him.
The sense of reality that shows forth in Welles's best work can
be seen as an expression of that condition, as well as his
attempt to cope with it.

As a director, Welles used cinematography that is so clever
and so artfully conceived as to dazzle us with its visual
innovations. Being a leading actor cast in the role of one or
another kinglike figure, he stupefies us with a show of strength
or weakness in that character, or, more often, a combination of
the two. Even in *The Lady from Shanghai*, where he narrates as
well as plays the role of an ordinary fellow who is duped in
love but ultimately survives, he stands apart in the climactic
mirror sequence as a detached individual whose own drama
may never be accessible to others. Where Renoir celebrates
both communal oneness and personal freedom for people who
wish to live in nature more directly, Welles vacillates between
those alternatives as only an alienated intellectual would. In all
his filmic capacities, the Welles who parades before us remains
an extraordinary artist whose virtuosity alone erects barriers
that make us wonder whether conversation with personae
such as his is even possible.

Perhaps in recognition of this fact, Welles appears as himself in his essayistic films *F for Fake* and *Don Quijote*. In both of them he looks as he might have looked in everyday life, though still occasionally relying on makeup to some extent. In any event, we always see him as Orson Welles playing Orson Welles the famous director, actor, magician, and the rest. In *Don Quijote* he is even shown receiving an official honor bestowed on him in Spain by a local dignitary. In *F for Fake* he illustrates the nature of fakery by reproducing his youthful coup on radio with the *The War of the Worlds*. His narration throughout *F for Fake* conveys a sense of informality, and yet it too seems to issue from an aesthetic realm of being as distant and impalpable as the photographic images on the screen. One cannot fail to notice the difference between Welles's self-presentation and the casual manner that Renoir projects in his movie roles and in his introductions to the segments of *Le Petit Théâtre de Jean Renoir*.

In Henry Jaglom's film *Someone to Love*, where Welles fluently talks about the world from his perspective, he does come through as an honest and seasoned warrior in the arts with whom one could very well converse. But he was speaking then as a guest in Jaglom's movie, not his own. From this cameo appearance, and from his interviews, we can see how great a raconteur and lover of good conversation he was in life. His films are not like that.

❀

As a further indication of differences among these cineastes, it is worth comparing—more thoroughly than I have thus far—their attitudes toward improvisation. As we've seen, Renoir made it central to his method, while Hitchcock considered it unnecessary, usually unwise, and to be avoided as a matter of

principle. Having worked diligently on the written prepara-
tions and the storyboard, Hitchcock claimed that he never had
to look at the script during the actual shooting. But he also tells
us that the making of *The Birds* was an exception in this regard.

In a long and splendid analysis, Hitchcock depicts the
many changes he created on the set of that film. They show his
fertility of mind as well as his remarkable insight into the way
that technical nuances—the slightly altered size of the image,
for instance—affect an audience's "emotion," as he calls it.[6] In
his account of these successful experiments, however,
Hitchcock does not indicate, or even suggest, an interest in any
deeper significance that may pertain to his improvisations. For
him they just afforded a rare opportunity to do at the time of
filming what he ordinarily did beforehand. For Renoir and
Welles, improvisation meant much more than that.

For these two, the use of improvisation provided a spontaneity and unforeseeability that would itself express the
nature of whatever reality they chose to represent. Unless we
keep this in mind, it becomes hard to appreciate adequately the
nature of Renoir's achievement throughout his career. For
instance, consider *Boudu sauvé des eaux*, released in 1932. Bazin,
who greatly admired Renoir's talent, calls attention to its
"carefully contrived dramatic disharmonies" and its ironic
"incongruity."[7] Without denying the validity of Bazin's
analysis, I think one might also study this film from a slightly
different angle. If one compares its craftsmanship with that of
contemporary movies being made by René Clair—*À Nous La
Liberté*, *Le Million*, and others—*Boudu* could seem oddly inept
and lacking in finesse. Near the beginning we observe the
scruffy hobo as he shuffles across the Pont des Arts, a bridge in
Paris. He has lost his dog in the Bois de Boulogne and has been

searching fruitlessly for him. Suddenly he puts his leg over a railing; there is an abrupt cut; then we see him thrashing about in the River Seine. Has he jumped because of suicidal despair? Has he fallen in by accident? And what exactly is he doing when he is in the water?

As this sequence progresses, a crowd of spectators gathers on the bridge. Presumably they are watching a possible drowning. But some of them don't look over the railing, and some are chatting idly or peering at the camera or fooling with each other as if nothing special is happening. Obviously they have not been minutely instructed about how they should act as extras in this movie. Something similar recurs throughout the film, for instance at the end, when Boudu accidentally over-turns a boat on a river in the countryside after his marriage. Everyone else scrambles to the shore, but he stays in the water. The shots of his bride and her entourage, interspersed with glimpses of him floating with the stream, appear gauche and impromptu. We can be sure that Clair's cinematography would have been more elegant. How then can we justify Renoir's improvisational methodology in these and other scenes?

His procedure makes sense once we treat it as a manifes-tation of his belief that life itself is chaotic and even "absurd," in the meaning that existentialist philosophers were already giving that term in the 1930s. If all human reality, and every-thing that we can know, is improvised rather than derived from some prior pattern, why can't the camera make its own state-ment to that effect by the way it films whatever event it wishes to address? The fuzzy images and casual views that cinéma vérité and la nouvelle vague would later cultivate had their origin in conscious efforts along these lines that Renoir made throughout his oeuvre. He in turn may have been inspired by predecessors such as Vertov in *Man with a Movie Camera*, though that kaleidoscopic documentary is much more stylized in its editing than *Boudu* and the other Renoir movies.

On the other hand, Renoir's method avoids the non-committal implications of either purely realistic cinéma vérité or the often random camera in the nouvelle vague. As if in preparation for the peasant whose playing of the panpipe creates sexual desire in *Le Déjeuner sur l'herbe*, a Parisian neighbor in *Boudu*, an incredible flutist who has no other role in the movie, performs a solo recital whenever the characters engage in the rites of lovemaking. Through this "poetic" motif, Renoir reminds us that in their imperious intervention our libidinal instincts regularly, though unforeseeably, shatter all our conventional notions about rectitude or rationality. His direction and his camerawork seek to vindicate this view. They never aspire to pure verisimilitude, nor submissively limit themselves to whatever images their shutter closes on adventitiously. They are means of communicating Renoir's conviction that human nature does not conform to traditional expectations about its affective being.

In *Citizen Kane*, Welles approximates the absurdist dimension in Renoir by the frequent cutting that was required by this film's large number of flashbacks. They do not provide a uniform or orderly image of a person's existence in its linear progression from birth to death. Welles believed that our reality precludes any such interpretation. Similarly, the striking low-angle shots that he and Gregg Toland so often used are meaningful not only in showing something we might encounter in ordinary existence—the oppressiveness of Kane or the unsteadiness of Leland when he is tipsy or just the presence of ceilings that we hardly notice in everyday life—but also in intimating that the common head-on mode of perception to which we are accustomed brings us no closer to ultimate reality than this expressionistic, and even weird, way of seeing things.

Moreover, as Welles points out in *Filming "Othello,"* and in many interviews, that Shakespearean movie was stitched together with improvised filming that often resorted to a stand-in's back for scenes in which the face of the original actor could not be photographed because he was no longer on the set. When costumes for the enactment of Rodrigo's murder failed to arrive, Welles placed the sequence in a turkish bath and clothed the men in bath towels. Finding at the last minute that some of the voices in *The Trial* would sound better if he dubbed them with his own imitation, Welles did that with seven of the characters.

For Welles, as for Renoir, improvisation of this sort was more than just expedient surmounting of the normal crises that occur in moviemaking. Far from consisting of merely technical arrangements, it was also a revelation of how the world appeared to each of them. The same might be said about Hitchcock, and yet the significance for him was not identical. In one place Hitchcock says: "I practice absurdity quite religiously!" He is responding to Truffaut's idea that in *North by Northwest* it is absurd to have the crop duster dust fields where there are no crops. Truffaut concludes that "the fantasy of the absurd is a key ingredient" in Hitchcock's filmmaking, but so deliberate in its "planned incongruity" that it works for him.[8] This is true, and Hitchcock's reply about his "religious" adherence is wholly appropriate. Even so, one has to realize that his incongruities are *planned*, conceived in advance by him and then preserved as architectural blueprints that everyone must follow on the set.

That alone defeats the more radical principle of improvisation as productive anarchy, which is basic in the methodology of Welles and Renoir because they thought the world itself is like that. This absurdist belief did not preclude Renoir's continual affirmations of nature or Welles's meticulous and sometimes mannerist concern about choreographic movement throughout a scene, minutely calculated lighting, and precision in estimating the aperture of the lens at all times. On the contrary, it provided a framework for their inventiveness.

In his discussions with Hitchcock, Truffaut mentions that while the master always identifies with characters in his films who are innocent victims they are less interesting persons than those who are not innocent.[9] I think this is correct, and I consider it congruent with my claim that Hitchcock mainly views his protagonists as living magnets that are designed to draw our attention from one episode to the next. We identify with these characters because we all feel that, regardless of what others may assume, we ourselves are fundamentally innocent and not infrequently unjustifiable casualties in life. Schopenhauer believed that merely in being alive each of us is a victim of the metaphysical force he called the will to live.

Hitchcock might very well agree. His innocent victims, ordinary people who sometimes end up doing heroic acts, rarely behave as they do because of abstract thought or sensory need or even passional impulse. They flee from imminent danger or engage in a secretive and solitary mission that pits them against something that is determined to destroy them. The drama concludes when they succeed, for then nothing perilous remains to prolong suspense.

Do we really care about the happy married life that the threatened couples will now presumably enter into? Not at all. We were fascinated by them only because they were surrogates of ourselves as imperfect human beings, and of all other persons who also have so much to fear in mere existence, which seems forever poised to victimize every finite creature. To some degree we even identify with Hitchcock's beguiling villains. They manifest the selfish, even ruthless assertiveness that we too might like to have. Simply in being what they are, they pose the question of how much anyone can get away with in life by acting immorally as they do. In this context, Hitchcock asserts that the audience always sides with the criminals when the police are closing in.

In several places Hitchcock tells us that he tries to give his villains a pleasant, often suave and seductive, appearance as opposed to his innocent protagonists, who run the risk of being too bland or unconvincing (as in *Frenzy*). This attitude toward good and evil comports with his blending of comedy with melodrama, and it also explains his proclaimed concern to keep his thrillers from degenerating into horror films.

That Truffaut should be the one who states the idea that Hitchcock identifies with his innocent victims is itself revelatory, since Truffaut's own movies frequently sought to transcend the traditional distinction between good and evil which Hitchcock normally presupposes. In his films Truffaut portrays instead a social and human condition in which no one is really to blame for the network of harm that occurs. In that regard, as well as others, Truffaut can be seen as responding to the differences between Hitchcock and Renoir. When Welles remarks that he always tries to elicit our sympathy for the heavies, however guilty they may be, he too

speaks as someone whose moral perspective is different from
Hitchcock's.

Truffaut having been a devotee of all three of these
filmmakers, it is worth noting that his movies often register a
level of compassion for hapless victims that is much more
pronounced than in theirs, even Renoir's. *The 400 Blows, Small
Change,* and *The Wild Child* are directed toward the plight of
youngsters who were badly brought up, as Truffaut had been
himself. In *The 400 Blows* all the adults are unable to understand the feeling and behavior of the children with whom they
live, while we perceive from the fashion in which this film has
been made that the filmmaker himself is the very opposite. In
Small Change Truffaut celebrates the gratuitous diversity of
children and uses the camera to show how interesting they can
be in relation to someone like himself who is willing to
disregard their frequent nastiness. In *The Wild Child* the tutor
succeeds in civilizing the twelve-year-old savage by means of
the compassion that he bestows upon him. Apart from the
housekeeper, the tutor, played by Truffaut, is the only one who
really cares about the boy.

In one place Truffaut tells Hitchcock he feels that *Rear
Window*, which he considers "probably your very best screenplay in all respects," has "a rather compassionate approach."
He amplifies this by saying that what James Stewart sees,
looking out his window, "is not horrible but simply a display
of human weaknesses and people in pursuit of happiness."
Hitchcock replies: "Definitely."[10] Be this as it may, one can argue
that compassion involves much more as well. Welles resembles
Truffaut, and differs from Hitchcock, in wanting to present his
principal characters—whether or not they are criminal—as
people who are burdened by the hardships of reality just as

their victims are. But in a manner that is foreign to Truffaut, Welles has ambivalent ideas about his protagonists, as I mentioned earlier. While admiring them as grandiose individuals, though morally flawed or out of touch with current society, as Falstaff and George Amberson are, he firmly rejects whatever political or personal philosophy they invoke to justify their egregious way of life.

One might call this a Shakespearean strand in everything Welles did. Shakespeare evinces the same ambivalence, and in fact more overtly. Welles's ethical posture is so highly modulated that it registers in the audience as a pervasive ambiguity. Is Kane a scheming liar out to delude the populace, as Welles tells Bogdanovich some forty years later? Despite his selfishness and petty crimes, is Falstaff one of the truly good men in Western literature, as Welles asserts in the discussion with Bogdanovich I have quoted? Is K as "guilty as hell," or is he the victim of a legal system that is itself unjust? Is Quinlan a tragic figure, a lousy cop but some kind of man, as Tania says, or is he simply a hideous monster?

Bazin recognizes the importance of ambiguity and paradox in all of Welles's movies, and he depicts how artfully they are conveyed in the mise en scène. In the case of *Citizen Kane*, for instance, Bazin argues that "the stretching of the image in depth, combined with the nearly constant use of low angles, produces throughout the film an impression of tension and conflict . . . the gaze upward seems to come out of the earth, while the ceilings, forbidding any escape within the décor, complete the fatality of this curse. Kane's lust for power crushes us, but is itself crushed by the décor. Through the camera, we are capable in a way of perceiving Kane's failure at the same time we experience his power."[11]

Searching for information about the failure and the power of Welles himself, I recently benefited from a firsthand account of the stage production of *King Lear* that marked his return to the United States in 1956. My informant, the acclaimed actor Alvin Epstein, who played alongside Welles in an important role on that occasion, emphasized how complicated it was to work with him. Though Welles wished to be in charge of every-thing—acting the leading part, directing, heavily collaborating with the stage and lighting designers, and so forth—his boundless energy resulted in one calamity after another. After carefully devising the set but not sufficiently rehearsing its intricacies, he sprained an ankle during one of the previews and then at the end of the performance on opening night he tripped and broke the other one. All this left the cast confused and disoriented. His co-performer concluded, in words that I took to be relevant to Welles as a human being as well as the artist he remained throughout his life: "He was just too self-destructive!"

Without presuming to analyze or evaluate at length that opinion, I think it might provide an insight into the Welles phenomenon. The price one pays for the ambiguous perspec-tive on life is a lack of security, recurrent doubt about one's mettle and the goodness of what one has achieved. Having experienced a meteoric rise in his early twenties, Welles could hardly have known how to deal with such great success in a world that is eager to punish anyone who has had it. "I began at the top, and I've been working my way down since then," Welles confesses in *F for Fake*. Two years before he died, he tells an interviewer that he thinks he "made essentially a mistake in staying in movies" and that his life as a moviemaker consisted in 98 percent hustling for money and only about 2 percent in actually making films.[12]

Though Welles rightly scorned naive psychoanalytical inferences about the permanent effect of his having lost his mother when he was nine years old, the fact remains that she was a music teacher who had guided his musical development, to which he never returned after she died, despite his innate talent. That alone bespeaks a self-destructiveness that can begin in childhood as a result of painful feelings of guilt at the time. The ambiguities in Welles's later life and work may all be tied to this condition, without being reducible to it alone. He himself recognized the lasting influence of his free-living but unstable father, who died when Welles was still in adolescence. The source of Welles's ability to transform his personal problems into an aesthetic resource may be hopelessly obscure, at least very difficult to unearth, but it is surely correlative to his perception of the ambiguities of human experience.

For Renoir, the ambiguous view of life—his own and everyone else's—could not have had the same dependence on guilt feelings or a self-destructive fear of success. Though as a young man he thought himself inferior to his father, the lifelong affection between them remained intact throughout the years. From Renoir's book about his father and himself, one also gleans that his mother was a good-natured peasant type. She was often painted and sculpted as such by his father, and Renoir used his memory of her in the carefree rural scenes of *Le Déjeuner sur l'herbe*. We have no reason to think that Welles's mother, or Hitchcock's, was as warm-hearted and supportive as Renoir's. Where Hitchcock identifies with some individual who fears quasi-parental authorities and is pursued by them because they are sure he is guilty, or else by evil people who want to harm him, and sometimes both, and where Welles sympathetically represents murderers and the like while also morally deconstructing them, repudiating the very turpitude that he represents with gusto, Renoir progressively and persistently searches for tolerance and a humanistic love that neither of the other two elaborate to any comparable extent.

Hitchcock had a long and productive marriage to the same woman, and no extensive dalliances with others. But he rarely draws upon this benign marital experience in his films—except for minor vignettes or slight humorous touches as in *Family Plot* or *Frenzy* (the detective and his loopy wife) or, as I mention in this chapter, *The 39 Steps*. Though the growth of married love did serve as a linking thread within *Rich and Strange* (1932), on which his wife Alma was the principal scenarist, that motif was submerged in the tepid romantic adventures that also predominate. Nor is it ever fully realized in the later productions that are characteristically Hitchcockean.

In the early work of Welles there are no happy marriages, or even instances of happy love. In his last wholly finished film, *F for Fake*, his adoration for gorgeous Oja Kodar shows forth from beginning to end. This final and perhaps "essential" love—to appropriate the phrase that Sartre and Simone de Beauvoir used to describe their relationship—may be seen as a subtext in that movie, but it is represented only obliquely there, and it does not exist in any other film that Welles made. In the output of both Hitchcock and Welles there are numerous love affairs, sometimes even love that is an endless pursuit (as in *Vertigo*). Yet love as a transcendent value, a human good that need not be damaging but can possibly give meaning to life, does not serve for them as a primary theme, which it often was for Renoir.

Since he was so proficient an actor, Welles could widen his perspective through individual performances that show love as more than just the sensuous or the passionate. I am thinking, for instance, of the loving-kindness that suffuses his delivery of Father Mapple's sermon in *Moby Dick*, and also of his pathetically gentle and introspective reading of Othello's agony at times when the verbal evidence of it could be, and generally is, screamed or shouted operatically. I discussed this compassionate aspect of Welles's mentality in my chapter on him, but here I want to reemphasize the importance it has in his work as a whole. I find its consummate expression in *The Magnificent Ambersons*, when George visits his mother's empty room near the end of the movie, after she has died and their mansion has been sold to pay off the family debts. He falls on his knees next to what had been her bed and begs her spirit, and then God, to forgive him. The scene is a condensation of what occurs in Tarkington but does not exist in the television remake. Welles himself wrote the voiceover at the scene's closing moments. Talking as the narrator, he speaks the following lines with great feeling: "Something had happened, a thing which years ago had been the eagerest hope of many, many good citizens of the town. And now it came at last. George Amberson Minafer had got his comeuppance. He got it three times filled, and running over. But those who had so longed for it were not there to see it, and they never knew it. Those who were still living had forgotten all about it, and all about him."

This compassionate comment effects a glorious peak in the history of cinema. Renoir must have approved wholeheartedly, though he wished to go further and to consider, more thoroughly than Welles does, what the nature and varieties of love or fellow feeling might be. Renoir's pluralistic approach precludes any unitary solutions, but his continuous probing

into human affect enlivens everything he did. In his introduction to Bazin's book on Renoir, Truffaut says that Renoir's
work "has always been guided by a philosophy of life which
expresses itself with the aid of something much like a trade
secret: *sympathy*."[13] I take that as a fitting tribute to what
Truffaut learned from Renoir and carried further. But, as I have
suggested in the previous chapter, there is in Renoir's
philosophy of life much more than this reference to sympathy
alone might indicate.

❀

In an essay on *North by Northwest*, Stanley Cavell states that it
is "the only one of Hitchcock's romantic thrillers in which the
adventurous pair are actually shown to have married." Since a
pair (but are they "adventurous"?) are shown to have married
in *Suspicion*, for example, I assume that Cavell is referring to
previous marriages. He claims that *North by Northwest* both
"derives from the genre of remarriage" and is about "the
legitimizing of marriage."[14] It is true that Thornhill, the Cary
Grant character, has been married twice before he marries Eve
Kendall (Eva Marie Saint) at the end of the movie. For her,
however, this is a first marriage, despite what we take to be her
multiple affairs, including her longstanding relationship as the
bad guy's girlfriend. But even that cannot justify calling her
subsequent bonding to Thornhill either a remarriage or a
legitimizing of marriage.

For one thing, no marital experience enters into *North by
Northwest*. When he and Eve are exchanging facts about themselves once they realize they have become a romantic couple,
Thornhill says ironically that his previous wives divorced him
because the life he led was so dull. That, however, is all he says

about those marriages. Nor do we learn anything about the new one to Eve that will come later on. We only see him lift her into his upper bunk on the train after addressing her as "Mrs. Thornhill." The train then goes through its tunnel—"the phallic symbol," as Hitchcock spoke of it—and the curtain comes down, terminating our prying as well as the movie itself.[15]

Though *North by Northwest* is not about the legitimizing of marriage, one could say, however, that both it and *The 39 Steps* are about the legitimization of their protagonists *with respect to the ideals of marriage*. In the latter film the hero creates a real woman out of a puristic and even alabaster spinster—in variation of the Pygmalion theme—while in the former he makes an honest person of her since she has already descended into the realm of both sexual and criminal experience.

Thornhill acts because of love, sex on the train having proved that Eve is the right woman for him. Hannay engages in a quest for sheer manliness, as in Buchan's novel. He goes to Scotland to find the murderer of the flighty Annabella Smith; in the course of that, he encounters the beautiful but emotionally unawakened female who is sitting by herself in the train. When he kisses her in the hope of deceiving the police who are looking for him, her glasses fall off her face. They are a token of her marmoreal condition and never recur in this film about her newfound womanhood. By bringing his life to her, Hannay brings out the life in her. While she is being kissed, however, her struggling right eye reveals her virginal fear.[16]

These idealizational motives, different as they are in the two movies, intertwine with the man's attempt to escape wrongful arrest in each case. Having participated in the plot against Thornhill, Eve appears at first to be devoid of the rectitude that we normally deem prerequisite for marital oneness.

She is finally revealed to be on the side of the angels, not only as a dedicated Mata Hari but also as a woman able to feel love for the elected man who truly reciprocates it.

Within the Romantic ideology that permeates this film, like so many others in the first century of cinema, handsome features and sexual allure are not enough to redeem a woman like Eve. As with the Barbara Stanwyck character in Preston Sturges's comedy *The Lady Eve*, the cleansing of her soiled and shady past requires more than that. Both Eves must find a way to surmount the sinfulness of the primordial female in the Bible whose name they bear.[17] It is their latent capacity for love that makes the difference, above all when it is love that eventuates in marriage. Something of this sort, but diversely adapted to the overall narrative of each film, is true of the leading ladies in *Notorious*, *Marnie*, *Vertigo*, and *The Birds*, among other Hitchcock thrillers. In each of these films the male protagonist has to justify his dominant role by somehow enabling the choice but impure or incomplete female to find her proper legitimization. In *Vertigo* the effort does not succeed.

If that movie "remains, unchallengeably, Hitchcock's masterpiece," as Robin Wood suggests, perhaps this is partly because Hitchcock defies in it the erotic conclusion he routinely accepted.[18] In *Psycho* the pattern was also defeated, but there the flawed woman is murdered before she can rejoin her legitimizing boyfriend. In *Frenzy* the former husband of the murdered woman who had divorced him is not entirely acceptable as a mate. In *Notorious*, however, the Romantic principle shows forth in all its magnificence.

Notorious is about a fallen woman who craves redemption through an authentic love that leads to conventional marriage. The Cary Grant protagonist is prevented from accomplishing that feat by his professional commitment as a government agent who must follow another path. He finally overcomes all obstacles when his unreliable love for Ingrid Bergman coalesces with his duty to save her from the Nazi bad guys who are poisoning her. Once the nasties have been defeated and the man assures the woman of his love in a definitive statement he has withheld until then, her culminating trip to the hospital signifies that she will be purged not only of the murderous fluids but also of the sexual past that has been poisoning her access to desirable marriage.

One can see *Notorious* as well as *North by Northwest* and *Marnie* as roseate revisions of the theme in *La Dame aux camélias*, the play by Alexandre Dumas *fils* that became Verdi's libretto for *La Traviata* (*The Wayward One* in the English translation, not often used). In that story Violetta transcends the social waywardness of her earlier life through her experience of romantic love but then dies before she can attain matrimonial reparation. In *Vertigo* her counterpart is literally a fallen woman who plunges to her death after being pulled by the man she loves to the heights of a church that might have sanctified their intimacy through an appropriate marriage. In bypassing such versions of the myth, *Notorious* serves as a benign alteration of the legend of Tristan and Iseult. Like Tristan, Cary Grant's character is a go-between who maneuvers Ingrid Bergman into a marriage with an older man she does not love. Like Tristan, Grant behaves this way for reasons of state rather than love. When Grant liberates Bergman from the misalliance, they do not die tragically as the medieval man and woman do but go on to a remarriage that rewards her for having bravely smoldered her amatory sentiments in conformity with the mission he has lured her into.

In *North by Northwest*, Eve's name gives us a further clue to her mythological status. Like her biblical predecessor, who exists as an extension of Adam's rib, this one is a projection of the masculine fantasy about a freely accessible and fully compliant recipient of his sexuality. In the last quarter of the nineteenth century, "the new woman" was a person of that gender who had emancipated herself from conventional restraints on nonsexual as well as sexual conduct. In the late 1950s when the movie was made, the Eve that Eva Marie Saint portrays is emancipated in both respects. But she cannot get a complete legitimization by herself. She requires the sustenance of a man who will function as her suitable partner.

North by Northwest shows how Thornhill, who also is in need of legitimization, rises to the occasion by ascending Mount Rushmore. As a twice divorced and hard-drinking inhabitant of Madison Avenue, he formerly had little to recommend him aside from his good looks and humorous lack of false vanity. That's the point in the exchange on the train about "R O T." Those letters are his initials, printed on the matchbook he hands to Eve. When she wonders what they stand for, he forcefully replies with the word *rot* as a mock confession that he himself is rotten, or a rotter. When she persists by asking about the meaning of the middle initial, since she knows what his name is, though he is unaware that she does know, he says: "Nothing." In other words, the O signifying zero, he claims to lack all of the qualities that make a life valuable and worthy of redemption.

The rest of the plot consists in their achieving double legitimization—hers by fulfilling the assignment she has undertaken and by entering into marriage with the right man; his by proving that not only is he not nothing but instead a hero who saves the endangered female, helping her moreover to succeed in her meritorious endeavor. The MacGuffin in *North by Northwest* is the microfilm with its ultrasecret message, and the ordinary man, now having enlisted as a patriot like the woman he loves, retrieves that important artifact and thereby thwarts the country's enemies. In the process he has turned into a different man while also changing Eve into a different and more reputable woman. This creative deed outdoes the original Pygmalion since Hitchcock's hero gives himself a new existence as well as giving one to the object of his erotic imagination.

Hitchcock called *North by Northwest* his American remake of *The 39 Steps*. Some of the elements exploited in each are indeed very much alike: the innocent citizen who is victimized by being erroneously accused of murder, his being chased by the criminals as well as by the police, his courageously performing feats of strength and cunning that enable him to acquire a desirable consort as a byproduct of his valiant action. Beyond these resemblances, however, and the fact that both films are thrillers with ample ingredients of comedy and romance, they belong to alternate versions of the Pygmalion myth. Since Pamela, the female lead in *The 39 Steps*, is not at first a liberated person, she does not have to be legitimized in the way that Eve Kendall does. Like her equivalent in *Suspicion*, Pamela (played by Madeleine Carroll) must only develop an ability to shed her pupillary stage and enter into consummational maturity. She gains legitimacy not by being rehabilitated, as in *North by Northwest* and its sibling films, but rather through her immersion into the realities of her sexual potential.

In *Suspicion* (and also *Rebecca*, where the unnamed bride faces a comparable ordeal), inexperience changes into enlightened consciousness as the outcome of matrimony. In *The 39 Steps* the requisite transmutation occurs in the courtship period that precedes marriage. The woman starts out as a schoolmarm type reading a book on the train—not making love in it like Eve in *North by Northwest*—but after she has been dragged through the anguish of her great adventure, she emerges as a helpmate in her man's heroic effort.

The male protagonist in *The 39 Steps* is correspondingly unlike the Cary Grant of *North by Northwest*. As conceived in Hitchcock's rendition of the Buchan novel, and as played by Robert Donat, Hannay is a hunter of big game who just naturally rushes off to capture those elusive culprits in Scotland who have caused the murder for which he has been accused. Far from being, or thinking of himself as, a rotter or nothing at all, he is a person whose virility we all regard with admiration. In the music hall sequence at the beginning, when he is identified as a Canadian, the audience applauds approvingly, as if his nationality alone (or is it his presence in England?) provides assurance of his sterling character. While stripping away the phony veneer of Buchan's imperialist tale and replacing it with a humorous romance that puts the story in a totally different category, Hitchcock hewed to the basic idealization of the underlying fantasy.

Since Madeleine Carroll typified the apparently cool and distanced woman that Hitchcock had such strongly ambivalent feelings about—adulating the depth of passion that he thinks she has, while simultaneously wanting to vitalize this creature by knocking her off her pedestal—it is not surprising that the Pamela she enacts does not exist in Buchan. She nevetheless fits in perfectly with the affective mythology that propels that book. Being a glorification of the male, Buchan's tale views men as enterprising animals who fight one another for supremacy and then marry some female they have collaterally subdued into passivity. At first, the Hannay in Hitchcock's film exhibits this kind of attitude toward the women—initially Annabella and then Pamela—that circumstances have thrust upon him. But through his premarital exploits with the second one, he too develops as a human being. That is evident in the montage with which Hitchcock ends the movie.

In the closing sequence the camera stands behind Hannay and Pamela, showing their backs in a way that returns to the opening shot of Hannay buying a ticket at the box office except that now he is accompanied by her. At the beginning, and until he took his seat in the theater, we saw Hannay only from the back and wearing a hat that obscures his face. Together with the low-angle shots, the dark lighting, and the strident chords of ominous music, the cinematic effect is reminiscent of the German films in which Hitchcock had first learned his trade. It made Hannay appear like a man of mystery, thereby telling us that the movie we are going to watch is probably a thriller. As soon as Hannay sits down, however, the film noir atmosphere transitions quickly into the gaiety of the music hall with its bright lights and vaudeville acts. By blending in this manner our expectations of both melodrama and comedy, Hitchcock creates suspense about the particular type of thriller this movie is, while also assuring us that it will not be too heavy-handed.

Having fulfilled his promise, Hitchcock at the end puts us behind the two protagonists as they listen to Mr. Memory recite the formula that has indirectly engendered the comedy as well as the thrills that have been delighting us. It is the formula Mr. Memory was to take out of England. With the hand that has remained handcuffed throughout the latter half of the film,

Hannay reaches around and grasps the hand of the woman who has been through it all with him. We take that as a sign that they will now become full-fledged lovers and go on to marry each other as lovers are supposed to do.

Focusing on the dangling handcuffs, Cavell interprets the shot as "suggesting that marriage is a kind of voluntary handcuffing (a portable vèrsion of the ball and chain)."[19] There may be some truth in this, the filmmaker concluding with a skeptical commentary on the long history of fictional romance that normally leads up to the moment of exhilaration when courtship ends prior to the awesome difficulties in marriage that are likely to ensue. Hitchcock's films do occasionally evince some such wry and even sardonic view about the married state. But in this movie, with its sympathetic inclusion of the doting innkeeper's wife and her sweetly tractable husband, the two of whom connive to shelter what they take to be a runaway couple madly in love with each other, everything has led us to expect the connubial outcome of the usual romantic comedy. Just before they got to the inn, as they were walking together at the edge of the moor, Hannay and Pamela were already bickering with each other in the cozy manner of happily married people.

For that reason alone, we cheapen the plenitude that has preceded the last image in *The 39 Steps* if we treat it only as Cavell recommended. Holding hands has always symbolized the joining of hearts and minds and bodies of persons who profess love for each other. Hannay makes this gesture as a resolute male who must convince the hesitant female to cooperate. The handcuffs that were forced upon him were also forced upon her by their mutual adversaries. The two of them having now escaped, he offers his unifying embrace in remembrance of what they have endured together. Beyond any suggestion of marriage as a ball and chain, which may itself be interpreted as just an acceptance of spousal responsibilities, the ending resolves the wholly Romantic quest that has filled every frame in this engaging movie.

Indeed what other choices can there be for the kind of Pygmalion and Galatea that the principals are in *The 39 Steps*? After being tested in the fire of their mythic trial, and having survived its hardships because and in spite of each other, they are ready to undertake the marital condition of most men and women in their society. In the play by George Bernard Shaw, Eliza Doolittle—Galatea as a flower girl—is deflowered in her relation to Pygmalion, but then surmounts that by opening a flower shop as she had dreamt of doing before he succeeded so well in making a lady of her. In the movie version of *Pygmalion* and in *My Fair Lady*, this denouement is deleted and the maturated woman returns to her male creator as a cooperative handmaid. That is the option that Hitchcock presupposes in *The 39 Steps*, and, more convincingly than either of those versions of *Pygmalion*, he presents Hannay as equally amenable to the matrimonial bond. As it is impossible for Hitchcock's Galatea to climb back upon her pedestal, so too is his Pygmalion incapable of reverting to bachelorhood now that he has moved beyond it with the assistance of this woman he has been so matey with. They both have no desire to do anything but share whatever burdens lurk within the binding handcuffs.

In this conclusion of *The 39 Steps*, the genres of romance and comedic thriller are fully resolved by the death scene of Mr. Memory. He is a professional who has dedicated his brain to the British Museum. He has lived up to his high calling by answering all "serious" questions put to him, even when they revealed his involvement in a treasonous conspiracy and even though he knew that he might be killed by the leader of the gang who has come to fetch him. The mystery that centers on Mr. Memory, embedded in the tune that Hannay keeps whistling without him or the audience realizing its significance, is transformed into something like Arkadin's anecdote about the frog and the scorpion. Dying as he does, Mr. Memory remains true to his character.

That itself consists in his being a performing artist whose talent arises from the kind of memory that he has, and that cameras also have—what we term a "photographic" memory, though we could just as well call it cinematic. As Hitchcock uses landmarks and famous monuments to fixate his audience's attention to what is happening in a scene, so too does he deploy in this finale an extended and triumphant display of Mr. Memory's artistic prowess. Mr. Memory's recital of the formula is comparable to Violetta's rebirth of energy just before she drops dead in the last moment of *La Traviata*. In his case, the concluding scena occurs in the wings of the Palladium, and throughout his grandly operatic performance we see in the background a chorus of lightly clad young women dancing onstage in a loud and vivacious music hall number. While the orchestra blares forth, the chorus line kicks rhythmically and joyously, offering in perfect unison the inviting fleshiness of their libidinal regions.

Hitchcock's use of this conjunction between death and the vibrancy of life—this "counterbalance" as Renoir would describe it—underlines the slightly ambiguous but residually positive implications of Hannay's outstretched arm. It is a directorial communication that we may take as similar to Welles's telling us in *F for Fake* that we all will die and our songs will all be silenced, "but what of it! Go on singing." ("And dancing," as he would surely say.) Not only in *French Cancan* but in many other films as well, Renoir too leaves us with that as his most fundamental message.

❁

Truffaut states that Hitchcock was "a neurotic."[20] In view of what I have been saying about Welles as possibly self-destructive, one might want to affix that label on him also. He seems to identify with, not just feel compassionate toward, the heavies in his films, whether they are evil (Quinlan, Arkadin, the Stranger in the movie with that title) or vile (the lawyer in *The Trial*) or pitiful losers who have had their day (Falstaff) or spoiled brats like George Amberson or monstrous tyrants like Kane and Mr. Clay. In the interviews he gave when he was approaching seventy years of age, Welles often speaks regretfully about his painful career, like someone who thinks that his own comeuppance may well have been justified and so he must warn young people not to follow his example. At the same time as he tells us that he himself will always be faithful to his girl (the camera), he never wavers in his belief that committed artists like him are doomed by modern civilization when it first encourages them to express their wondrous talents and then punishes them for doing so.

Welles could never reconcile with any equanimity these contrasting feelings that he had about his own career. The inner torments and the outer excesses that filled his existence may warrant his being called neurotic. But I am more greatly persuaded by the summary comment that Jeanne Moreau makes at the end of the BBC documentary about Welles and his life in films. "And to me, Orson is so much like a destitute King," she says: "A destitute King not because he was thrown away from the kingdom, but on this earth, the way the world is, there's no kingdom that is good enough for Orson Welles."[21] I likewise relish the remark by Marlene Dietrich to the effect that whenever she met Orson she felt like a flower that has been watered.

In a documentary about Stanley Kubrick, Woody Allen puts him and Welles in "the pantheon of the absolute top film directors that the world has seen." He speaks of them as "two major artists . . . in terms of being, you know, genuine no holds barred artists."[22] The combining of these two is felicitous, I believe. Welles and Kubrick are very much alike. They are comparable in their defiance of purely commercial interests, in their fidelity to high cinematic standards, in their refined pictorial sensibility, and in their understanding of the kinship between film and literature. As early as 1965, Welles told an interviewer that among filmmakers of the "younger generation" Kubrick was "a giant," indeed "a great director who has not yet made his great film."[23]

One can imagine Welles making films as Kubrick did if only the world had allowed him. On the set Welles may not have been as much of a perfectionist as Kubrick, but he was masterful in his ability to adapt to problematic circumstances and unforeseen hurdles. Although he spent years, sometimes decades, on ventures like *Don Quijote* (which he quipped that he would retitle *When Are You Going to Finish Don Quijote?*), he lacked the final fortitude, and the monetary sustenance, that was needed for their conclusion. If Welles had been more of a perfectionist, he might have managed to complete these projects, that being requisite to their inherent goodness. Twenty-one years before he died without releasing *Don Quijote*, he is quoted as having said that it was "really finished" and needed only three more weeks of work. He then added: "What makes me nervous is launching it: I know that this film will please no one. This will be an execrated film. I need a big success before putting it in circulation. If *The Trial* had been a complete critical success, then I would have had the courage to bring out my *Don Quijote.* Things being what they are, I don't know what to do: everyone will be enraged by this film."[24]

Kubrick also lamented not having brought to fruition many of the projects that remained in the planning stage. But his history as a filmmaker was different from Welles's history. Kubrick had commercial successes from the start, more or less, and the studios could count on his ability to make money for them in the long run. Welles's first movie was a financial disaster, and its being hailed in later years as possibly the best film ever made only solidified his desire to follow his own artistic bent regardless of the consequences. The aesthetic taste of Welles varied in quality: for the most part excellent—in *Chimes at Midnight* for instance—but often poor (in the film version of *Macbeth*) and only partly good (in *Othello*), though the latter two were much impaired by money matters beyond his control.

Kubrick was a great photographer who learned how to transform the beauty of static images into the dramatic potential of moving pictures, and sometimes, as in *Barry Lyndon*, vice versa. Kubrick's achievement in this area was exceptional, but Welles had a more wide-ranging intellect than Kubrick did, and he had unmatchable knowledge of radio and the stage, both of which he could use as only a very gifted writer would. If Welles can be studied for the breadth of his philosophic mind, which I have tried to do in this book, Kubrick has to be treated as a storyteller who had the analytical power of a logician or mathematician, or even chess master, with a few ideas about life, but not many. In his own mesmerizing way, Kubrick is closer to Hitchcock than either Welles or Renoir was.

❋

With their long strings of consecutive work, Hitchcock and Renoir differ from both Welles and Kubrick. Hitchcock could prevail in the typical American strategy for success because he played, as well as anyone has, the game of producing a viable commodity for mass consumption. His movies were, and still are, financial winners that were manufactured to satisfy the emotional needs of an immense audience. Renoir escaped the treatment of someone like Welles because French culture still had its favorable disposition toward humanistic art, into which Renoir's mentality fitted perfectly. One can hardly imagine what movies Renoir would be making today. But in his time he was close enough to the adoration of the Belle Epoque that the French, at least, retained until the period just after World War II. Itself a contributor to that adoration, his father's painting had flourished as an expression of the broadly prevalent love of vitality, sensory pleasure, and the goodness of a life in nature, while also trying to subjugate any harmful or mawkish passions that might intervene though likewise coming out of nature.

Auguste Renoir, who hated Beethoven for having shamefully inserted personal feelings into his music, was staunchly anti-Romantic. As I have been saying, Jean Renoir was ambivalent about this; but that helped give the sophisticated ambiguities in his films their attunement with the vacillating mood of the early twentieth century. More than Welles or Hitchcock, Renoir was also fully responsive to the idealization of "the common man," which has had such importance in contemporary civilization. Welles sided with this attitude in his left-wing politics, but he himself was so uncommon, so kingly and "aristocratic," as Renoir said about his works, that he regularly used ideas and techniques that offended many in the public by alienating them from their own experience of the commonplace. Hitchcock had no problem of that sort. He treated his birth in the lower middle class as a touch of nature that he could, and did, channel through skillful cinematic manipulations—a type of social climbing from the outside, characteristic of artists, rather than the usual type from within.

⚜

This question about acceptance or rejection of commonality should be recognized as different from two other issues I have discussed—one about the ordinary, and the other about an artist's recourse to improvisation of some sort. Truffaut maintains that "Hitchcock loathe[d] the 'ordinary'" and always sought to "keep banality off the screen." He says that Hitchcock did this by "introducing [a] disturbing note, a feeling of apprehension and anxiety . . . that invests [an] ordinary situation with potential drama."[25] Correct as this statement surely is, I take it as only a partial truth. Couched within Hitchcock's formalist effort to create suspense and a beneficial experience of fear, there lingers a conception of the ordinary as the human framework in which the terrible things that it can often harbor must be exposed as vividly as possible. The banality that Hitchcock found repugnant was only the self-deceiving acquiescence in the commonplace. Audiences had to be led out of that by perceiving how much of life is suspenseful as well as frightening, and therefore liable to his type of dramatic presentation. The complementary element of shock that Hitchcock regularly employed served as a means of keeping the viewer alert throughout the process.

If we interpret Hitchcock's filmmaking in this fashion, we can see how coherent it is with the varied approaches of Welles and Renoir. Like other filmmakers who subscribe in some vague way to the doctrine of realism but then go beyond it in treating film as "poetry" or "magic" or pictorial "orchestration," they too wanted to remain faithful to what is ordinary in nature while excluding any boring reenactment of it. Their reliance upon improvisation was a step in that direction. The statements they made about elaborate plans they discarded once they arrived on the set and realized that everything had to be changed are more than just autobiographical accounts. They embody a conception of creativity that all artists probably share to some extent. The ordinary comes to everyone as the given aspect of our reality. To portray it with the inventive agility that imagination can provide, an artist must somehow filter out the dreary sediment of what is *only* commonplace. Welles and Renoir both teach us that the inspired doing of this has to be largely unforeseen (*l'imprévu*, as in Stendhal's philosophy of love and of art). Improvisation accommodates that necessity.

Furthermore, we also know that Hitchcock's customary refusal to improvise on the set was not the totality of what went into his cinematography. He spent a great amount of time on special effects that required one or another experimentation with the camera, and often intricate angle shots for whatever mise en scène he wanted at some point. In addition, his comments about his films, frequently long after they were finished, show how much he revised his earlier opinions about how to shoot and edit them. The type of improvisation that came to Welles and Renoir while they stood behind the camera would seem to have arisen and evolved in Hitchcock's mind over a period of years before and after each production.

This variance as related to cineastic creativity is compounded by the fact that Welles and Renoir themselves did not improvise in identical ways or for the same reasons. For Welles improvisation was mainly a means of being spontaneous in how one saw the world and then reliving the spontaneity in an act of representing it. His view of that is based on his notion that moviemakers should not emulate the achievements of their forerunners, even the greatest ones, but rather create their own films "innocently"—as he puts it: "The way Adam named the animals on the first day in the Garden."[26] While this Wellesean belief conformed to Renoir's ideas about improvisation, and largely reflects a similar philosophy of life, it is less extensive than what Renoir intended.

Above all in *The Rules of the Game*, but also in most of his other movies, Renoir continually defeats the expectations he has been setting up not only in the plot but also in the characterization of the protagonists, and even in the physical appearance of his actors. He resembles Buñuel in this respect. As an example that I touched on in my book *Reality Transformed*, notice the camera's fixation on the relatively unattractive back of Nora Grégor in her bedroom scene near the beginning of *The Rules*. In itself the ungainly expanse of flesh undermines the flirtatiousness that she will manifest at the chateau later in this film. This combination of divergent effects contributes to those counterweights that Renoir was seeking throughout and on which he rightly prided himself. In the scene I have chosen here as an illustration, and in many others, the cinematography was surely improvised during the

actual shooting and not thought out in advance. It was something that occurred to Renoir on the spot, and as a reaction at
the moment to what the actors were displaying to the camera
unawares.

Renoir defends his procedure by telling us again and again
that clichés are always boring and must be avoided at any cost.
Welles (and certainly Hitchcock) would have agreed. But
Renoir is also motivated by his conviction that reality is
unfathomable. Even when he makes his perfunctory bow to
Zola's determinism in *La Bête humaine*, he does so only in the
prologue and then goes on to depict the life of his characters as
mainly fortuitous happenstance. His realistic naturalism
conveys a sense of the cosmos as just a complex enactment of
forces that are themselves improvisations of what will come
next in time and space. While Hitchcock and Welles may show
lasting signs of the Catholicism in which they were raised,
there is no inkling of that or any other traditional metaphysics
in the films of Renoir.

❈

As a final note, I want to state that in my own pantheon of
greatness, these three filmmakers are not placed in any order of
rank. I respect their genuine differences. As a pluralist and
humanistic philosopher, I delight in the explorations of Renoir.
Even at their least successful, his movies have deep meaning
for me. But as an American intellectual who is familiar with the
sense of alienation, even isolation, that so rare and audacious
an artist as Welles experienced in his life, I respond to his vision
and to his fate with feelings of protectiveness as well as
indignation. For Hitchcock's technical skill I have endless
admiration. It's how I feel about the grandeur of modern

technology, and about those who produce and comprehend its arcane but godlike achievements. I see no point in grading the three filmmakers as better or worse among themselves.

In the conclusion of his book *Three Philosophical Poets: Lucretius, Dante, Goethe,* Santayana says: *"Onorate l'altissimo poeta"* (Let us honor the highest poet).[27] He thinks of this exemplar, still unborn, as an ideal poet who combines the virtues of the three great artists Santayana studies in that book. I myself am content to honor the filmmakers in the present effort for what they are respectively and as uniquely original creators. The concept of *l'altissimo* seems vacuous to me.

Notes

Some Preliminary Remarks

1. *Orson Welles: Interviews*, ed. Mark W. Estrin (Jackson: University Press of Mississippi, 2002), interview with Juan Cobos, Miguel Rubio, and J. A. Pruneda, 99.

Alfred Hitchcock

1. BBC Television, *Reputations: Alfred Hitchcock*, 1999; and also *Destination Hitchcock: The Making of North by Northwest*, a film by Peter Fitzgerald, 2000.

2. *Hitchcock on Hitchcock: Selected Writings and Interviews*, ed. Sidney Gottlieb (Berkeley: University of California Press, 1995), 186–187.

3. Gottlieb, *Hitchcock on Hitchcock*, 186.

4. Gottlieb, *Hitchcock on Hitchcock*, 187.

5. Peter Bogdanovich, *Who The Devil Made It: Conversations with . . .* (New York: Knopf, 1997), 522.

6. Gottlieb, *Hitchcock on Hitchcock*, 288.

7. Gottlieb, *Hitchcock on Hitchcock*, 289.

8. Bogdanovich, *Who The Devil Made It*, 533.

9. Estrin, ed., *Orson Welles: Interviews*, xxii and 135.

10. Gottlieb, *Hitchcock on Hitchcock*, 118.

11. Gottlieb, *Hitchcock on Hitchcock*, 117.

12. Gottlieb, *Hitchcock on Hitchcock*, 109.

13. Gottlieb, *Hitchcock on Hitchcock*, 111.

14. For a discussion of the extent to which *Psycho* in particular should or should not be classified as a horror film, see Noël Carroll, *The Philosophy of Horror or Paradoxes of the Heart* (New York: Routledge, 1990), 38–39. See also Carroll on horror and suspense in his "Film, Emotion, and Genre," in *Passionate Views: Film, Cognition, and Emotion*, ed. Carl Plantinga and Greg M. Smith (Baltimore: Johns Hopkins University Press, 1999), 38–46. On the concept of suspense in Hitchcock, see Deborah Knight and George McKnight, "Suspense and Its Master," in *Alfred Hitchcock: Centenary Essays*, ed. Richard Allen and S. Ishii-Gonzalès (London: *bfi*, 1999), 107–121. See also Dolf Zillman, "The Psychology of Suspense in Dramatic Exposition," in *Suspense: Conceptualizations, Theoretical Analyses, and Empirical Explorations*, ed. Peter Vorderer et al. (Mahwah, NJ: Lawrence Erlbaum, 1996), 199–231; and, in the same volume, Noël Carroll, "The Paradox of Suspense," 71–91.

15. Gottlieb, *Hitchcock on Hitchcock*, 125–126.

16. Gottlieb, *Hitchcock on Hitchcock*, 129.

17. Gottlieb, *Hitchcock on Hitchcock*, 128.

18. Gottlieb, *Hitchcock on Hitchcock*, 115.

19. On Herrmann's scores for Hitchcock and Welles movies, see Steven C. Smith, *A Heart at Fire's Center: The Life and Music of Bernard Herrmann* (Berkeley: University of California Press, 1991), 219–222, 236–241, and passim; and 77–84, 91–94, and passim.

20. Gottlieb, *Hitchcock on Hitchcock*, 248.

21. Gottlieb, *Hitchcock on Hitchcock*, 313–314.

22. Gottlieb, *Hitchcock on Hitchcock*, 311.

23. Gottlieb, *Hitchcock on Hitchcock*, 312.

24. Gottlieb, *Hitchcock on Hitchcock*, 312.

25. Gottlieb, *Hitchcock on Hitchcock*, 313.

26. Gottlieb, *Hitchcock on Hitchcock*, 256.

27. Gottlieb, *Hitchcock on Hitchcock*, 257.

28. Gottlieb, *Hitchcock on Hitchcock*, 257.

29. *The Illustrated Hitchcock*, Camera Three interview with Pia Lindstrom, 1972.

30. Gottlieb, *Hitchcock on Hitchcock*, 174.

31. Gottlieb, *Hitchcock on Hitchcock*, 56.

32. Gottlieb, *Hitchcock on Hitchcock*, 248.

33. On this, see BBC Television, *Reputations: Alfred Hitchcock*.

34. Gottlieb, *Hitchcock on Hitchcock*, 257.

35. Gottlieb, *Hitchcock on Hitchcock*, 140. For "Let 'Em Play God," see 113–115.

Orson Welles

Material in this chapter appeared, in a revised format, as "*The Dead: Story and Film*," in *The Hudson Review* 56, no. 4.

1. Bogdanovich, *Who The Devil Made It*, 502.

2. Orson Welles and Peter Bogdanovich, *This Is Orson Welles* (Cambridge, MA: Da Capo 1998), 82.

3. Welles and Bogdanovich, *This Is Orson Welles*, 278–279.

4. Welles and Bogdanovich, *This Is Orson Welles*, 284.

5. *Talking with Ingmar Bergman*, ed. G. William Jones (Dallas: SMU Press, 1983), 28.

6. Welles and Bogdanovich, *This Is Orson Welles*, 17.

7. Welles and Bogdanovich, *This Is Orson Welles*, 100.

8. Welles and Bogdanovich, *This Is Orson Welles*, 101.

9. Welles and Bogdanovich, *This Is Orson Welles*, viii.

10. Welles and Bogdanovich, *This Is Orson Welles*, 93.

11. Welles and Bogdanovich, *This Is Orson Welles*, 96.

12. Welles and Bogdanovich, *This Is Orson Welles*, 173.

13. James Joyce, *Stephen Hero*, ed. Theodore Spencer (New York: New Directions, 1959), 211.

14. Joyce, *Stephen Hero*, 213.

15. *James Joyce: The Dead*, ed. Daniel R. Schwarz (Boston: Bedford/St. Martin's, 1994), 49.

16. Schwarz, ed., *James Joyce: The Dead*, 58–59.

17. Schwarz, ed., *James Joyce: The Dead*, 35.

18. Welles and Bogdanovich, *This Is Orson Welles*, 33.

19. Welles and Bogdanovich, *This Is Orson Welles*, 114.

20. Welles and Bogdanovich, *This Is Orson Welles*, 130.

21. Welles and Bogdanovich, *This Is Orson Welles*, 132.

22. Welles and Bogdanovich, *This Is Orson Welles*, 463.

23. On this, see William Johnson, "Orson Welles: Of Time and Loss," in *Perspectives on Orson Welles*, ed. Morris Beja (New York: G. K. Hall, 1995), 75–89.

24. Welles and Bogdanovich, *This Is Orson Welles*, 214–215.

25. Welles and Bogdanovich, *This Is Orson Welles*, 212.

26. BBC Television, *With Orson Welles: Stories from a Life in Film*, interview with Leslie Megahey, 1989.

27. Welles and Bogdanovich, *This Is Orson Welles*, xxxv.

28. Welles and Bogdanovich, *This Is Orson Welles*, 198.

29. Welles and Bogdanovich, *This Is Orson Welles*, 282–283.

30. Welles and Bogdanovich, *This Is Orson Welles*, 286–287.

31. Welles and Bogdanovich, *This Is Orson Welles*, 301.

32. Welles and Bogdanovich, *This Is Orson Welles*, 51.

33. Welles and Bogdanovich, *This Is Orson Welles*, 235.

34. For Welles's remarks about the meaning of *character* in relation to this anecdote, see Estrin, ed., *Orson Welles: Interviews*, interview with André Bazin, Charles Bitsch, and Jean Domarchi, 73–74.

35. Welles and Bogdanovich, *This Is Orson Welles*, 17.

36. Welles and Bogdanovich, *This Is Orson Welles*, 17–18.

37. See James Howard, *The Complete Films of Orson Welles*, (New York: Citadel, 1991), passim.

38. On this, see my book *Reality Transformed: Film as Meaning and Technique* (Cambridge, MA: MIT Press, 1998), 81–86.

39. Welles and Bogdanovich, *This Is Orson Welles*, xxxviii.

40. Welles and Bogdanovich, *This Is Orson Welles*, 174.

41. Welles and Bogdanovich, *This Is Orson Welles*, 182.

42. Welles and Bogdanovich, *This Is Orson Welles*, 182.

43. Welles and Bogdanovich, *This Is Orson Welles*, 72.

44. Welles and Bogdanovich, *This Is Orson Welles*, 309.

45. Welles and Bogdanovich, *This Is Orson Welles*, 88. On the influence of radio on Welles's use of sound in films, see Louis Giannetti, *Understanding Movies*, 7th ed. (Englewood Cliffs, NJ: Prentice Hall, 1996), 481.

46. Welles and Bogdanovich, *This Is Orson Welles*, 103.

47. Welles and Bogdanovich, *This Is Orson Welles*, 310.

48. Welles and Bogdanovich, *This Is Orson Welles*, 450–451. For further remarks of Welles about television, see Estrin, ed., *Orson Welles: Interviews*, interview with André Bazin and Charles Bitsch, 44–45.

49. Jones, ed., *Talking with Ingmar Bergman*, 47.

50. Quoted in André Bazin, *Orson Welles: A Critical View* (Los Angeles: Acrobat, 1991), 132–133.

51. Welles and Bogdanovich, *This Is Orson Welles*, 256.

52. Welles and Bogdanovich, *This Is Orson Welles*, 255.

53. Welles and Bogdanovich, *This Is Orson Welles*, 189.

54. See BBC Television, *With Orson Welles*.

55. See BBC Television, *With Orson Welles*, and the partial transcript of this telecast in Estrin, ed., *Orson Welles*, interview with Leslie Megahey, 198–199.

56. Welles and Bogdanovich, *This Is Orson Welles*, 448. See also BBC Television, *With Orson Welles*, and Estrin, ed., *Orson Welles*, interview with Leslie Megahey, where Welles says that Renoir "is I think the best director ever" (193).

57. Isak Dinesen, "The Immortal Story," in her *Anecdotes of Destiny* (New York: Random House, 1958), 229.

58. Welles and Bogdanovich, *This is Orson Welles*, 526–527.

59. Welles and Bogdanovich, *This is Orson Welles*, 232.

60. Welles and Bogdanovich, *This is Orson Welles*, 258.

61. Welles and Bogdanovich, *This is Orson Welles*, 258–259.

Jean Renoir

1. Jean Renoir, *Renoir on Renoir: Interviews, Essays, and Remarks*, trans. Carol Volk (Cambridge: Cambridge University Press, 1989), 250.

2. James Joyce, *A Portrait of the Artist as a Young Man* (New York: Bantam, 1992), 209.

3. Renoir, *Renoir on Renoir*, 250. On Renoir's vision of his craft as an auteur seeking to make contact, see his *Renoir on Renoir*, 251, and also Martin O'Shaughnessy, *Jean Renoir* (Manchester: Manchester University Press, 2000), 23–25 and 30–61.

4. Renoir, *Renoir on Renoir*, 251.

5. Renoir, *Renoir on Renoir*, 251.

6. Renoir, *Renoir on Renoir*, 6.

7. Renoir, *Renoir on Renoir*, 39–40.

8. Renoir, *Renoir on Renoir*, 191.

9. Renoir, *Renoir on Renoir*, 186, 188.

10. Renoir, *Renoir on Renoir*, 188.

11. Renoir, *Renoir on Renoir*, 189.

12. Renoir, *Renoir on Renoir*, 4.

13. Renoir, *Renoir on Renoir*, 152.

14. Renoir, *Renoir on Renoir*, 46. On this, and on Renoir's ideas in general about the relation between the director and the actors, see Jean Renoir, *An Interview* (København: Green Integer, 1998), 27–43.

15. Bogdanovich, *Who The Devil Made It*, 441.

16. Renoir, *Renoir on* Renoir, 244.

17. Renoir, *Renoir on* Renoir, 250.

18. Renoir, *Renoir on Renoir*, 21–22.

19. Renoir, *Renoir on Renoir*, 239–240.

20. Renoir, *Renoir on Renoir*, 37.

21. Renoir, *Renoir on Renoir*, 115.

22. Renoir, *Renoir on Renoir*, 116.

23. Singer, *Reality Transformed*, 155–189.

24. Renoir, *Renoir on Renoir*, 52.

25. Renoir, *Renoir on Renoir*, 49. For Renoir's attack on "progress" and his defense of "imperfection," see also his *My Life and My Films*, trans. Norman Denny (New York: Atheneum, 1974), 204–206.

26. See André Bazin, *What Is Cinema?*, trans. Hugh Gray (Berkeley: University of California Press, 1967), 1: 9–16 and 17–22.

27. Jean Renoir, "André Bazin's Little Beret," in André Bazin, *Jean Renoir*, ed. François Truffaut, trans. W. W. Halsley II and William H. Simon (New York: Da Capo, 1992), 11–12.

28. Renoir, *Renoir on Renoir*, 157.

29. Renoir, *Renoir on Renoir*, 157.

30. Renoir, *My Life and My Films*, 278.

31. Renoir, *Renoir on Renoir*, 47–48.

32. Renoir, *Renoir on Renoir*, 49.

33. For excellent analyses of Renoir's cinematography, see Bazin, *Jean Renoir*, 43–46, 88–90, and passim.

34. Renoir, *Renoir on Renoir*, 97.

35. Renoir, *Renoir on Renoir*, 35.

36. Renoir, *Renoir on Renoir*, 96–97.

37. Renoir, *Renoir on Renoir*, 229.

38. Renoir, *Renoir on Renoir*, 229.

39. Renoir, *Renoir on Renoir*, 182.

40. Renoir, *Renoir on Renoir,* 182–183.

41. Renoir, *Renoir on Renoir,* 251.

A Family Portrait

1. François Truffaut, *Hitchcock*, rev. ed. (New York: Simon and Schuster, 1983), 101–102.

2. Truffaut, *Hitchcock*, 165.

3. Truffaut, *Hitchcock*, 287.

4. Truffaut, *Hitchcock*, 288.

5. Truffaut, *Hitchcock*, 48.

6. Truffaut, *Hitchcock*, 289–291.

7. Bazin, *Jean Renoir*, 31–32.

8. Truffaut, *Hitchcock*, 256

9. Truffaut, *Hitchcock*, 346.

10. Truffaut, *Hitchcock*, 222–223.

11. Bazin, *Orson Welles*, 74–75. For an extended analysis of both form and content in *Citizen Kane*, see the comprehensive "Synthesis" that explains all the aspects of filmmaking by reference to that film alone in Giannetti, *Understanding Movies*, 467–501. For a somewhat dubious judgment about Welles's movie in relation to the myth of the past, see Jean-Paul Sartre, "*Citizen Kane*," in *Perspectives on Citizen Kane*, ed. Ronald Gottesman (New York: G. K. Hall, 1996), 58, where Sartre remarks that in that film "everything is analyzed, dissected, presented in an intellective order . . . everything is dead." In the same anthology Adrienne Rich's words about "the / cold blue of the past," in her poem "Amnesia" about the snow scene in *Citizen Kane*, are more insightful (586). See also several other noteworthy entries, among them: André Bazin, "The Technique of *Citizen Kane*," trans. Alain Piette and Bert Cardullo, 229–237; Bert Cardullo, "The Real Fascination of *Citizen Kane*," 242–253; and Noël Carroll, "Interpreting *Citizen Kane*," 254–267.

12. BBC Television, *With Orson Welles*, and Estrin, ed., *Orson Welles*, interview with Leslie Megahey, 209.

13. François Truffaut, "Introduction" to Bazin, *Jean Renoir*, 8.

14. Stanley Cavell, *"North by Northwest,"* in *A Hitchcock Reader*, ed. Marshall Deutelbaum and Leland Poague (Ames, IA: Iowa State University Press, 1986), 250.

15. Truffaut, *Hitchcock*, 150.

16. On this, see also Charles L. P. Silet, "Through a Woman's Eyes: Sexuality and Memory in *The Steps*," in Deutelbaum and Poague, eds., *A Hitchcock Reader*, 11.

17. For a comparison of Hitchcock and Sturges, see Lesley Brill, "Redemptive Comedy in the Films of Alfred Hitchcock and Preston Sturges: 'Are Snakes Necessary?,' " in Allen and Ishii-Gonzalès, eds., *Alfred Hitchcock: Centenary Essays*, 205–219.

18. Robin Wood, "Retrospective," in Deutelbaum and Poague, eds., *A Hitchcock Reader*, 38.

19. Cavell, *"North by Northwest,"* in Deutelbaum and Poague, eds., *A Hitchcock Reader*, 254–255.

20. Truffaut, *Hitchcock*, 346.

21. BBC Television, *With Orson Welles*, and Estrin, ed., *Orson Welles*, interview with Leslie Megahey, 209. For detailed and definitive accounts of the life and works of Orson Welles, see also *The Encyclopedia of Orson Welles*, ed. Chuck Berg and Tom Erskine, with others (New York: Facts On File, 2003).

22. *Stanley Kubrick: A Life in Pictures*, a film by Jan Harlan, 2001.

23. Estrin, ed., *Orson Welles*, interview with Juan Cobos, Miguel Rubio, and J. A. Pruneda, 122.

24. Estrin, ed., *Orson Welles*, interview with Juan Cobos, Miguel Rubio, and J. A. Pruneda, 124. Spelling of film's title altered to match what appears on screen.

25. Truffaut, *Hitchcock*, 15–16.

26. BBC Television, *With Orson Welles*, and Estrin, ed., *Orson Welles*, interview with Leslie Megahey, 209. For further Welles remarks about improvisation, see Estrin, ed., *Orson Welles*, interview with André Bazin and Charles Bitsch, 38–39.

27. George Santayana, *Three Philosophical Poets: Lucretius, Dante, Goethe* (New York: Cooper Square, 1970), 215.

Index